The Complete Diabetic Cookbook for Beginners

800 Affordable and Healthy Recipes for The New Diagnozed and Busy People on Type 2 Diabetes

Juliette Villegas

Table of Contents

Chapter 4 Beef, Pork, and Lamb 30

Chapter 5 Fish and Seafood 42

INTRODUCTION

I remember when my grandfather was diagnosed with diabetes. We were all afraid for him and went out of our way to help him make the necessary changes for his new lifestyle. We didn't know it then, but he was miserable. All he had to eat were steamed veggies, flavorless meat, and brown rice. He missed being able to enjoy my grandmother's cooking.

Life has changed a lot since then; research and new discoveries in medicine are making it possible for people with diabetes to enjoy a good quality of life without having to let go of the meals they hold dear.

Once we find out we have diabetes, our first thought is often that eating all our favorite foods is a thing of the past. It doesn't have to be! This book is full of carefully crafted, tried and true recipes that are 100% safe for people with diabetes.

Each recipe comes with step-by-step instructions that make it easy to prepare and uses well-known ingredients that are easily locatable at farmer's markets and grocery stores.

The nutritional analysis is included in each recipe so that you will know the amount of carbohydrates, fat, protein, and sodium in every meal.

Eating with diabetes doesn't have to be complicated, so whether you've just been diagnosed or have known you suffer from diabetes for years, this book is for you!

Chapter 1: Key Things to Know About Diabetes

What Is Diabetes?

Diabetes is a chronic condition that impacts the way our bodies turn nutrients into energy. There are several types of diabetes, but what they all have in common is that they cause high levels of glucose in the blood.

Glucose is what gives us energy. After we eat or drink something, our bodies break the carbohydrates down and then release glucose into our blood. The pancreas then releases a hormone called insulin. Insulin allows the glucose in our blood to penetrate our cells and fuel our bodies.

When a person doesn't suffer from diabetes, their pancreas can sense when there is glucose in the bloodstream and it's able to release the right amount of insulin to allow glucose into our cells. For someone with diabetes, their system doesn't work the same way.

Someone who has type 1 diabetes cannot produce insulin at all. Someone with type 2 diabetes produces insulin, but it either doesn't work effectively or it just isn't enough. In both cases, glucose can't penetrate your cells, so it starts to build up in your blood.

Having too much glucose in your blood over a long period of time can damage your heart, eyes, kidneys, and feet.

Symptoms and Causes

Symptoms

Some common symptoms that one might experience when they have diabetes include:

- Frequent urination
- Constant thirst
- Weight loss
- Hunger
- Blurred vision
- A tingling sensation in the hands and feet
- Fatigue
- Dry Skin
- Being more prone to infection
- Slow-healing wounds

Causes of Type 1 Diabetes

Type 1 diabetes is also referred to as autoimmune diabetes, as it's believed to be caused by an autoimmune reaction in the body. The reaction recognizes the beta cells in the pancreas that make insulin as foreign bodies and then destroys them.

Some people inherit genes that increase their likelihood of developing type 1 diabetes. While many people carry these genes, they can still go unaffected by diabetes. Environmental factors like viruses can trigger a response in the body that leads to developing the disease.

Causes of Type 2 Diabetes

Type 2 diabetes used to be called adult-onset diabetes because it's more common in older people. There are a host of risk factors that contribute to it. These include:

> ♦ Being overweight: This increases the risk of high blood pressure, unhealthy cholesterol and high blood glucose.
> ♦ Uneven fat distribution: When a lot of our body fat is concentrated in our abdomen, we're at greater risk of developing Type 2 diabetes.
> ♦ Inactivity: When we are inactive, we put ourselves at a higher risk of developing diabetes because being active helps us use up a lot of the glucose in our blood, which then makes our cells more sensitive to insulin.
> ♦ Family history: If one or more of our direct family members has diabetes, we're at a higher risk for developing it.
> ♦ Race and ethnicity: Studies have shown that people of Black, Hispanic, Asian, and Pacific Islander descent have a greater chance of developing type 2 diabetes than people of Caucasian heritage.
> ♦ Age: The older we become, the more likely we are to develop the disease. Type 2 diabetes is most prevalent in people over the age of 45.

One of the biggest causes of type 2 diabetes is insulin resistance. This happens when the cells in your fat, muscles, and liver don't respond to insulin and become unable to use the glucose in your blood. Your pancreas ends up making more insulin to compensate. After a while, your blood sugar levels start to rise and this can lead to organ damage.

Preventing Type 2 Diabetes

Prediabetes occurs when your blood sugar is higher than normal, but isn't high enough to be considered diabetes. Making some necessary changes to your lifestyle can lessen your risk of developing type 2 diabetes.

The best way to prevent diabetes, especially for those who have been diagnosed as prediabetic, is to adopt healthier habits such as:

Decreasing Inactivity

It sounds crazy, but sitting still for long periods of time can increase the risk of developing type 2 diabetes. It's important to be on your feet for a few minutes at least every half hour.

Becoming More Active

Incorporating a moderate workout regimen into your schedule can prevent you from developing diabetes. Aim for a 30 minute workout at least 2-3 times per week.

Eating Healthy Food

Eat foods with a little to no saturated fat and opt for healthy fats like omega-3s. Foods that are higher in fiber, like fruits, veggies, and grains, are good for you. Lean protein is essential, because it helps to rebuild your muscles but has less calories.

Losing Weight

Losing weight and keeping it off can slow down the progression from prediabetes to type 2 diabetes.

Managing Diabetes

Following the news that you've been diagnosed with diabetes, you'll want to pay attention to a few things. Among them are the ABCs of diabetes.

The ABCs of diabetes are A1c, blood pressure, cholesterol, and stop smoking. In order to gauge your risk for diabetic complications, you need to know your numbers so that you can better manage your condition.

A1c

The HbA1c or A1c test is used by medical professionals to measure your blood glucose levels over a period of 2-3 months. It's mostly used to diagnose prediabetes and diabetes. Once you've been diagnosed with diabetes, it's best to take this test at least twice a year, because it's also used to aid in the management of your diabetes. If your A1c levels are high, you might begin to experience diabetic complications.

The ideal A1c level for someone with diabetes is 7%. Even the slightest change in that percentage can either increase or decrease your risk of experiencing complications. If you're able to lower your A1c level by 1%, your risk for complications goes down by as much as 35%. Just a single percentage point above 7% can as much as double your risk for complications.

Most people with diabetes are able to monitor their blood glucose levels at home so that they can get an idea of whether they're doing the right things to keep those levels controlled.

Doctors can give their patients plasma-calibrated blood glucose meters to use at home. The device allows you to check your blood sugar levels daily before and after meals. The ideal level before a meal is around 70-130 mg/dl and less than 180 mg/dl at least an hour after a meal.

Blood Pressure

Blood pressure is the force that our blood exerts against the walls of our arteries. When our hearts beat, they pump blood into our arteries; the pressure is at its highest when the heart contracts. When pressure is high, our arteries become more resistant to the flow of blood and our hearts end up pumping harder than normal in order to circulate the blood.

Blood pressure is measured using two numbers. The systolic pressure is the number on the top, which refers to the pressure inside the artery when the heart contracts and pumps blood. The diastolic pressure is the number on the bottom, which refers to the pressure inside the artery when the heart is at rest and filling with blood. Both these numbers are recorded as millimeters of mercury or mm Hg.

When you have diabetes, your ideal blood pressure is anything below 140/80 mm Hg.

Cholesterol

Cholesterol is a fat-like substance that's made in our livers and travels throughout our bloodstream. It can build up in our arteries and harden over time. If this happens, the arteries can become narrow, stiff, and hinder blood flow. This makes the heart pump harder and

increases the chances of heart attack and stroke.

People with diabetes should have yearly blood tests to measure their triglycerides, low-density lipoprotein (LDL), and high-density lipoprotein (HDL) cholesterol levels. This is because they often have lower HDL (good) cholesterol levels and higher LDL (bad) cholesterol levels than people without the disease.

Everyone is different, so our risk profiles will differ too. But the general consensus is that our LDL levels should be under 100 mg/dl (milligrams/deciliter), our HDL levels should be under 40 mg/dl, and our triglycerides under 150 mg/dl.

Stop Smoking

Smoking can lead to type 2 diabetes. The more you smoke, the higher your chances of developing diabetes. Smokers with diabetes have a harder time dosing their insulin and managing the illness. They also are at higher risk of developing other health issues like:

♦ Kidney disease

♦ Heart disease

♦ Decreased blood flow in the legs and feet. This often leads to ulcers, infection, and sometimes amputation.

♦ Retinopathy (causes blindness)

♦ Peripheral neuropathy (the nerves in the arms and legs become damaged, causing numbness, weakness and poor coordination.

Following your meal plan is another factor that can help with managing diabetes.

A meal plan helps you keep your blood sugar at a healthy level by letting you know when, what, and how much to eat. The best way to keep to a meal plan is by formulating one that caters to your tastes and fits your lifestyle.

♦ Try to incorporate a lot of green veggies into your diet, like broccoli, green beans, and spinach.

♦ Try to exclude foods with added sugars and refined grains.

♦ Try to stay away from processed foods and focus more on whole foods.

The more carbohydrates we consume, the higher our blood sugar levels will be. There's no way to avoid carbs altogether, but we can mitigate their effects on our blood sugar. We can lessen the pace at which our blood sugar rises by opting for healthier options. Another way to slow things down is to pair our carbs with fat, fiber, or protein.

Your meals should always be balanced and have more or less the same amount of carbs each time, so that your sugar levels never go too high or low.

Diabetic Food List

The rule of thumb when you have diabetes is to eat foods that have healthy carbohydrates, healthy fats, fiber, and lean protein.

In movies, characters always seem to be trying to cut carbs out of their diet completely. People with diabetes seem to want to do this too but carbs in moderation are actually good for you. Healthy carbohydrates give you energy, help you burn fat, aid with sleep, improve your muscle mass, and lower your risk of developing cardiac problems.

Healthy fats are good for your cholesterol and your heart. They decrease your LDL levels while raising your HDL levels. They also lower your blood pressure and triglyceride levels. Healthy fats actually promote weight loss because they make you feel fuller for longer and stop you from overeating.

Fiber helps to improve your blood sugar levels by slowing down the absorption of sugar. It also reduces inflammation and blood pressure.

Lean protein can help to increase your body's response to insulin without raising your blood glucose levels. Proteins also improve your immunity, which can be compromised when you have diabetes.

Food to Recommend

Here is a list of recommended foods to add to your diet:

♦ Beans: Half a cup of beans contains as much protein as an ounce of meat, but without any saturated fat. This helps to offset the carbohydrate content. Canned beans work just as well as fresh beans, but they need to be drained and rinsed to get rid of any excess salt. The best kinds of beans to use are black, kidney, and pinto beans because they are high in magnesium and potassium.

♦ Berries: Whenever we think about a diabetic diet we usually think—no sweets. Berries can satisfy your craving for something sweet. They are packed with vitamins C and K, fiber, manganese, and potassium.

♦ Citrus: Citrus fruits can also fulfill your sweet cravings. They've got vitamin C, fiber, folate, and potassium.

♦ Fish: People with diabetes should eat fatty fish at least twice a week. Fatty fish refers to fish high in omega-3s. These fats are good for reducing inflammation and preventing heart disease. Examples of fish high in omega-3 include: albacore tuna, herring, mackerel, salmon, and sardines.

♦ Leafy greens: Leafy green vegetables are low in carbohydrates and packed with vitamins A, C, E, and K, and minerals like calcium, iron, and potassium. For variety, try adding collards, kale, or spinach into your salads, soups, and stews.

♦ Nonfat or low-fat dairy: Dairy products are synonymous with calcium and strong bones. In addition to this, they are fortified, which makes them high in vitamin D. While nonfat milk and low-fat milk do contain carbohydrates, you can opt to buy the kinds that have lower fat and sugar content.

♦ Nuts and seeds: Nuts contain a lot of healthy fats and they are also good for curbing hunger pangs. They're high in fiber and contain magnesium. Walnuts and flax seeds are high in omega-3 fatty acids.

♦ Tomatoes: Tomatoes contain vitamins C and E and potassium.

♦ Whole grains: Whole grains contain vitamin B and minerals like chromium, folate, and iron. They're also packed with fiber. Some examples of whole grains are: farro, quinoa, whole grain barley, and whole oats.

While all of these foods are great, they can put a strain on your budget and they aren't all available year-round. To lower your costs you can buy and cook what's in season, or opt for frozen veggies and canned beans and fish.

Foods to Limit

Type 2 diabetes does not require a person to give up their favorite foods. It's commonly assumed that there's a long list of foods to avoid at all costs, but this isn't the case. Some foods are just higher in nutritional value and contain less fat, sugar, and carbs. Most foods can be included in a diabetic eating plan, but people with diabetes may need to eat smaller portions of certain foods. You'll be in a better position to avoid diabetic complications if you can reduce your consumption of foods high in trans fat, saturated fat, and sugar. Here are some of the foods you should limit:

- ◆ Full fat dairy (butter, cheese, full cream milk, and sour cream)
- ◆ Fatty meats (dark meat poultry, fatty pork cuts, and poultry skin)
- ◆ Processed foods (chips, microwave popcorn, processed meats, and ready-made meals)
- ◆ Sweets (baked goods, candies, dessert, and ice cream)
- ◆ Sweetened beverages (juice, energy drinks, soda, and sweet tea)
- ◆ Trans fats (fried foods, coffee creamer, hydrogenated oils, and vegetable shortening)

3 Ways to Formulate a Diabetic Diet

Counting Carbs

Keeping track of the carbs we consume is beneficial. If we set a limit and keep track of how many carbs we're consuming, it's easier to keep our blood sugar levels in check. It's safest to work on your meal plan with a doctor or a registered dietician so that you know how many carbs you can consume and how frequently.

The Plate Method

Depending on the size of the plate or bowl we use to eat, we can overeat without realizing it. With the plate method, you can ensure that you're getting enough greens and proteins while limiting your carb intake.

This method works best when using a 9-inch plate.

- ♦ Fill half the plate with greens.
- ♦ Put protein in one quarter of the plate.
- ♦ Fill the other quarter of the plate with foods that contain carbs.

The Glycemic Index

People on a glycemic index diet eat food based on how it's going to affect their blood sugar level. The glycemic index (GI) assigns numbers to foods that contain carbohydrates according to how much they increase blood sugar. It's used mostly during meal prep, because the index doesn't specify the number of calories to consume and it doesn't advise on portion size either.

The index's main purpose is to allow people with diabetes to eat carbs that aren't going to raise their blood sugar levels too high. Following a low GI diet can result in weight loss and lessen your chances of developing cardiovascular disease.

GI values are assigned based on how food raises your blood sugar in comparison to pure glucose. They are divided into three categories:

- ♦ Low GI: 1-55
- ♦ Medium GI: 56-69
- ♦ High GI: 70 or higher

Once you're able to compare these values, you can make the healthiest choices for yourself. One of the drawbacks to looking only at GI levels is that while you may know the overall GI value of any given food, you may not know how the amount you eat changes that value.

For example, a whole watermelon has a GI value of 80. You would want to avoid eating the entire watermelon, but it's also low in carbohydrates and isn't likely to raise your blood glucose level significantly if just a small amount is consumed.

Glycemic load, or GL, was then formulated to show how your blood sugar changes when you eat a regular serving of a specific food. A 4.2 oz serving of watermelon has a GL value of 5. This means that it's safe to eat in small portions despite its high overall GI value.

Like GI values, GL values are divided into three categories:

- Low: 1-10
- Medium: 11-19
- High: 20 or higher

Here are some examples of foods and where they fall in the glycemic index:

- Low GI value: bran cereals, beans, chickpeas, kidney, leafy greens, lentils, and raw carrots
- Medium GI value: bananas, oat breakfast cereals, raw pineapples, and rye bread
- High GI value: white rice and white bread

People with diabetes are recommended to stick with a low GI diet, which is also good for appetite control. High GI foods cause a spike in blood glucose, which results in a fast insulin response that leaves you feeling hungry all over again.

The long-term effect of a low GI diet should be weight loss, because if your appetite is suppressed you're less likely to overeat.

Being Active Matters

When you have diabetes, physical activity makes your body more sensitive to insulin, which can help you manage the disease better. It also helps control your blood sugar levels and lessens the likelihood that you will develop heart disease and nerve damage.

Other benefits of physical activity include:

- Lowering LDL and raising HDL
- Losing weight
- Maintaining a healthy weight
- Better control of your blood pressure
- Improved sleep

The best way to benefit from physical activity is by getting at least 150 minutes of moderately intense exercise per week. Some of the best forms of exercise are:

- Brisk walking
- Cycling
- Dancing
- Jogging
- Swimming

There are a few things that people with diabetes should especially consider when exercising. Drink a good amount of water during activity to avoid dehydration. If you take insulin, be sure to check your blood sugar before engaging in any physical activity. If your blood sugar is below 100 mg/dl, it's best to eat a small snack to raise it a little bit so that it doesn't get too low. If your blood sugar is measuring above 240 mg/dl, then it might be too high for you to exert yourself safely.

Always check your blood glucose level after exercise as well. This will demonstrate how your body responds to exercise, which can assist you in avoiding potentially dangerous blood sugar fluctuations. Lastly, consider wearing cotton socks and a pair of athletic shoes every time you exercise. The socks keep your feet dry and warm; they also prevent the restriction of blood flow. Once your workout is complete, check your feet for any abrasions and call your doctor if abrasions don't start to show signs of healing after two days.

Now that you have an in-depth knowledge of type 2 diabetes and how to manage it, you are more than ready to start cooking up a storm!

Spaghetti Squash Fritters

Prep time: 15 minutes | Cook time: 8 minutes | Serves 4

2 cups cooked spaghetti squash
2 tablespoons unsalted butter, softened
1 large egg
¼ cup blanched finely ground

almond flour
2 stalks green onion, sliced
½ teaspoon garlic powder
1 teaspoon dried parsley

1. Remove excess moisture from the squash using a cheesecloth or kitchen towel. 2. Mix all ingredients in a large bowl. Form into four patties. 3. Cut a piece of parchment to fit your air fryer basket. Place each patty on the parchment and place into the air fryer basket. 4. Adjust the temperature to 400ºF (204ºC) and set the timer for 8 minutes. 5. Flip the patties halfway through the cooking time. Serve warm.

Per Serving:

calories: 146 | fat: 12g | protein: 4g | carbs: 7g | sugars: 3g | fiber: 2g | sodium: 36mg

Coddled Eggs and Smoked Salmon Toasts

Prep time: 5 minutes | Cook time: 10 minutes | Serves 4

2 teaspoons unsalted butter
4 large eggs
4 slices gluten-free or whole-grain rye bread
½ cup plain 2 percent Greek yogurt
4 ounces cold-smoked salmon, or 1 medium avocado, pitted,

peeled, and sliced
2 radishes, thinly sliced
1 Persian cucumber, thinly sliced
1 tablespoon chopped fresh chives
¼ teaspoon freshly ground black pepper

1. Pour 1 cup water into the Instant Pot and place a long-handled silicone steam rack into the pot. (If you don't have the long-handled rack, use the wire metal steam rack and a homemade sling) 2. Coat each of four 4-ounce ramekins with ½ teaspoon butter. Crack an egg into each ramekin. Place the ramekins on the steam rack in the pot. 3. Secure the lid and set the Pressure Release to Sealing. Select the Steam setting and set the cooking time for 3 minutes at low pressure. (The pot will take about 5 minutes to come up to pressure before the cooking program begins.) 4. While eggs are cooking, toast the bread in a toaster until golden brown. Spread the yogurt onto the toasted slices, put the toasts onto plates, and then top each toast with the smoked salmon, radishes, and cucumber. 5. When the cooking program ends, let the pressure release naturally for 5 minutes, then move the Pressure Release to Venting to release any remaining steam. Open the pot and, wearing heat-resistant mitts, grasp the handles of the steam rack and lift it out of the pot. 6. Run a knife around the inside edge of each ramekin to loosen the egg

and unmold one egg onto each toast. Sprinkle the chives and pepper on top and serve right away. 7. Note 8. The yolks of these eggs are fully cooked through. If you prefer the yolks slightly less solid, perform a quick pressure release rather than letting the pressure release naturally for 5 minutes.

Per Serving:

calories: 275 | fat: 12g | protein: 21g | carbs: 21g | sugars: 4g | fiber: 5g | sodium: 431mg

Griddle Corn Cakes

Prep time: 5 minutes | Cook time: 10 minutes | Serves 6

1 cup whole-wheat flour
2 teaspoons baking powder
1 tablespoon fructose
¾ cup low-fat buttermilk

1 egg white
2 tablespoons canola oil
1 cup corn kernels (frozen or fresh; if frozen, defrost)

1. In a medium bowl, combine the flour, baking powder, and fructose. 2. In another bowl, combine the buttermilk, egg white, and oil. Stir in the corn kernels. Slowly add the wet mixture to the dry ingredients, just to blend. A few lumps will remain. 3. On a heated nonstick griddle, pour ¼ cup batter per cake. Cook cakes for about 3 minutes, flip them over, and cook 1-2 minutes more, until golden brown. Serve.

Per Serving:

calories: 160 | fat: 6g | protein: 5g | carbs: 25g | sugars: 5g | fiber: 3g | sodium: 71mg

Sweet Quinoa Cereal

Prep time: 5 minutes | Cook time: 20 minutes | Serves 4

1 cup water
1 cup skim milk
1 cup uncooked quinoa, well rinsed
½ teaspoon ground cinnamon
Pinch sea salt

2 tablespoons granulated sweetener
1 teaspoon pure vanilla extract
¼ cup toasted chopped almonds
½ cup sliced strawberries

1. Put the water, milk, quinoa, cinnamon, and salt in a medium saucepan over medium-high heat. 2. Bring the mixture to a boil, then reduce the heat to low. 3. Simmer the quinoa cereal until most of the liquid is gone, about 15 minutes. 4. Remove the cereal from the heat and stir in the sweetener and vanilla. 5. Spoon the cereal into four bowls and top with the almonds and strawberries.

Per Serving:

calories: 243 | fat: 6g | protein: 9g | carbs: 39g | sugars: 9g | fiber: 4g | sodium: 30mg

Spinach and Feta Egg Bake

Prep time: 7 minutes | Cook time: 23 to 25 minutes | Serves 2

Avocado oil spray
⅓ cup diced red onion
1 cup frozen chopped spinach, thawed and drained
4 large eggs
¼ cup heavy (whipping) cream

Sea salt and freshly ground black pepper, to taste
¼ teaspoon cayenne pepper
½ cup crumbled feta cheese
¼ cup shredded Parmesan cheese

1. Spray a deep pan with oil. Put the onion in the pan, and place the pan in the air fryer basket. Set the air fryer to 350ºF (177ºC) and bake for 7 minutes. 2. Sprinkle the spinach over the onion. 3. In a medium bowl, beat the eggs, heavy cream, salt, black pepper, and cayenne. Pour this mixture over the vegetables. 4. Top with the feta and Parmesan cheese. Bake for 16 to 18 minutes, until the eggs are set and lightly brown.

Per Serving:

calories: 366 | fat: 26g | protein: 25g | carbs: 8g | fiber: 3g | sodium: 520mg

Low-Carb Peanut Butter Pancakes

Prep time: 10 minutes | Cook time: 10 minutes | Serves 2

1 cup almond flour
½ teaspoon baking soda
Pinch sea salt
2 large eggs
¼ cup sparkling water (plain,

unsweetened)
2 tablespoons canola oil, plus more for cooking
4 tablespoons peanut butter

1. Heat a nonstick griddle over medium-high heat. 2. In a small bowl, whisk together the almond flour, baking soda, and salt. 3. In a glass measuring cup, whisk together the eggs, water, and oil. 4. Pour the liquid ingredients into the dry ingredients, and mix gently until just combined. 5. Brush a small amount of canola oil onto the griddle. 6. Using all of the batter, spoon four pancakes onto the griddle. 7. Cook until set on one side, about 3 minutes. Flip with a spatula and continue cooking on the other side. 8. Before serving, spread each pancake with 1 tablespoon of the peanut butter.

Per Serving:

calories: 516 | fat: 43g | protein: 25g | carbs: 21g | sugars: 5g | fiber: 6g | sodium: 580mg

Breakfast Millet with Nuts and Strawberries

Prep time: 0 minutes | Cook time: 30 minutes | Serves 8

2 tablespoons coconut oil or unsalted butter
1½ cups millet
2⅔ cups water
½ teaspoon fine sea salt

1 cup unsweetened almond milk or other nondairy milk
1 cup chopped toasted pecans, almonds, or peanuts
4 cups sliced strawberries

1. Select the Sauté setting on the Instant Pot and melt the oil. Add the millet and cook for 4 minutes, until aromatic. Stir in the water and salt, making sure all of the grains are submerged in the liquid. 2. Secure the lid and set the Pressure Release to Sealing. Press the Cancel button to reset the cooking program, then select the Porridge, Pressure Cook, or Manual setting and set the cooking time for 12 minutes at high pressure. (The pot will take about 10 minutes to come up to pressure before the cooking program begins.) 3. When the cooking program ends, let the pressure release naturally for 10 minutes, then move the Pressure Release to Venting to release any remaining steam. Open the pot and use a fork to fluff and stir the millet. 4. Spoon the millet into bowls and top each serving with 2 tablespoons of the almond milk, then sprinkle with the nuts and top with the strawberries. Serve warm.

Per Serving:

calories: 270 | fat: 13g | protein: 6g | carbs: 35g | sugars: 4g | fiber: 6g | sodium: 151mg

Fresh Blueberry Pancakes

Prep time: 5 minutes | Cook time: 10 minutes | Serves 8

1 cup whole-wheat flour
1½ teaspoon baking powder
Zest of 1 lemon
1 teaspoon cinnamon
1 egg white

¾ cup low-fat buttermilk
¼ cup fat-free vanilla yogurt
1 tablespoon canola oil
½ cup fresh blueberries, washed and drained

1. In a medium bowl, combine the flour, baking powder, lemon zest, and cinnamon; set aside. 2. In a small bowl, combine the egg white, buttermilk, yogurt, and oil, and mix well. Add the wet mixture to the dry ingredients, stirring until moistened. Then gently fold in the blueberries. 3. Coat a griddle or skillet with cooking spray. Pour 2 tablespoons of batter for each pancake onto a hot griddle. Turn the pancakes when the tops are covered with tiny bubbles and the edges are golden brown.

Per Serving:

calories: 92 | fat: 2g | protein: 4g | carbs: 15g | sugars: 3g | fiber: 2g | sodium: 57mg

Plum Smoothie

Prep time: 5 minutes | Cook time: 0 minutes | Serves 2

4 ripe plums, pitted
1 cup skim milk
6 ounces 2 percent plain Greek

yogurt
4 ice cubes
¼ teaspoon ground nutmeg

1. Put the plums, milk, yogurt, ice, and nutmeg in a blender and blend until smooth. 2. Pour into two glasses and serve.

Per Serving:

calories: 144 | fat: 1g | protein: 14g | carbs: 20g | sugars: 17g | fiber: 2g | sodium: 82mg

Brussels Sprouts and Egg Scramble

Prep time: 5 minutes | Cook time: 20 minutes | Serves 4

Avocado oil cooking spray
4 slices low-sodium turkey bacon
20 Brussels sprouts, halved

lengthwise
8 large eggs
¼ cup crumbled feta, for garnish

1. Heat a large skillet over medium heat. When hot, coat the cooking surface with cooking spray and cook the bacon to your liking. 2. Carefully remove the bacon from the pan and set it on a plate lined with a paper towel to drain and cool. 3. Place the Brussels sprouts in the skillet cut-side down, and cook for 3 minutes. 4. Reduce the heat to medium-low. Flip the Brussels sprouts, move them to one side of the skillet, and cover. Cook for another 3 minutes. 5. Uncover. Cook the eggs to over-medium alongside the Brussels sprouts, or to your liking. 6. Crumble the bacon once it has cooled. 7. Divide the Brussels sprouts into 4 portions and top each portion with one-quarter of the crumbled bacon and 2 eggs. Add 1 tablespoon of feta to each portion.

Per Serving:

calories: 314 | fat: 22g | protein: 20g | carbs: 10g | sugars: 3g | fiber: 4g | sodium: 373mg

Bacon-and-Eggs Avocado

Prep time: 5 minutes | Cook time: 17 minutes | Serves 1

1 large egg
1 avocado, halved, peeled, and pitted
2 slices bacon

Fresh parsley, for serving (optional)
Sea salt flakes, for garnish (optional)

1. Spray the air fryer basket with avocado oil. Preheat the air fryer to 320ºF (160ºC). Fill a small bowl with cool water. 2. Soft-boil the egg: Place the egg in the air fryer basket. Air fry for 6 minutes for a soft yolk or 7 minutes for a cooked yolk. Transfer the egg to the bowl of cool water and let sit for 2 minutes. Peel and set aside. 3. Use a spoon to carve out extra space in the center of the avocado halves until the cavities are big enough to fit the soft-boiled egg. Place the soft-boiled egg in the center of one half of the avocado and replace the other half of the avocado on top, so the avocado appears whole on the outside. 4. Starting at one end of the avocado, wrap the bacon around the avocado to completely cover it. Use toothpicks to hold the bacon in place. 5. Place the bacon-wrapped avocado in the air fryer basket and air fry for 5 minutes. Flip the avocado over and air fry for another 5 minutes, or until the bacon is cooked to your liking. Serve on a bed of fresh parsley, if desired, and sprinkle with salt flakes, if desired. 6. Best served fresh. Store extras in an airtight container in the fridge for up to 4 days. Reheat in a preheated 320ºF (160ºC) air fryer for 4 minutes, or until heated through.

Per Serving:

calories: 605 | fat: 54g | protein: 17g | carbs: 18g | sugars: 2g | fiber: 14g | sodium: 329mg

Breakfast Panini

Prep time: 10 minutes | Cook time: 10 minutes | Serves 2

2 eggs, beaten
½ teaspoon salt-free seasoning blend
2 tablespoons chopped fresh chives
2 whole wheat thin bagels

2 slices tomato
2 thin slices onion
4 ultra-thin slices reduced-sodium deli ham
2 thin slices reduced-fat Cheddar cheese

1 Spray 8-inch skillet with cooking spray; heat skillet over medium heat. In medium bowl, beat eggs, seasoning and chives with fork or whisk until well mixed. Pour into skillet. As eggs begin to set at bottom and side, gently lift cooked portions with spatula so that thin, uncooked portion can flow to bottom. Avoid constant stirring. Cook 3 to 4 minutes or until eggs are thickened throughout but still moist and creamy; remove from heat. 2 Meanwhile, heat closed contact grill or panini maker 5 minutes. 3 For each panini, divide cooked eggs evenly between bottom halves of bagels. Top each with 1 slice each tomato and onion, 2 ham slices, 1 cheese slice and top half of bagel. Transfer filled panini to heated grill. Close cover, pressing down lightly. Cook 2 to 3 minutes or until browned and cheese is melted. Serve immediately.

Per Serving:

1 Panini: calories: 260 | fat: 7g | protein: 15g | carbs: 32g | sugars: 5g | fiber: 2g | sodium: 410mg

Easy Buckwheat Crêpes

Prep time: 5 minutes | Cook time: 15 minutes | Makes 12 crêpes

1 cup buckwheat flour
1¾ cups milk
⅛ teaspoon kosher salt
1 tablespoon extra-virgin olive

oil
½ tablespoon ground flaxseed (optional)

1. Combine the buckwheat flour, milk, salt, extra-virgin olive oil, and flaxseed (if using), in a bowl and whisk thoroughly, or in a blender and pulse until well combined. 2. Heat a nonstick medium skillet over medium heat. Once it's hot, add a ¼ cup of batter to the skillet, spreading it out evenly. Cook until bubbles appear and the edges crisp like a pancake, 1 to 3 minutes, then flip and cook for another 2 minutes. 3. Repeat until all the batter is used up, and the crêpes are cooked. Layer parchment paper or tea towels between the crêpes to keep them from sticking to one another while also keeping them warm until you're ready to eat. 4. Serve with the desired fillings. 5. Store any leftovers in an airtight container in the refrigerator for up to 3 days.

Per Serving:

1 crêpes: calories: 56 | fat: 2g | protein: 2g | carbs: 9g | sugars: 2g | fiber: 1g | sodium: 46mg

Blueberry Oat Mini Muffins

Prep time: 12 minutes | Cook time: 10 minutes | Serves 7

½ cup rolled oats
¼ cup whole wheat pastry flour or white whole wheat flour
½ tablespoon baking powder
½ teaspoon ground cardamom or ground cinnamon
⅛ teaspoon kosher salt
2 large eggs

½ cup plain Greek yogurt
2 tablespoons pure maple syrup
2 teaspoons extra-virgin olive oil
½ teaspoon vanilla extract
½ cup frozen blueberries (preferably small wild blueberries)

1. In a large bowl, stir together the oats, flour, baking powder, cardamom, and salt. 2. In a medium bowl, whisk together the eggs, yogurt, maple syrup, oil, and vanilla. 3. Add the egg mixture to oat mixture and stir just until combined. Gently fold in the blueberries. 4. Scoop the batter into each cup of the egg bite mold. 5. Pour 1 cup of water into the electric pressure cooker. Place the egg bite mold on the wire rack and carefully lower it into the pot. 6. Close and lock the lid of the pressure cooker. Set the valve to sealing. 7. Cook on high pressure for 10 minutes. 8. When the cooking is complete, allow the pressure to release naturally for 10 minutes, then quick release any remaining pressure. Hit Cancel. 9. Lift the wire rack out of the pot and place on a cooling rack for 5 minutes. Invert the mold onto the cooling rack to release the muffins. 10. Serve the muffins warm or refrigerate or freeze.

Per Serving:

calories: 117 | fat: 4g | protein: 5g | carbs: 15g | sugars: 4g | fiber: 2g | sodium: 89mg

Sweet Potato Breakfast Bites

Prep time: 5 minutes | Cook time: 17 to 18 minutes | Makes 12 bites

1½ cups precooked and cooled sweet potato
½ cup pure maple syrup
1 teaspoon pure vanilla extract
1¼ cups rolled oats
1 cup oat flour
½ teaspoon cinnamon
½ teaspoon pumpkin pie spice

(optional; can substitute another ½ teaspoon cinnamon)
2 teaspoons baking powder
¼ teaspoon sea salt
2-3 tablespoons raisins or sugar-free nondairy chocolate chips (optional)

1. Preheat the oven to 350°F and line a baking sheet with parchment paper. 2. In a medium bowl, mash the sweet potato. Add the syrup and vanilla and stir to combine. Add the oats, oat flour, cinnamon, pumpkin pie spice (if using), baking powder, and salt, and mix until well combined. Add the raisins or chips (if using), and stir to combine. Refrigerate for 5 to 10 minutes. Scoop 1½ tablespoon rounds of the mixture onto the parchment, spacing them 1 to 2 inches apart. Bake for 17 to 18 minutes, or until set to the touch. Remove from the oven, and let cool.

Per Serving:

calorie: 215 | fat: 2g | protein: 6g | carbs: 52g | sugars: 19g | fiber: 5g | sodium: 281mg

Spinach and Mushroom Mini Quiche

Prep time: 10 minutes | Cook time: 15 minutes | Serves 4

1 teaspoon olive oil, plus more for spraying
1 cup coarsely chopped mushrooms
1 cup fresh baby spinach, shredded

4 eggs, beaten
½ cup shredded Cheddar cheese
½ cup shredded Mozzarella cheese
¼ teaspoon salt
¼ teaspoon black pepper

1. Spray 4 silicone baking cups with olive oil and set aside. 2. In a medium sauté pan over medium heat, warm 1 teaspoon of olive oil. Add the mushrooms and sauté until soft, 3 to 4 minutes. 3. Add the spinach and cook until wilted, 1 to 2 minutes. Set aside. 4. In a medium bowl, whisk together the eggs, Cheddar cheese, Mozzarella cheese, salt, and pepper. 5. Gently fold the mushrooms and spinach into the egg mixture. 6. Pour ¼ of the mixture into each silicone baking cup. 7. Place the baking cups into the air fryer basket and air fry at 350°F (177°C) for 5 minutes. Stir the mixture in each ramekin slightly and air fry until the egg has set, an additional 3 to 5 minutes.

Per Serving:

calories: 156 | fat: 10g | protein: 14g | carbs: 2g | fiber: 1g | sodium: 411mg

Potato-Bacon Gratin

Prep time: 20 minutes | Cook time: 40 minutes | Serves 8

1 tablespoon olive oil
6-ounce bag fresh spinach
1 clove garlic, minced
4 large potatoes, peeled or unpeeled, divided
6-ounce Canadian bacon slices,

divided
5-ounce reduced-fat grated Swiss cheddar, divided
1 cup lower-sodium, lower-fat chicken broth

1. Set the Instant Pot to Sauté and pour in the olive oil. Cook the spinach and garlic in olive oil just until spinach is wilted (5 minutes or less). Turn off the instant pot. 2. Cut potatoes into thin slices about ¼" thick. 3. In a springform pan that will fit into the inner pot of your Instant Pot, spray it with nonstick spray then layer ⅓ the potatoes, half the bacon, ⅓ the cheese, and half the wilted spinach. 4. Repeat layers ending with potatoes. Reserve ⅓ cheese for later. 5. Pour chicken broth over all. 6. Wipe the bottom of your Instant Pot to soak up any remaining oil, then add in 2 cups of water and the steaming rack. Place the springform pan on top. 7. Close the lid and secure to the locking position. Be sure the vent is turned to sealing. Set for 35 minutes on Manual at high pressure. 8. Perform a quick release. 9. Top with the remaining cheese, then allow to stand 10 minutes before removing from the Instant Pot, cutting and serving.

Per Serving:

calories: 220 | fat: 7g | protein: 14g | carbs: 28g | sugars: 2g | fiber: 3g | sodium: 415mg

Breakfast Hash

Prep time: 10 minutes | Cook time: 30 minutes | Serves 6

Oil, for spraying
3 medium russet potatoes, diced
½ yellow onion, diced
1 green bell pepper, seeded and
diced

2 tablespoons olive oil
2 teaspoons granulated garlic
1 teaspoon salt
½ teaspoon freshly ground black
pepper

1. Line the air fryer basket with parchment and spray lightly with oil. 2. In a large bowl, mix together the potatoes, onion, bell pepper, and olive oil. 3. Add the garlic, salt, and black pepper and stir until evenly coated. 4. Transfer the mixture to the prepared basket. 5. Air fry at 400°F (204°C) for 20 to 30 minutes, shaking or stirring every 10 minutes, until browned and crispy. If you spray the potatoes with a little oil each time you stir, they will get even crispier.
Per Serving:
calories: 133 | fat: 5g | protein: 3g | carbs: 21g | fiber: 2g | sodium: 395mg

Instant Pot Hard-Boiled Eggs

Prep time: 10 minutes | Cook time: 5 minutes | Serves 7

1 cup water

6-8 eggs

1. Pour the water into the inner pot. Place the eggs in a steamer basket or rack that came with pot. 2. Close the lid and secure to the locking position. Be sure the vent is turned to sealing. Set for 5 minutes on Manual at high pressure. (It takes about 5 minutes for pressure to build and then 5 minutes to cook.) 3. Let pressure naturally release for 5 minutes, then do quick pressure release. 4. Place hot eggs into cool water to halt cooking process. You can peel cooled eggs immediately or refrigerate unpeeled.

Per Serving:
calories: 72 | fat: 5g | protein: 6g | carbs: 0g | sugars: 0g | fiber: 0g | sodium: 71mg

Cinnamon French Toast

Prep time: 10 minutes | Cook time: 20 minutes | Serves 8

3 eggs
2 cups low-fat milk
2 tablespoons maple syrup
15 drops liquid stevia
2 teaspoons vanilla extract
2 teaspoons cinnamon

Pinch salt
16-ounce whole wheat bread,
cubed and left out overnight to
go stale
1½ cups water

1. In a medium bowl, whisk together the eggs, milk, maple syrup, Stevia, vanilla, cinnamon, and salt. Stir in the cubes of whole wheat bread. 2. You will need a 7-inch round baking pan for this. Spray the inside with nonstick spray, then pour the bread mixture into the pan. 3. Place the trivet in the bottom of the inner pot, then pour in the water. 4. Make foil sling and insert it onto the trivet. Carefully

place the 7-inch pan on top of the foil sling/trivet. 5. Secure the lid to the locked position, then make sure the vent is turned to sealing. 6. Press the Manual button and use the "+/-" button to set the Instant Pot for 20 minutes. 7. When cook time is up, let the Instant Pot release naturally for 5 minutes, then quick release the rest

Per Serving:
calories: 75 | fat: 3g | protein: 4g | carbs: 7g | sugars: 6g | fiber: 0g | sodium: 74mg

Tropical Steel Cut Oats

Prep time: 5 minutes | Cook time: 5 minutes | Serves 4

1 cup steel cut oats
1 cup unsweetened almond milk
2 cups coconut water or water
¾ cup frozen chopped peaches
¾ cup frozen mango chunks

1 (2-inch) vanilla bean, scraped
(seeds and pod)
Ground cinnamon
¼ cup chopped unsalted
macadamia nuts

1. In the electric pressure cooker, combine the oats, almond milk, coconut water, peaches, mango chunks, and vanilla bean seeds and pod. Stir well. 2. Close and lock the lid of the pressure cooker. Set the valve to sealing. 3. Cook on high pressure for 5 minutes. 4. When the cooking is complete, allow the pressure to release naturally for 10 minutes, then quick release any remaining pressure. Hit Cancel. 5. Once the pin drops, unlock and remove the lid. 6. Discard the vanilla bean pod and stir well. 7. Spoon the oats into 4 bowls. Top each serving with a sprinkle of cinnamon and 1 tablespoon of the macadamia nuts.

Per Serving:
calories: 127 | fat: 7g | protein: 2g | carbs: 14g | sugars: 8g | fiber: 3g | sodium: 167mg

Cinnamon-Almond Green Smoothie

Prep time: 4 minutes | Cook time: 0 minutes | Serves 2

1½ cups nonfat milk
2 tablespoons finely ground
flaxseed
1 tablespoon almond butter
1 (8-ounce) container plain
nonfat Greek yogurt
1 cup frozen spinach

1 small apple, peeled, cored,
and finely chopped
1 teaspoon vanilla extract
1 teaspoon cinnamon
Stevia, for sweetening
4 to 6 ice cubes (optional)

1. In a blender, combine the milk, flaxseed, and almond butter. Blend for 10 seconds on medium. 2. Add the yogurt, spinach, apple, vanilla, cinnamon, stevia, and ice cubes (if using). Blend for about 1 minute, or until smooth and creamy. 3. Pour into 2 glasses and sip to your health!

Per Serving:
calories: 292 | fat: 9g | protein: 24g | carbs: 32g | sugars: 18g | fiber: 8g | sodium: 200mg

Orange-Berry Pancake Syrup

Prep time: 5 minutes | Cook time: 0 minutes | Serves 8

2 cups raspberries, fresh or frozen
½ cup fresh orange juice

¼ cup pure maple syrup
Pinch of sea salt

1. In a blender, combine the raspberries, juice, syrup, and salt. Puree until smooth, stopping to scrape down the blender as needed. If the mixture is too thick (particularly if using frozen berries), you may need to scrape down more often or add a tablespoon or two of water to assist with the blending. Once it's smooth, transfer the syrup to a jar or other airtight container and store it in the refrigerator. It keeps for about a week in the fridge.

Per Serving:

calorie: 65 | fat: 0.4g | protein: 1g | carbs: 16g | sugars: 10g | fiber: 4g | sodium: 38mg

Ginger Blackberry Bliss Smoothie Bowl

Prep time: 5 minutes | Cook time: 0 minutes | Serves 2

½ cup frozen blackberries
1 cup plain Greek yogurt
1 cup baby spinach
½ cup unsweetened almond

milk
½ teaspoon peeled and grated fresh ginger
¼ cup chopped pecans

1. In a blender or food processor, combine the blackberries, yogurt, spinach, almond milk, and ginger. Blend until smooth. 2. Spoon the mixture into two bowls. 3. Top each bowl with 2 tablespoons of chopped pecans and serve.

Per Serving:

calories: 211 | fat: 11g | protein: 10g | carbs: 18g | sugars: 13g | fiber: 4g | sodium: 149mg

Berry Almond Smoothie

Prep time: 5 minutes | Cook time: 0 minutes | Serves 4

2 cups frozen berries of choice
1 cup plain low-fat Greek yogurt

1 cup unsweetened vanilla almond milk
½ cup natural almond butter

1. Put the berries, yogurt, almond milk, and almond butter into a blender and blend until smooth. If the smoothie is too thick, add more almond milk to thin. 2. Complete the meal: Pair this smoothie with Simple Grain-Free Biscuits, Coconut Pancakes, or Orange Muffins for a proper portion of calories and carbs.

Per Serving:

calories: 293 | fat: 19g | protein: 10g | carbs: 19g | sugars: 12g | fiber: 6g | sodium: 84mg

Cinnamon Bun Oatmeal

Prep time: 5 minutes | Cook time: 15 minutes | Serves 3

1½ cups rolled oats
⅓ cup chopped dates
1 teaspoon cinnamon
Pinch of sea salt (optional)
2 cups water
3 tablespoons raisins

¾ cup + 1-2 tablespoons low-fat nondairy milk
Sprinkle of cinnamon
3 teaspoons coconut sugar (optional)

1. In a pot over high heat, combine the oats, dates, cinnamon, salt, and water, and bring to a boil. Reduce the heat to low and let simmer for 7 to 8 minutes, until the water is absorbed and the oats are softening. Add the raisins and ¾ cup of the milk, and cook for another 6 to 7 minutes, or until the raisins have softened. Remove from the heat and let stand for a few minutes. The oatmeal will thicken more as it sits, so add the remaining 1 to 2 tablespoons of milk if needed to thin. Top each serving with the cinnamon and 1 teaspoon of the coconut sugar (if using).

Per Serving:

calorie: 251 | fat: 3 | protein: 7g | carbs: 51g | sugars: 18g | fiber: 7g | sodium: 34mg

Avocado-Tofu Scramble with Roasted Potatoes

Prep time: 5 minutes | Cook time: 25 minutes | Serves 4

1½ pounds small potatoes, cut into bite-size pieces
4 tablespoons plant-based oil (safflower, olive, or grapeseed), divided
Kosher salt
Freshly ground black pepper
1 ounce water
2 teaspoons ground cumin

2 teaspoons turmeric
¼ teaspoon paprika
1 yellow onion, finely chopped
1 bell pepper, finely chopped
3 cups kale, torn into bite-size pieces
3 ounces firm tofu, drained and crumbled
1 avocado, diced, for garnish

1. Preheat the oven to 425°F. Line a baking sheet with parchment paper. 2. Combine the potatoes with 2 tablespoons of oil and a pinch each of salt and pepper on the baking sheet, then toss them to coat. Roast for 20 to 25 minutes or until tender and golden brown. 3. Meanwhile, stir together the water, cumin, turmeric, and paprika until well mixed to make the sauce. Set aside. 4. Heat the remaining 2 tablespoons of oil in a large skillet over medium heat. Add the onion and bell pepper and sauté for 3 to 5 minutes. Season with a pinch of salt and pepper. 5. Add the kale to the skillet, cover, and allow the steam to cook the kale for about 2 minutes. 6. Remove the lid and, using a spatula, push the vegetables to one side of the skillet and place the tofu and sauce on the empty side. Stir until the tofu is heated through, 3 to 5 minutes. Stir the tofu and vegetables. 7. Serve the tofu scramble with the roasted potatoes on the side and garnished with avocado.

Per Serving:

calories: 385 | fat: 23g | protein: 8g | carbs: 42g | sugars: 3g | fiber: 9g | sodium: 25mg

Brussels Sprout Hash and Eggs

Prep time: 15 minutes | Cook time: 15 minutes | Serves 4

3 teaspoons extra-virgin olive oil, divided
1 pound Brussels sprouts, sliced
2 garlic cloves, thinly sliced
¼ teaspoon salt
Juice of 1 lemon
4 eggs

1. In a large skillet, heat 1½ teaspoons of oil over medium heat. Add the Brussels sprouts and toss. Cook, stirring regularly, for 6 to 8 minutes until browned and softened. Add the garlic and continue to cook until fragrant, about 1 minute. Season with the salt and lemon juice. Transfer to a serving dish. 2. In the same pan, heat the remaining 1½ teaspoons of oil over medium-high heat. Crack the eggs into the pan. Fry for 2 to 4 minutes, flip, and continue cooking to desired doneness. Serve over the bed of hash.

Per Serving:

calories: 158 | fat: 9g | protein: 10g | carbs: 12g | sugars: 4g | fiber: 4g | sodium: 234mg

Grain-Free Apple Cinnamon Cake

Prep time: 10 minutes | Cook time: 50 minutes | Serves 8

2 cups almond flour
½ cup Lakanto Monkfruit Sweetener Golden
1½ teaspoons ground cinnamon
1 teaspoon baking powder
½ teaspoon fine sea salt
½ cup plain 2 percent Greek yogurt
2 large eggs
½ teaspoon pure vanilla extract
1 small apple, chopped into small pieces

1. Pour 1 cup water into the Instant Pot. Line the base of a 7 by 3-inch round cake pan with parchment paper. Butter the sides of the pan and the parchment or coat with nonstick cooking spray. 2. In a medium bowl, whisk together the almond flour, sweetener, cinnamon, baking powder, and salt. In a smaller bowl, whisk together the yogurt, eggs, and vanilla until no streaks of yolk remain. Add the wet mixture to the dry mixture and stir just until the dry ingredients are evenly moistened, then fold in the apple. The batter will be very thick. 3. Transfer the batter to the prepared pan and, using a rubber spatula, spread it in an even layer. Cover the pan tightly with aluminum foil. Place the pan on a long-handled silicone steam rack, then, holding the handles of the steam rack, lower it into the Instant Pot. (If you don't have the long-handled rack, use the wire metal steam rack and a homemade sling) 4. Secure the lid and set the Pressure Release to Sealing. Select the Cake, Pressure Cook, or Manual setting and set the cooking time for 40 minutes at high pressure. (The pot will take about 10 minutes to come up to pressure before the cooking program begins.) 5. When the cooking program ends, let the pressure release naturally for 10 minutes, then move the Pressure Release to Venting to release any remaining steam. Open the pot and, wearing heat-resistant mitts, grasp the handles of the steam rack and lift it out of the pot. Uncover the pan, taking care not to get burned by the steam or to drip condensation onto the cake. Let the cake cool in the pan on a cooling rack for about 5 minutes. 6. Run a butter knife around the edge of the pan to loosen the cake from the pan sides. Invert the cake onto the rack, lift off the pan, and peel off the parchment. Let cool for 15 minutes, then invert the cake onto a serving plate. Cut into eight wedges and serve.

Per Serving:

calories: 219 | fat: 16g | protein: 9g | carbs: 20g | sugars: 8g | fiber: 16g | sodium: 154mg

Smoked Salmon and Asparagus Quiche Cups

Prep time: 15 minutes | Cook time: 15 minutes | Serves 2

Nonstick cooking spray
4 asparagus spears, cut into ½-inch pieces
2 tablespoons finely chopped onion
3 ounces (85 g) smoked salmon
(skinless and boneless), chopped
3 large eggs
2 tablespoons 2% milk
¼ teaspoon dried dill
Pinch ground white pepper

1. Pour 1½ cups of water into the electric pressure cooker and insert a wire rack or trivet. 2. Lightly spray the bottom and sides of the ramekins with nonstick cooking spray. Divide the asparagus, onion, and salmon between the ramekins. 3. In a measuring cup with a spout, whisk together the eggs, milk, dill, and white pepper. Pour half of the egg mixture into each ramekin. Loosely cover the ramekins with aluminum foil. 4. Carefully place the ramekins inside the pot on the rack. 5. Close and lock the lid of the pressure cooker. Set the valve to sealing. 6. Cook on high pressure for 15 minutes. 7. When the cooking is complete, hit Cancel and quick release the pressure. 8. Once the pin drops, unlock and remove the lid. 9. Carefully remove the ramekins from the pot. Cool, covered, for 5 minutes. 10. Run a small silicone spatula or a knife around the edge of each ramekin. Invert each quiche onto a small plate and serve.

Per Serving:

calories: 180 | fat: 9g | protein: 20g | carbs: 3g | sugars: 1g | fiber: 1g | sodium: 646mg

High-Protein Oatmeal

Prep time: 2 minutes | Cook time: 8 minutes | Serves 1

8 ounces vanilla soy milk
½ cup oats
1 tablespoon chia seeds
¼ cup blueberries
1 tablespoon sliced and toasted almonds

1. In a medium saucepan over medium-high heat, stir together the soy milk and oats. 2. Bring to a boil, reduce the heat to low, and simmer, stirring frequently, until cooked and tender, 5 to 8 minutes. 3. Remove the oatmeal from the heat and serve topped with chia seeds, blueberries, and almonds. 4. Store any leftovers in an airtight container in the refrigerator for up to 5 days.

Per Serving:

calories: 480 | fat: 14g | protein: 22g | carbs: 70g | sugars: 5g | fiber: 13g | sodium: 147mg

Veggie-Stuffed Omelet

Prep time: 15 minutes | Cook time: 10 minutes | Serves 1

1 teaspoon olive or canola oil
2 tablespoons chopped red bell pepper
1 tablespoon chopped onion
¼ cup sliced fresh mushrooms
1 cup loosely packed fresh baby spinach leaves, rinsed

½ cup fat-free egg product or 2 eggs, beaten
1 tablespoon water
Pinch salt
Pinch pepper
1 tablespoon shredded reduced-fat Cheddar cheese

1 In 8-inch nonstick skillet, heat oil over medium-high heat. Add bell pepper, onion and mushrooms to oil. Cook 2 minutes, stirring frequently, until onion is tender. Stir in spinach; continue cooking and stirring just until spinach wilts. Transfer vegetables from pan to small bowl. 2 In medium bowl, beat egg product, water, salt and pepper with fork or whisk until well mixed. Reheat same skillet over medium-high heat. Quickly pour egg mixture into pan. While sliding pan back and forth rapidly over heat, quickly stir with spatula to spread eggs continuously over bottom of pan as they thicken. Let stand over heat a few seconds to lightly brown bottom of omelet. Do not overcook; omelet will continue to cook after folding. 3 Place cooked vegetable mixture over half of omelet; top with cheese. With spatula, fold other half of omelet over vegetables. Gently slide out of pan onto plate. Serve immediately.

Per Serving:

calorie: 140 | fat: 5g | protein: 16g | carbs: 6g | sugars: 3g | fiber: 2g | sodium: 470mg

Eggplant Breakfast Sandwich

Prep time: 5 minutes | Cook time: 20 minutes | Serves 2 to 4

2 tablespoons extra-virgin olive oil, divided
1 eggplant, cut into 8 (½-inch-thick) rounds
¼ teaspoon kosher salt
¼ teaspoon freshly ground black

pepper
4 large eggs
1 garlic clove, minced
4 cups fresh baby spinach
Hot sauce or harissa (optional)

1. Heat 1 tablespoon of extra-virgin olive oil in a large skillet over medium heat. Add the eggplant in a single layer and cook until tender and browned on both sides, 4 to 5 minutes per side. Transfer the eggplant from the skillet to a plate and season it with salt and pepper. Wipe out the skillet and set aside. 2. Meanwhile, place a large saucepan filled three-quarters full with water over medium-high heat and bring it to a simmer. Carefully break the eggs into small, individual bowls and pour slowly into a fine-mesh strainer over another bowl. Allow the excess white to drain, then lower the strainer into the water. Tilt the egg out into the water. Repeat with the remaining eggs. Swirl the water occasionally as the eggs cook and whites set, about 4 minutes. Remove the eggs with a slotted spoon, transfer them to a paper towel, and drain. 3. Heat the remaining 1 tablespoon of extra-virgin olive oil over medium heat in the large skillet and add the garlic and spinach. Cook until the spinach is wilted, about 1 minute. 4. Place one eggplant round on each of four plates and evenly divide the spinach among the rounds.

Top the spinach with a poached egg on each sandwich and place the remaining eggplant round on the egg. Serve with hot sauce or harissa (if using).

Per Serving:

calories: 174 | fat: 12g | protein: 9g | carbs: 10g | sugars: 5g | fiber: 5g | sodium: 243mg

Veggie-Loaded All-American Breakfast

Prep time: 10 minutes | Cook time: 15 minutes | Serves 1

1 teaspoon cooking oil
½ small sweet potato, cut into small cubes
1 cup (67 g) coarsely chopped kale leaves, stems removed
2 ounces (57 g) cooked low-sodium chicken sausage

2 large eggs
1 cup (125 g) fresh berries of choice
1 slice whole-grain bread
2 tablespoons (22 g) mashed avocado

1. Heat the oil in a large skillet over medium heat. Tilt and turn the skillet to coat the bottom with the oil. 2. Add the sweet potato, kale, and chicken sausage to the skillet. Sauté them for 10 to 15 minutes, or until the sweet potato is tender and the kale is soft. 3. Transfer the veggie mixture to a plate and return the skillet to the heat. Crack the eggs into the skillet and prepare them as desired to your preferred doneness. Once they are cooked, serve them with the veggie mixture, berries, bread, and avocado.

Per Serving:

calorie: 561 | fat: 25g | protein: 29g | carbs: 10g | sugars: 21g | fiber: 10g | sodium: 820mg

Broccoli-Mushroom Frittata

Prep time: 10 minutes | Cook time: 20 minutes | Serves 2

1 tablespoon olive oil
1½ cups broccoli florets, finely chopped
½ cup sliced brown mushrooms
¼ cup finely chopped onion

½ teaspoon salt
¼ teaspoon freshly ground black pepper
6 eggs
¼ cup Parmesan cheese

1. In a nonstick cake pan, combine the olive oil, broccoli, mushrooms, onion, salt, and pepper. Stir until the vegetables are thoroughly coated with oil. Place the cake pan in the air fryer basket and set the air fryer to 400°F (204°C). Air fry for 5 minutes until the vegetables soften. 2. Meanwhile, in a medium bowl, whisk the eggs and Parmesan until thoroughly combined. Pour the egg mixture into the pan and shake gently to distribute the vegetables. Air fry for another 15 minutes until the eggs are set. 3. Remove from the air fryer and let sit for 5 minutes to cool slightly. Use a silicone spatula to gently lift the frittata onto a plate before serving.

Per Serving:

calories: 329 | fat: 23g | protein: 24g | carbs: 6g | fiber: 0g | sodium: 793mg

Spicy Tomato Smoothie

Prep time: 5 minutes | Cook time: 0 minutes | Serves 2

1 cup tomato juice
2 tomatoes, diced
¼ English cucumber

Juice of 1 lemon
1 teaspoon hot sauce
4 ice cubes

1. Put the tomato juice, tomatoes, cucumber, lemon juice, hot sauce, and ice cubes in a blender and blend until smooth. 2. Pour into two glasses and serve.

Per Serving:

calories: 51 | fat: 1g | protein: 2g | carbs: 11g | sugars: 7g | fiber: 2g | sodium: 34mg

Easy Sweet Potato and Egg Sandwiches

Prep time: 5 minutes | Cook time: 10 minutes | Serves 2

1 large sweet potato, sliced into
4 (¼-inch [6-mm]-thick) rounds
2 ounces (57 g) shredded

mozzarella cheese
Cooking oil spray, as needed
2 large eggs

1. Preheat the oven to broil. Line a large baking sheet with parchment paper. 2. Arrange the sweet potato rounds evenly on the prepared baking sheet. Broil the sweet potatoes for 4 to 6 minutes, until they are beginning to brown. Make sure to keep an eye on them so they don't burn. 3. Remove the sweet potatoes from the oven and add 1 ounce (28 g) of mozzarella cheese per sweet potato round to two of the rounds. Remove the plain sweet potato rounds from the baking sheet, and return the baking sheet with the cheese-topped sweet potatoes to the oven. Broil the rounds for 1 to 2 minutes, until the cheese begins to brown. 4. Remove the baking sheet from the oven and set it aside with the other sweet potato rounds. 5. Heat a medium skillet over medium heat. Spray it with the cooking oil spray and add the eggs. Scramble the eggs to your preferred doneness. 6. Top the cheesy sweet potato rounds with some of the scrambled eggs and the remaining sweet potato rounds. Slice the sandwiches and serve them.

Per Serving:

calorie: 222 | fat: 9g | protein: 15g | carbs: 20g | sugars: 4g | fiber: 3g | sodium: 297mg

White Bean-Oat Waffles

Prep time: 10 minutes | Cook time: 20 minutes | Serves 2

1 large egg white
2 tablespoons finely ground flaxseed
½ cup water
¼ teaspoon salt
1 teaspoon vanilla extract
½ cup cannellini beans, drained

and rinsed
1 teaspoon coconut oil
1 teaspoon liquid stevia
½ cup old-fashioned rolled oats
Extra-virgin olive oil cooking spray

1. In a blender, combine the egg white, flaxseed, water, salt, vanilla, cannellini beans, coconut oil, and stevia. Blend on high for 90 seconds. 2. Add the oats. Blend for 1 minute more. 3. Preheat the waffle iron. The batter will thicken to the correct consistency while the waffle iron preheats. 4. Spray the heated waffle iron with cooking spray. 5. Add ¾ cup of batter. Close the waffle iron. Cook for 6 to 8 minutes, or until done. Repeated with the remaining batter. 6. Serve hot, with your favorite sugar-free topping.

Per Serving:

calories: 294 | fat: 10g | protein: 13g | carbs: 38g | sugars: 4g | fiber: 9g | sodium: 404mg

Butternut Squash and Ricotta Frittata

Prep time: 10 minutes | Cook time: 33 minutes | Serves 2 to 3

1 cup cubed (½-inch) butternut
squash (5½ ounces / 156 g)
2 tablespoons olive oil
Kosher salt and freshly ground
black pepper, to taste

4 fresh sage leaves, thinly sliced
6 large eggs, lightly beaten
½ cup ricotta cheese
Cayenne pepper

1. In a bowl, toss the squash with the olive oil and season with salt and black pepper until evenly coated. Sprinkle the sage on the bottom of a cake pan and place the squash on top. Place the pan in the air fryer and bake at 400°F (204°C) for 10 minutes. Stir to incorporate the sage, then cook until the squash is tender and lightly caramelized at the edges, about 3 minutes more. 2. Pour the eggs over the squash, dollop the ricotta all over, and sprinkle with cayenne. Bake at 300°F (149°C) until the eggs are set and the frittata is golden brown on top, about 20 minutes. Remove the pan from the air fryer and cut the frittata into wedges to serve.

Per Serving:

calories: 289 | fat: 22g | protein: 18g | carbs: 5g | fiber: 1g | sodium: 184mg

Cottage Cheese Almond Pancakes

Prep time: 10 minutes | Cook time: 20 minutes | Serves 4

2 cups low-fat cottage cheese
4 egg whites
2 eggs

1 tablespoon pure vanilla extract
1½ cups almond flour
Nonstick cooking spray

1. Place the cottage cheese, egg whites, eggs, and vanilla in a blender and pulse to combine. 2. Add the almond flour to the blender and blend until smooth. 3. Place a large nonstick skillet over medium heat and lightly coat it with cooking spray. 4. Spoon ¼ cup of batter per pancake, 4 at a time, into the skillet. Cook the pancakes until the bottoms are firm and golden, about 4 minutes. 5. Flip the pancakes over and cook the other side until they are cooked through, about 3 minutes. 6. Remove the pancakes to a plate and repeat with the remaining batter. 7. Serve with fresh fruit.

Per Serving:

calories: 441 | fat: 32g | protein: 30g | carbs: 9g | sugars: 3g | fiber: 5g | sodium: 528mg

Summer Veggie Scramble

Prep time: 10 minutes | Cook time: 10 minutes | Serves 4

1 teaspoon extra-virgin olive oil
1 scallion, white and green parts, finely chopped
½ yellow bell pepper, seeded and chopped
½ zucchini, diced
8 large eggs, beaten

1 tomato, cored, seeded, and diced
2 teaspoons chopped fresh oregano
Sea salt
Freshly ground black pepper

1. Place a large skillet over medium heat and add the olive oil. 2. Add the scallion, bell pepper, and zucchini to the skillet and sauté for about 5 minutes. 3. Pour in the eggs and, using a wooden spoon or spatula, scramble them until thick, firm curds form and the eggs are cooked through, about 5 minutes. 4. Add the tomato and oregano to the skillet and stir to incorporate. 5. Serve seasoned with salt and pepper.

Per Serving:

calories: 170 | fat: 11g | protein: 14g | carbs: 4g | sugars: 1g | fiber: 1g | sodium: 157mg

Savory Grits

Prep time: 5 minutes | Cook time: 7 minutes | Serves 4

2 cups water
1 cup fat-free milk

1 cup stone-ground corn grits

1. In a heavy-bottomed pot, bring the water and milk to a simmer over medium heat. 2. Gradually add the grits, stirring continuously. 3. Reduce the heat to low, cover, and cook, stirring often, for 5 to 7 minutes, or until the grits are soft and tender. Serve and enjoy.

Per Serving:

calories: 166 | fat: 1g | protein: 6g | carbs: 34g | sugars: 3g | fiber: 1g | sodium: 35mg

Shredded Potato Omelet

Prep time: 15 minutes | Cook time: 20 minutes | Serves 6

3 slices bacon, cooked and crumbled
2 cups shredded cooked potatoes
¼ cup minced onion
¼ cup minced green bell pepper
1 cup egg substitute

¼ cup fat-free milk
¼ teaspoon salt
⅛ teaspoon black pepper
1 cup 75%-less-fat shredded cheddar cheese
1 cup water

1. With nonstick cooking spray, spray the inside of a round baking dish that will fit in your Instant Pot inner pot. 2. Sprinkle the bacon, potatoes, onion, and bell pepper around the bottom of the baking dish. 3. Mix together the egg substitute, milk, salt, and pepper in mixing bowl. Pour over potato mixture. 4. Top with cheese. 5. Add

water, place the steaming rack into the bottom of the inner pot and then place the round baking dish on top. 6. Close the lid and secure to the locking position. Be sure the vent is turned to sealing. Set for 20 minutes on Manual at high pressure. 7. Let the pressure release naturally. 8. Carefully remove the baking dish with the handles of the steaming rack and allow to stand 10 minutes before cutting and serving.

Per Serving:

calories: 130 | fat: 3g | protein: 12g | carbs: 13g | sugars: 2g | fiber: 2g | sodium: 415mg

Peaches and Cream Yogurt Bowl

Prep time: 5 minutes | Cook time: 0 minutes | Serves 1

6 ounces (170 g) plain Greek yogurt
½ teaspoon pure vanilla extract
½ teaspoon ground cinnamon
1 medium peach, sliced to

desired thickness, or 1 cup (250 g) frozen sliced peaches
1 tablespoon (15 g) almond butter
1 teaspoon honey (optional)

1. In a small bowl, stir together the yogurt, vanilla, and cinnamon. Add the peach slices and drizzle the yogurt bowl with the almond butter and honey (if using).

Per Serving:

calorie: 361 | fat: 19g | protein: 24g | carbs: 27g | sugars: 21g | fiber: 6g | sodium: 91mg

Whole-Grain Strawberry Pancakes

Prep time: 30 minutes | Cook time: 10 minutes | Serves 7

1½ cups whole wheat flour
3 tablespoons sugar
1 teaspoon baking powder
½ teaspoon baking soda
½ teaspoon salt
3 eggs or ¾ cup fat-free egg product
1 container (6 ounces) vanilla

low-fat yogurt
¾ cup water
3 tablespoons canola oil
1¾ cups sliced fresh strawberries
1 container (6 ounces) strawberry low-fat yogurt

1 Heat griddle to 375°F or heat 12-inch skillet over medium heat. Grease with canola oil if necessary (or spray with cooking spray before heating). 2 In large bowl, mix flour, sugar, baking powder, baking soda and salt; set aside. In medium bowl, beat eggs, vanilla yogurt, water and oil with egg beater or whisk until well blended. Pour egg mixture all at once into flour mixture; stir until moistened. 3 For each pancake, pour slightly less than ¼ cup batter onto hot griddle. Cook pancakes 1 to 2 minutes or until bubbly on top, puffed and dry around edges. Turn; cook other sides 1 to 2 minutes or until golden brown. 4 Top each serving with ¼ cup sliced strawberries and 1 to 2 tablespoons strawberry yogurt.

Per Serving:

calories: 260 | fat: 9g | protein: 8g | carbs: 34g | sugars: 13g | fiber: 4g | sodium: 380mg

Ratatouille Baked Eggs

Prep time: 20 minutes | Cook time: 50 minutes | Serves 4

2 teaspoons extra-virgin olive oil
½ sweet onion, finely chopped
2 teaspoons minced garlic
½ small eggplant, peeled and diced
1 green zucchini, diced
1 yellow zucchini, diced
1 red bell pepper, seeded and diced

3 tomatoes, seeded and chopped
1 tablespoon chopped fresh oregano
1 tablespoon chopped fresh basil
Pinch red pepper flakes
Sea salt
Freshly ground black pepper
4 large eggs

1. Preheat the oven to 350°F. 2. Place a large ovenproof skillet over medium heat and add the olive oil. 3. Sauté the onion and garlic until softened and translucent, about 3 minutes. Stir in the eggplant and sauté for about 10 minutes, stirring occasionally. Stir in the zucchini and pepper and sauté for 5 minutes. 4. Reduce the heat to low and cover. Cook until the vegetables are soft, about 15 minutes. 5. Stir in the tomatoes, oregano, basil, and red pepper flakes, and cook 10 minutes more. Season the ratatouille with salt and pepper. 6. Use a spoon to create four wells in the mixture. Crack an egg into each well. 7. Place the skillet in the oven and bake until the eggs are firm, about 5 minutes. 8. Remove from the oven. Serve the eggs with a generous scoop of vegetables.

Per Serving:
calories: 164 | fat: 8g | protein: 10g | carbs: 16g | sugars: 8g | fiber: 5g | sodium: 275mg

Cauliflower Scramble

Prep time: 5 minutes | Cook time: 5 minutes | Serves 3

1 package (12-16 ounces) medium or medium-firm tofu
3½-4 cups steamed cauliflower florets, lightly mashed
½ teaspoon onion powder
½ teaspoon garlic powder
½ teaspoon sea salt
¼ teaspoon prepared mustard

½ teaspoon black salt (or another ¼ teaspoon sea salt)
½ tablespoon tahini
2½-3 tablespoons nutritional yeast
2-3 cups chopped spinach or kale

1. In a large nonstick skillet, use your fingers to crumble the tofu, breaking it up well. Place the skillet over medium heat. Add the cauliflower, onion powder, garlic powder, sea salt, mustard, and black salt. Cook for 3 to 4 minutes, then add the tahini and nutritional yeast and stir to combine thoroughly. If the mixture is sticking, add 1 to 2 tablespoons water. Add the spinach or kale during the final minutes of cooking, stirring until just nicely wilted and still bright green. Taste, season as desired, and serve.
Per Serving:
calorie: 196 | fat: 9g | protein: 21g | carbs: 16g | sugars: 3g | fiber: 10g | sodium: 862mg

Breakfast Egg Bites

Prep time: 10 minutes | Cook time: 25 minutes | Serves 8

Nonstick cooking spray
6 eggs, beaten
¼ cup unsweetened plain almond milk
1 red bell pepper, diced
1 cup chopped spinach

¼ cup crumbled goat cheese
½ cup sliced brown mushrooms
¼ cup sliced sun-dried tomatoes
Salt
Freshly ground black pepper

1. Preheat the oven to 350°F. Spray 8 muffin cups of a 12-cup muffin tin with nonstick cooking spray. Set aside. 2. In a large mixing bowl, combine the eggs, almond milk, bell pepper, spinach, goat cheese, mushrooms, and tomatoes. Season with salt and pepper. 3. Fill the prepared muffin cups three-fourths full with the egg mixture. Bake for 20 to 25 minutes until the eggs are set. Let cool slightly and remove the egg bites from the muffin tin. 4. Serve warm, or store in an airtight container in the refrigerator for up to 5 days or in the freezer for up to 1 month.

Per Serving:
calories: 68 | fat: 4g | protein: 6g | carbs: 3g | sugars: 2g | fiber: 1g | sodium: 126mg

Mini Spinach-Broccoli Quiches

Prep time: 5 minutes | Cook time: 35 minutes | Serves 2

Extra-virgin olive oil cooking spray
1 cup frozen broccoli florets
½ cup frozen spinach
2 large eggs
2 large egg whites
¼ cup unsweetened almond

milk, or nonfat dairy milk
Salt, to season
Freshly ground black pepper, to season
2 tablespoons fresh dill, divided
Shredded nonfat cheese, for garnish (optional)

1. Preheat the oven to 400°F. 2. Spray two (8-ounce) ramekins with cooking spray. 3. In a small microwave-safe dish, mix together the broccoli and spinach. Place in the microwave and thaw on high for 30 seconds. Remove from the microwave and drain off any excess liquid. 4. Fill each ramekin with half of the vegetable mixture. 5. In a medium bowl, beat the eggs and egg whites with the almond milk. Season with salt and pepper. 6. Evenly divide the egg mixture between the ramekins. 7. Top each with 1 tablespoon of dill. Garnish with the shredded cheese (if using). 8. Place the ramekins on a baking sheet. Carefully transfer the sheet to the preheated oven. Bake for about 35 minutes, or until the center is firm and the top is golden brown.

Per Serving:
calories: 151 | fat: 6g | protein: 16g | carbs: 11g | sugars: 3g | fiber: 5g | sodium: 188mg

Chorizo Mexican Breakfast Pizzas

Prep time: 15 minutes | Cook time: 15 minutes | Serves 4

6 ounces chorizo sausage, casing removed, crumbled, or 6 ounces bulk chorizo sausage

2 (10-inch) whole-grain lower-carb lavash flatbreads or tortillas

¼ cup chunky-style salsa

½ cup black beans with cumin and chili spices (from 15-ounce can)

½ cup chopped tomatoes

½ cup frozen whole-kernel corn, thawed

¼ cup reduced-fat shredded Cheddar cheese (1 ounce)

1 tablespoon chopped fresh cilantro

2 teaspoons crumbed cotija (white Mexican) cheese

1 Heat oven to 425°F. In 8-inch skillet, cook sausage over medium heat 4 to 5 minutes or until brown; drain. 2 On 1 large or 2 small cookie sheets, place flatbreads. Spread each with 2 tablespoons salsa. Top each with half the chorizo, beans, tomatoes, corn and Cheddar cheese. 3 Bake about 8 minutes or until cheese is melted. Sprinkle each with half the cilantro and cotija cheese; cut into wedges. Serve immediately.

Per Serving:

calories: 330 | fat: 2g | protein: 20g | carbs: 19g | sugars: 2g | fiber: 6g | sodium: 1030mg

Chapter 3 Beans and Grains

Rice with Spinach and Feta

Prep time: 10 minutes | Cook time: 15 minutes | Serves 4

¾ cup uncooked brown rice
1½ cups water
1 tablespoon extra-virgin olive oil
1 medium onion, diced
1 cup sliced mushrooms
2 garlic cloves, minced
1 tablespoon lemon juice
½ teaspoon dried oregano
9 cups fresh spinach, stems trimmed, washed, patted dry, and coarsely chopped
⅓ cup crumbled fat-free feta cheese
⅛ teaspoon freshly ground black pepper

1. In a medium saucepan over medium heat, combine the rice and water. Bring to a boil, cover, reduce heat, and simmer for 15 minutes. Transfer to a serving bowl. 2. In a skillet, heat the oil. Sauté the onion, mushrooms, and garlic for 5-7 minutes. Stir in the lemon juice and oregano. Add the spinach, cheese, and pepper, tossing until the spinach is slightly wilted. 3. Toss with rice and serve.

Per Serving:

calorie: 205 | fat: 5g | protein: 7g | carbs: 34g | sugars: 2g | fiber: 4g | sodium: 129mg

Pressure-Stewed Chickpeas

Prep time: 10 minutes | Cook time: 25 minutes | Serves 5

3 tablespoons water
2 large or 3 small to medium onions, chopped (3-3½ cups)
1½ tablespoons smoked paprika
½ teaspoon ground cumin
⅛-¼ teaspoon ground allspice
Rounded ½ teaspoon sea salt
2 cans (15 ounces each) chickpeas, rinsed and drained
⅔ cup chopped, pitted dates
1 jar (24 ounces) strained tomatoes

1. In the instant pot set on the sauté function, combine the water, onions, paprika, cumin, allspice, and salt. Cook for 6 to 7 minutes, stirring occasionally. If the mixture is sticking, add another tablespoon or two of water. Add the chickpeas, dates, and tomatoes, and stir well. Turn off the sauté function, and put on the lid. Manually set to pressure cook on high for 18 minutes. Release the pressure or let the pressure release naturally. Stir, taste, season as desired, and serve.

Per Serving:

calorie: 258 | fat: 4g | protein: 10g | carbs: 50g | sugars: 23g | fiber: 13g | sodium: 742mg

Edamame-Tabbouleh Salad

Prep time: 20 minutes | Cook time: 10 minutes | Serves 6

Salad
1 package (5.8 ounces) roasted garlic and olive oil couscous mix
1¼ cups water
1 teaspoon olive or canola oil
1 bag (10 ounces) refrigerated fully cooked ready-to-eat shelled edamame (green soybeans)
2 medium tomatoes, seeded, chopped (1½ cups)
1 small cucumber, peeled, chopped (1 cup)
¼ cup chopped fresh parsley
Dressing
1 teaspoon grated lemon peel
2 tablespoons lemon juice
1 teaspoon olive or canola oil

1 Make couscous mix as directed on package, using the water and oil. 2 In large bowl, mix couscous and remaining salad ingredients. In small bowl, mix dressing ingredients. Pour dressing over salad; mix well. Serve immediately, or cover and refrigerate until serving time.

Per Serving:

calorie: 200 | fat: 5g | protein: 10g | carbs: 28g | sugars: 3g | fiber: 4g | sodium: 270mg

Colorful Rice Casserole

Prep time: 5 minutes | Cook time: 20 minutes | Serves 12

1 tablespoon extra-virgin olive oil
1½ pounds zucchini, thinly sliced
¾ cup chopped scallions
2 cups corn kernels (frozen or fresh; if frozen, defrost)
One 14.5-ounce can no-salt-
added chopped tomatoes, undrained
¼ cup chopped parsley
1 teaspoon oregano
3 cups cooked brown (or white) rice
⅛ teaspoon freshly ground black pepper

1. In a large skillet, heat the oil. Add the zucchini and scallions, and sauté for 5 minutes. 2. Add the remaining ingredients, cover, reduce heat, and simmer for 10-15 minutes or until the vegetables are heated through. Season with salt, if desired, and pepper. Transfer to a bowl, and serve.

Per Serving:

calorie: 109 | fat: 2g | protein: 3g | carbs: 21g | sugars: 4g | fiber: 3g | sodium: 14mg

Spicy Couscous and Chickpea Salad

Prep time: 20 minutes | Cook time: 10 minutes | Serves 4

Salad
½ cup uncooked whole wheat couscous
1½ cups water
¼ teaspoon salt
1 can (15 ounces) chickpeas (garbanzo beans), drained, rinsed
1 can (14.5 ounces) diced tomatoes with green chiles, undrained
½ cup frozen shelled edamame

(green soybeans) or lima beans, thawed
2 tablespoons chopped fresh cilantro
Green bell peppers, halved, if desired
Dressing
2 tablespoons olive oil
1 teaspoon ground coriander
½ teaspoon ground cumin
½ teaspoon ground cinnamon

1. Cook couscous in the water and salt as directed on package. 2. Meanwhile, in medium bowl, mix chickpeas, tomatoes, edamame and cilantro. In small bowl, mix dressing ingredients until well blended. 3. Add cooked couscous to salad; mix well. Pour dressing over salad; stir gently to mix. Spoon salad mixture into halved bell peppers. Serve immediately, or cover and refrigerate until serving time.

Per Serving:
calorie: 370 | fat: 11g | protein: 16g | carbs: 53g | sugars: 6g | fiber: 10g | sodium: 460mg

Tex-Mex Rice 'N' Beans

Prep time: 10 minutes | Cook time: 25 minutes | Serves 4

1½ cups chopped bell pepper
1-1½ cups chopped onion
1 tablespoon dried oregano
2 teaspoons chili powder
½ tablespoon paprika
½ tablespoon ground cumin
1 teaspoon garlic powder
½ teaspoon cinnamon
Rounded ½ teaspoon sea salt
2 tablespoons water + 2½ cups water (boiled, if using an instant

pot)
½ cup dried red lentils
1 cup uncooked brown rice (can substitute quinoa)
2 cans (15 ounces each) black beans, rinsed and drained
¼ cup tomato paste
1 bay leaf
2 tablespoons lime juice
Hot sauce to taste (optional)

1. In an instant pot, combine the bell pepper, onion, oregano, chili powder, paprika, cumin, garlic powder, cinnamon, salt, and 2 tablespoons of the water, and set to the sauté function. Cook for 3 to 4 minutes, stirring frequently. Turn off the sauté function and add the lentils, rice, beans, tomato paste, bay leaf, and the remaining 2½ cups water. Stir, cover the instant pot, and set to high pressure for 20 minutes. After 20 minutes, you can manually release the pressure or let it naturally release. Stir in the lime juice, taste, and season as desired. Add the hot sauce (if using), and serve.

Per Serving:
calorie: 525 | fat: 3g | protein: 24g | carbs: 103g | sugars: 7g | fiber: 25g | sodium: 898mg

Chicken-Wild Rice Salad with Dried Cherries

Prep time: 30 minutes | Cook time: 10 minutes | Serves 5

1 package (6.2 ounces) fast-cooking long-grain and wild rice mix
2 cups chopped cooked chicken or turkey
1 medium unpeeled apple, chopped (1 cup)
1 medium green bell pepper, chopped (1 cup)
1 medium stalk celery, chopped

(½ cup)
½ cup chopped dried apricots
⅓ cup chopped dried cherries
2 tablespoons reduced-sodium soy sauce
2 tablespoons water
2 teaspoons sugar
2 teaspoons cider vinegar
⅓ cup dry-roasted peanuts

1 Cook rice mix as directed on package, omitting butter. On large cookie sheet, spread rice evenly in thin layer. Let stand 10 minutes, stirring occasionally, until cool. 2 Meanwhile, in large bowl, mix chicken, apple, bell pepper, celery, apricots and cherries. In small bowl, mix soy sauce, water, sugar and vinegar until sugar is dissolved. 3 Add rice and soy sauce mixture to apple mixture; toss gently until coated. Add peanuts; toss gently.

Per Serving:
calorie: 380 | fat: 7g | protein: 24g | carbs: 54g | sugars: 21g | fiber: 4g | sodium: 760mg

Veggie Unfried Rice

Prep time: 15 minutes | Cook time: 25 minutes | Serves 4

1 tablespoon extra-virgin olive oil
1 bunch collard greens, stemmed and cut into chiffonade
½ cup store-bought low-sodium vegetable broth
1 carrot, cut into 2-inch matchsticks

1 red onion, thinly sliced
1 garlic clove, minced
2 tablespoons coconut aminos
1 cup cooked brown rice
1 large egg
1 teaspoon red pepper flakes
1 teaspoon paprika

1. In a large Dutch oven, heat the olive oil over medium heat. 2. Add the collard greens and cook for 3 to 5 minutes, or until the greens are wilted. 3. Add the broth, carrot, onion, garlic, and coconut aminos, then cover and cook for 5 to 7 minutes, or until the carrot softens and the onion and garlic are translucent. 4. Uncover, add the rice, and cook for 3 to 5 minutes, gently mixing all the ingredients together until well combined but not mushy. 5. Crack the egg over the pot and gently scramble the egg. Cook for 2 to 5 minutes, or until the eggs are no longer runny. 6. Remove from the heat and season with the red pepper flakes and paprika.

Per Serving:
calorie: 164 | fat: 4g | protein: 9g | carbs: 26g | sugars: 3g | fiber: 9g | sodium: 168mg

BBQ Lentils

Prep time: 10 minutes | Cook time: 55 minutes | Serves 5

2 cups dried green or brown lentils, rinsed
3 tablespoons balsamic vinegar
4½ cups water
½ cup tomato paste
2 tablespoons vegan Worcestershire sauce

2 teaspoons dried rosemary
1 teaspoon onion powder
½ teaspoon garlic powder
½ teaspoon allspice
¼ teaspoon sea salt
1 tablespoon coconut nectar or pure maple syrup

1. In a large saucepan over medium-high heat, combine the lentils with 2 tablespoons of the vinegar. Cook, stirring, for 5 to 7 minutes to lightly toast the lentils. Once the pan is getting dry, add the water, tomato paste, Worcestershire sauce, rosemary, onion powder, garlic powder, allspice, salt, nectar or syrup, and the remaining 1 tablespoon vinegar, and stir through. Bring to a boil, then reduce the heat to low, cover the pot, and cook for 37 to 40 minutes, or until the lentils are fully tender. Season to taste, and serve.

Per Serving:

calorie: 295 | fat: 1g | protein: 20g | carbs: 54g | sugars: 9g | fiber: 14g | sodium: 399mg

African Squash and Chickpea Stew

Prep time: 30 minutes | Cook time: 30 minutes | Serves 4

4 teaspoons olive oil
2 large onions, chopped (2 cups)
1 teaspoon ground coriander
1½ teaspoons ground cumin
½ teaspoon ground cinnamon
½ teaspoon ground turmeric
¼ teaspoon salt
¼ teaspoon ground red pepper (cayenne)
2 cups butternut squash, peeled, seeded, cut into 1-inch cubes
2 cups vegetable broth

1 can (14.5 ounces) low-sodium diced tomatoes, undrained
1 can (15 ounces) chickpeas (garbanzo beans), drained, rinsed
1½ cups thinly sliced okra
½ cup chopped fresh cilantro leaves
⅓ cup raw unsalted hulled pumpkin seeds (pepitas), toasted*

1 In 5-quart Dutch oven or saucepan, heat 3 teaspoons of the oil over medium heat. Add onions to oil; cook 10 minutes, stirring occasionally, until golden brown. Add all spices; stir until onions are well coated. Cook about 3 minutes, stirring frequently, until glazed and deep golden brown. Stir in squash; coat well with seasoned mixture. Stir in broth, tomatoes and chickpeas. Heat stew to boiling; reduce heat. Cover and simmer about 15 minutes or until squash is tender. 2 Meanwhile, in 8-inch skillet, heat remaining 1 teaspoon oil over medium-high heat; add okra to oil. Cook 3 to 5 minutes, stirring frequently, until tender and edges are golden brown; stir into stew. 3 Divide stew evenly among 4 bowls. For each serving, top stew with 2 tablespoons chopped cilantro and generous 1 tablespoon pumpkin seeds.

Per Serving:

calorie: 390 | fat: 13g | protein: 15g | carbs: 54g | sugars: 11g | fiber: 12g | sodium: 650mg

BBQ Bean Burgers

Prep time: 10 minutes | Cook time: 20 minutes | Makes 8 burgers

2 cups sliced carrots
1 medium-large clove garlic, quartered
1 can (15 ounces) kidney beans, rinsed and drained
1 cup cooked, cooled brown rice
¼ cup barbecue sauce
½ tablespoon vegan

Worcestershire sauce
½ tablespoon Dijon mustard
Scant ½ teaspoon sea salt
¼–½ teaspoon smoked paprika
1 tablespoon chopped fresh thyme
1¼ cups rolled oats

1. In a food processor, combine the carrots and garlic. Pulse until minced. Add the beans, rice, barbecue sauce, Worcestershire sauce, mustard, salt, paprika, and thyme. Puree until well combined. Once the mixture is fairly smooth, add the oats and pulse to combine. Chill the mixture for 30 minutes, if possible. 2. Preheat the oven to 400°F. Line a baking sheet with parchment paper. 3. Use an ice cream scoop to scoop the mixture onto the prepared baking sheet, flattening to shape it into patties. Bake for about 20 minutes, flipping the burgers halfway through. Alternatively, you can cook the burgers in a nonstick skillet over medium heat for 6 to 8 minutes Per side, or until golden brown.

Per Serving:

calorie: 152 | fat: 2g | protein: 6g | carbs: 29g | sugars: 6 | fiber: 5g | sodium: 247mg

Green Chickpea Falafel

Prep time: 10 minutes | Cook time: 11 to 12 minutes | Serves 4

1 bag (14 ounces) green chickpeas, thawed (about 3½ cups)
½ cup fresh flat-leaf parsley leaves
½ cup fresh cilantro leaves
1½ tablespoons freshly squeezed lemon juice

2 medium-large cloves garlic
2 teaspoons ground cumin
½ teaspoon turmeric
1 teaspoon ground coriander
1 teaspoon sea salt
¼–½ teaspoon crushed red-pepper flakes
1 cup rolled oats

1. In a food processor, combine the chickpeas, parsley, cilantro, lemon juice, garlic, cumin, turmeric, coriander, salt, and red-pepper flakes. (Use ¼ teaspoon if you like it mild and ½ teaspoon if you like it spicier.) Process until the mixture breaks down and begins to smooth out. Add the oats and pulse a few times to work them in. Refrigerate for 30 minutes, if possible. 2. Preheat the oven to 400°F. Line a baking sheet with parchment paper. 3. Use a cookie scoop to take small scoops of the mixture, 1 to 1½ tablespoons each. Place falafel balls on the prepared baking sheet. Bake for 11 to 12 minutes, until the falafel balls begin to firm (they will still be tender inside) and turn golden in spots.

Per Serving:

calorie: 253 | fat: 4g | protein: 12g | carbs: 43g | sugars: 5g | fiber: 10g | sodium: 601mg

Veggies and Kasha with Balsamic Vinaigrette

Prep time: 15 minutes | Cook time: 8 minutes | Serves 4

Salad
1 cup water
½ cup uncooked buckwheat kernels or groats (kasha)
4 medium green onions, thinly sliced (¼ cup)
2 medium tomatoes, seeded, coarsely chopped (1½ cups)
1 medium unpeeled cucumber, seeded, chopped (1¼ cups)

Vinaigrette
2 tablespoons balsamic or red wine vinegar
1 tablespoon olive oil
2 teaspoons sugar
½ teaspoon salt
¼ teaspoon pepper
1 clove garlic, finely chopped

1 In 8-inch skillet, heat water to boiling. Add kasha; cook over medium-high heat 7 to 8 minutes, stirring occasionally, until tender. Drain if necessary. 2 In large bowl, mix kasha and remaining salad ingredients. 3 In tightly covered container, shake vinaigrette ingredients until blended. Pour vinaigrette over kasha mixture; toss. Cover; refrigerate 1 to 2 hours to blend flavors.

Per Serving:

calorie: 120 | fat: 4g | protein: 2g | carbs: 19g | sugars: 6g | fiber: 3g | sodium: 310mg

Asian Fried Rice

Prep time: 5 minutes | Cook time: 20 minutes | Serves 4

2 tablespoons peanut oil
¼ cup chopped onion
1 cup sliced carrot
1 green bell pepper, diced
1 tablespoon grated fresh ginger
2 cups cooked brown rice, cold
½ cup water chestnuts, drained
½ cup sliced mushrooms
1 tablespoon light soy sauce
2 egg whites
½ cup sliced scallions

1. In a large skillet, heat the oil. Sauté the onion, carrot, green pepper, and ginger for 5-6 minutes. 2. Stir in the rice, water chestnuts, mushrooms, and soy sauce, and stir-fry for 8-10 minutes. 3. Stir in the egg whites, and continue to stir-fry for another 3 minutes. Top with the sliced scallions to serve.

Per Serving:

calorie: 223 | fat: 9g | protein: 6g | carbs: 32g | sugars: 5g | fiber: 4g | sodium: 151mg

Sage and Garlic Vegetable Bake

Prep time: 30 minutes | Cook time: 1 hour 15 minutes | Serves 6

1 medium butternut squash, peeled, cut into 1-inch pieces (3 cups)
2 medium parsnips, peeled, cut into 1-inch pieces (2 cups)
2 cans (14.5 ounces each) stewed tomatoes, undrained
2 cups frozen cut green beans
1 medium onion, coarsely chopped (½ cup)
½ cup uncooked quick-cooking barley
½ cup water
1 teaspoon dried sage leaves
½ teaspoon seasoned salt
2 cloves garlic, finely chopped

1 Heat oven to 375°F. In ungreased 3-quart casserole, mix all ingredients, breaking up large pieces of tomatoes. 2 Cover; bake 1 hour to 1 hour 15 minutes or until vegetables and barley are tender.
Per Serving:
calorie: 170 | fat: 0g | protein: 4g | carbs: 37g | sugars: 9g | fiber: 8g | sodium: 410mg

Beet Greens and Black Beans

Prep time: 10 minutes | Cook time: 20 minutes | Serves 4

1 tablespoon unsalted non-hydrogenated plant-based butter
½ Vidalia onion, thinly sliced
½ cup store-bought low-sodium vegetable broth
1 bunch beet greens, cut into ribbons
1 bunch dandelion greens, cut into ribbons
1 (15-ounce) can no-salt-added black beans
Freshly ground black pepper

1. In a medium skillet, melt the butter over low heat. 2. Add the onion, and sauté for 3 to 5 minutes, or until the onion is translucent. 3. Add the broth and greens. Cover the skillet and cook for 7 to 10 minutes, or until the greens are wilted. 4. Add the black beans and cook for 3 to 5 minutes, or until the beans are tender. Season with black pepper.

Per Serving:

calorie: 153 | fat: 3g | protein: 9g | carbs: 25g | sugars: 2g | fiber: 11g | sodium: 312mg

Texas Caviar

Prep time: 10 minutes | Cook time: 0 minutes | Serves 6

1 cup cooked black-eyed peas
1 cup cooked lima beans
1 ear fresh corn, kernels removed
2 celery stalks, chopped
1 red bell pepper, chopped
½ red onion, chopped
3 tablespoons apple cider vinegar
2 tablespoons extra-virgin olive oil
1 teaspoon paprika

1. In a large bowl, combine the black-eyed peas, lima beans, corn, celery, bell pepper, and onion. 2. In a small bowl, to make the dressing, whisk the vinegar, oil, and paprika together. 3. Pour the dressing over the bean mixture, and gently mix. Set aside for 15 to 30 minutes, allowing the flavors to come together.

Per Serving:

calorie: 142 | fat: 5g | protein: 6g | carbs: 19g | sugars: 3g | fiber: 6g | sodium: 10mg

Dirty Forbidden Rice

Prep time: 15 minutes | Cook time: 35 minutes | Serves 10

1 pound 90 percent lean ground beef
1 small red onion, chopped
1 medium tomato, chopped
1 garlic clove, minced
½ large red bell pepper, chopped
2 large carrots, peeled and

chopped
2⅔ cups (15-ounce) forbidden rice (black rice)
4¾ cups store-bought low-sodium chicken broth
1 tablespoon Creole seasoning

1. Heat a Dutch oven over medium heat. 2. Put the ground beef, onion, tomato, and garlic in the pot and cook for 5 minutes, or until the beef is browned. 3. Stir in the bell pepper, carrots, and rice. 4. Add the broth and Creole seasoning, cover, and cook over medium-low heat for 30 minutes, or until the rice is tender. 5. Serve with a plate of greens of your choice.

Per Serving:

calorie: 274 | fat: 4g | protein: 16g | carbs: 43g | sugars: 2g | fiber: 3g | sodium: 79mg

Thai Red Lentils

Prep time: 5 minutes | Cook time: 25 minutes | Serves 4

2 cups dried red lentils
1 can (13½ ounces) lite coconut milk
2 tablespoons red or yellow Thai curry paste

¼-½ teaspoon sea salt (use less if using more curry paste)
2-2¼ cups water
⅓ cup finely chopped fresh basil
3-4 tablespoons lime juice

1. In a large saucepan over high heat, combine the lentils, coconut milk, curry paste, salt, and 2 cups of the water. Stir and bring to a boil. Reduce the heat to low, cover, and cook for 20 minutes, or until the lentils are fully softened. Add the basil and 3 tablespoons of the lime juice, and stir. Season to taste with more salt and the remaining 1 tablespoon lime juice, if desired. Add the remaining ¼ cup water to thin, if desired.

Per Serving:

calorie: 389 | fat: 8g | protein: 25g | carbs: 58g | sugars: 4g | fiber: 16g | sodium: 441mg

Brown Rice-Stuffed Butternut Squash

Prep time: 30 minutes | Cook time: 50 minutes | Serves 4

2 small butternut squash (about 2 pounds each)
4 teaspoons olive oil
¼ teaspoon salt
½ teaspoon freshly ground pepper
⅓ cup uncooked brown basmati rice

1¼ cups reduced-sodium chicken broth
1 thyme sprig
1 bay leaf
2 links (3 ounces each) sweet Italian turkey sausage, casings removed
1 small onion, chopped (⅓ cup)

1 cup sliced cremini mushrooms
1 cup fresh baby spinach leaves

1 teaspoon chopped fresh or ¼ teaspoon dried sage leaves

1 Heat oven to 375°F. Cut each squash lengthwise in half; remove seeds and fibers. Drizzle cut sides with 3 teaspoons of the olive oil; sprinkle with salt and pepper. On cookie sheet, place squash, cut side down. Bake 35 to 40 minutes, until squash is tender at thickest portion when pierced with fork. When cool enough to handle, cut off long ends of squash to within ½ inch edge of cavities (peel and refrigerate ends for another use). 2 Meanwhile, in 1-quart saucepan, heat remaining 1 teaspoon oil over medium heat. Add rice to oil, stirring well to coat. Stir in chicken broth, thyme and bay leaf. Heat to boiling; reduce heat. Cover and simmer 30 to 35 minutes, until all liquid is absorbed and rice is tender. Remove from heat; discard thyme sprig and bay leaf. 3 In 10-inch nonstick skillet, cook sausage and onion over medium-high heat 8 to 10 minutes, stirring frequently, until sausage is thoroughly cooked. Add mushrooms. Cook 4 minutes or until mushrooms are tender. Stir in cooked rice, spinach and sage; cook about 3 minutes or until spinach is wilted and mixture is hot. Divide sausage-rice mixture between squash halves, pressing down on filling so it forms a slight mound over cavity.

Per Serving:

calorie: 350 | fat: 10g | protein: 14g | carbs: 50g | sugars: 14g | fiber: 5g | sodium: 670mg

Farmers' Market Barley Risotto

Prep time: 30 minutes | Cook time: 15 minutes | Serves 4

1 tablespoon olive oil
1 medium onion, chopped (½ cup)
1 medium bell pepper, coarsely chopped (1 cup)
2 cups chopped fresh mushrooms (4 ounces)
1 cup frozen whole-kernel corn
1 cup uncooked medium pearled barley
¼ cup dry white wine or

chicken broth
2 cups reduced-sodium chicken broth
3 cups water
1½ cups grape tomatoes, cut in half (if large, cut into quarters)
⅔ cup shredded Parmesan cheese
3 tablespoons chopped fresh or 1 teaspoon dried basil leaves
½ teaspoon pepper

1 In 4-quart Dutch oven or saucepan, heat oil over medium heat. Cook onion, bell pepper, mushrooms and corn in oil about 5 minutes, stirring frequently, until onion is crisp-tender. Add barley, stirring about 1 minute to coat. 2 Stir in wine and ½ cup of the broth. Cook 5 minutes, stirring frequently, until liquid is almost absorbed. Repeat with remaining broth and 3 cups water, adding ½ to ¾ cup of broth or water at a time and stirring frequently, until absorbed. 3 Stir in tomatoes, ¼ cup of the cheese, the basil and pepper. Cook until thoroughly heated. Sprinkle with remaining ¼ cup cheese.

Per Serving:

calorie: 370 | fat: 8g | protein: 15g | carbs: 55g | sugars: 6g | fiber: 11g | sodium: 520mg

Curried Rice with Pineapple

Prep time: 5 minutes | Cook time: 35 minutes | Serves 8

1 onion, chopped
1½ cups water
1¼ cups low-sodium chicken broth
1 cup uncooked brown basmati rice, soaked in water 20 minutes and drained before cooking
2 red bell peppers, minced

1 teaspoon curry powder
1 teaspoon ground turmeric
1 teaspoon ground ginger
2 garlic cloves, minced
One 8-ounce can pineapple chunks packed in juice, drained
¼ cup sliced almonds, toasted

1. In a medium saucepan, combine the onion, water, and chicken broth. Bring to a boil, and add the rice, peppers, curry powder, turmeric, ginger, and garlic. Cover, placing a paper towel in between the pot and the lid, and reduce the heat. Simmer for 25 minutes. 2. Add the pineapple, and continue to simmer 5-7 minutes more until rice is tender and water is absorbed. Taste and add salt, if desired. Transfer to a serving bowl, and garnish with almonds to serve.

Per Serving:

calorie: 144 | fat: 3g | protein: 4g | carbs: 27g | sugars: 6g | fiber: 3g | sodium: 16mg

Gingered Red Lentils with Millet

Prep time: 10 minutes | Cook time: 20 minutes | Serves 4

3 cups water
1 cup millet, rinsed
½ cup red lentils, rinsed
3 tablespoons extra-virgin olive oil, divided
Pinch kosher salt
1 onion, diced

3-inch piece ginger, grated (or minced)
4 cups cherry tomatoes, diced
3 tablespoons unsalted peanuts, chopped
2 limes, quartered
1 bunch mint leaves

1. In a medium saucepan over medium heat, stir together the water, millet, lentils, 1 tablespoon of extra-virgin olive oil, and the salt. Bring to a boil, reduce the heat to low, cover, and simmer until tender, about 15 minutes. Remove the saucepan from the heat and let the grains sit for a few minutes. 2. Meanwhile, in a small saucepan, heat the remaining 2 tablespoons of extra-virgin olive oil. Sauté the onion until translucent, about 3 minutes. Add the ginger, tomatoes, and peanuts. Cook for about 5 minutes, adjust the seasonings as desired, and allow to sit until the millet and lentils are finished. 3. Divide the millet and lentils among four bowls, and top them with the gingered onion mixture. Garnish with lime wedges and mint leaves. 4. Serve, and store any leftovers in an airtight container in the refrigerator for up to 3 days.

Per Serving:

calorie: 454 | fat: 17g | protein: 15g | carbs: 65g | sugars: 6g | fiber: 11g | sodium: 18mg

Lentil Bolognese

Prep time: 10 minutes | Cook time: 30 minutes | Serves 4

⅓ cup red wine
1 cup diced onion
½ cup minced carrot
1 tablespoon dried oregano leaves
1 teaspoon vegan Worcestershire sauce
¾ teaspoon smoked paprika
½ teaspoon sea salt
¼ teaspoon ground nutmeg
1½ cups cooked brown or green

lentils
¼ cup chopped sun-dried tomatoes
1 can (28 ounces) diced tomatoes (use fire-roasted, if you'd like a spicy kick)
2-3 tablespoons minced dates
1 pound dry pasta
½ cup almond meal (toast until lightly golden if you want extra flavor)

1. In a large pot over high heat, combine the wine, onion, carrot, oregano, Worcestershire sauce, paprika, salt, and nutmeg. Cook for 5 minutes, stirring frequently. Add the lentils, sun-dried tomatoes, diced tomatoes, and dates, and bring to a boil. Reduce the heat to low, cover, and cook for 20 to 25 minutes. 2. While the sauce is simmering, prepare the pasta according to package directions. Once the pasta is almost cooked (still having some "bite," not mushy), drain and return it to the cooking pot. 3. Add the almond meal to the sauce, stir to incorporate, and cook for a couple of minutes. Taste, season as desired, and toss with the pasta before serving.

Per Serving:

calorie: 754 | fat: 11g | protein: 31g | carbs: 132g | sugars: 14g | fiber: 17g | sodium: 622mg

Coconut-Ginger Rice

Prep time: 10 minutes | Cook time: 20 minutes | Serves 8

2½ cups reduced-sodium chicken broth
⅔ cup reduced-fat (lite) coconut milk (not cream of coconut)
1 tablespoon grated gingerroot
½ teaspoon salt
1⅓ cups uncooked regular long-

grain white rice
1 teaspoon grated lime peel
3 medium green onions, chopped (3 tablespoons)
3 tablespoons flaked coconut, toasted*
Lime slices

1 In 3-quart saucepan, heat broth, coconut milk, gingerroot and salt to boiling over medium-high heat. Stir in rice. Return to boiling. Reduce heat; cover and simmer about 15 minutes or until rice is tender and liquid is absorbed. Remove from heat. 2 Add lime peel and onions; fluff rice mixture lightly with fork to mix. Garnish with coconut and lime slices.

Per Serving:

calorie: 150 | fat: 2g | protein: 3g | carbs: 30g | sugars: 1g | fiber: 0g | sodium: 340mg

Chapter 4 Beef, Pork, and Lamb

Beef Roast with Onions and Potatoes

Prep time: 30 minutes | Cook time: 9 to 10 hours | Serves 6

1 large sweet onion, cut in half, then cut into thin slices
1 boneless beef bottom round roast (3 pounds), trimmed of excess fat
3 baking potatoes, cut into 1½- to 2-inch cubes
2 cloves garlic, finely chopped
1¾ cups beef-flavored broth
1 package (1 ounce) onion soup mix (from 2-ounce box)
¼ cup all-purpose flour

1. Spray 5- to 6-quart slow cooker with cooking spray. In slow cooker, place onion. If beef roast comes in netting or is tied, remove netting or strings. Place beef on onion. Place potatoes and garlic around beef. In small bowl, mix 1¼ cups of the broth and the dry soup mix; pour over beef. (Refrigerate remaining broth.) 2. Cover; cook on Low heat setting 9 to 10 hours. 3. Remove beef and vegetables from slow cooker; place on serving platter. Cover to keep warm. 4. In small bowl, mix remaining ½ cup broth and the flour; gradually stir into juices in slow cooker. Increase heat setting to High. Cover; cook about 15 minutes, stirring occasionally, until sauce has thickened. Serve sauce over beef and vegetables.
Per Serving:
calorie: 416 | fat: 9g | protein: 54g | carbs: 27g | sugars: 4g | fiber: 3g | sodium: 428mg

Beef Barley Soup

Prep time: 20 minutes | Cook time: 30 minutes | Serves 4

2 teaspoons extra-virgin olive oil
1 sweet onion, chopped
1 tablespoon minced garlic
4 celery stalks, with greens, chopped
2 carrots, peeled, diced
1 sweet potato, peeled, diced
8 cups low-sodium beef broth
1 cup cooked pearl barley
2 cups diced cooked beef
2 bay leaves
2 teaspoons hot sauce
2 teaspoons chopped fresh thyme
1 cup shredded kale
Sea salt
Freshly ground black pepper

1. Place a large stockpot over medium-high heat and add the oil. 2. Sauté the onion and garlic until softened and translucent, about 3 minutes. 3. Stir in the celery, carrot, and sweet potato, and sauté for a further 5 minutes. 4. Stir in the beef broth, barley, beef, bay leaves, and hot sauce. 5. Bring the soup to a boil, then reduce the heat to low. 6. Simmer until the vegetables are tender, about 15 minutes. 7. Remove the bay leaves and stir in the thyme and kale. 8. Simmer for 5 minutes, and season with salt and pepper.

Per Serving:
calorie: 652 | fat: 22g | protein: 45g | carbs: 76g | sugars: 9g | fiber: 6g | sodium: 252mg

Slow-Cooked Pork Burrito Bowls

Prep time: 15 minutes | Cook time: 8 to 10 hours | Serves 10

1 boneless pork shoulder (2 pounds), trimmed of excess fat
1 can (15 to 16 ounces) pinto beans, drained, rinsed
1 package (1 ounce) 40% less-sodium taco seasoning mix
1 can (4.5 ounces) diced green chiles, undrained
2 packages (7.6 ounces each) Spanish rice mix
5 cups water
1½ cups shredded Mexican cheese blend (6 ounces)
3 cups shredded lettuce
¾ cup chunky-style salsa

1 Spray 3- to 4-quart slow cooker with cooking spray. If pork comes in netting or is tied, remove netting or strings. Place pork in slow cooker. Pour beans around pork. Sprinkle taco seasoning mix over pork. Pour chiles over beans. 2 Cover; cook on Low heat setting 8 to 10 hours. 3 About 45 minutes before serving, in 3-quart saucepan, make rice mixes as directed on package, using water and omitting butter. 4 Remove pork from slow cooker; place on cutting board. Use 2 forks to pull pork into shreds. Return pork to slow cooker; gently stir to mix with beans. 5 To serve, spoon rice into each of 10 serving bowls; top each with pork mixture, cheese, lettuce and salsa.

Per Serving:
calories: 460 | fat: 17g | protein: 30g | carbs: 48g | sugars: 4g | fiber: 5g | sodium: 1030mg

Parmesan-Crusted Pork Chops

Prep time: 5 minutes | Cook time: 12 minutes | Serves 4

1 large egg
½ cup grated Parmesan cheese
4 (4-ounce / 113-g) boneless
pork chops
½ teaspoon salt
¼ teaspoon ground black pepper

1. Whisk egg in a medium bowl and place Parmesan in a separate medium bowl. 2. Sprinkle pork chops on both sides with salt and pepper. Dip each pork chop into egg, then press both sides into Parmesan. 3. Place pork chops into ungreased air fryer basket. Adjust the temperature to 400°F (204ºC) and air fry for 12 minutes, turning chops halfway through cooking. Pork chops will be golden and have an internal temperature of at least 145°F (63ºC) when done. Serve warm.

Per Serving:
calories: 218 | fat: 9g | protein: 32g | carbs: 1g | fiber: 0g | sodium: 372mg

Beef and Vegetable Shish Kabobs

Prep time: 15 minutes | Cook time: 20 minutes | Serves 8

2 teaspoons canola oil
¼ cup red wine vinegar
1 tablespoon light soy sauce
4 garlic cloves, minced
2 tablespoons freshly squeezed lemon juice
⅛ teaspoon freshly ground black pepper

1½ pounds boneless beef top sirloin steak, cut into 24 cubes
2 large bell peppers, red and green, cut into 1-inch pieces
1 pound mushrooms, stemmed
1 large tomato, cut into wedges
1 medium onion, quartered

1. In a small bowl, combine the oil, vinegar, soy sauce, garlic, lemon juice, and pepper. Pour over the beef cubes, and let marinate in the refrigerator 3-4 hours or overnight. 2. Place 3 beef cubes on 8 metal or wooden skewers (remember to soak the wooden skewers in water before using), alternating with peppers, mushroom caps, tomato wedges, and onions. 3. Grill over medium heat, turning often and basting with marinade until the meat is cooked through. Arrange the skewers on a platter to serve.

Per Serving:

calorie: 211 | fat: 11g | protein: 20g | carbs: 7g | sugars: 4g | fiber: 2g | sodium: 82mg

BBQ Ribs and Broccoli Slaw

Prep time: 10 minutes | Cook time: 50 minutes | Serves 6

BBQ Ribs
4 pounds baby back ribs
1 teaspoon fine sea salt
1 teaspoon freshly ground black pepper
Broccoli Slaw
½ cup plain 2 percent Greek yogurt
1 tablespoon olive oil
1 tablespoon fresh lemon juice
½ teaspoon fine sea salt
¼ teaspoon freshly ground black pepper

1 pound broccoli florets (or florets from 2 large crowns), chopped
10 radishes, halved and thinly sliced
1 red bell pepper, seeded and cut lengthwise into narrow strips
1 large apple (such as Fuji, Jonagold, or Gala), thinly sliced
½ red onion, thinly sliced
¾ cup low-sugar or unsweetened barbecue sauce

1. To make the ribs: Pat the ribs dry with paper towels, then cut the racks into six sections (three to five ribs per section, depending on how big the racks are). Season the ribs all over with the salt and pepper. 2. Pour 1 cup water into the Instant Pot and place the wire metal steam rack into the pot. Place the ribs on top of the wire rack (it's fine to stack them up). 3. Secure the lid and set the Pressure Release to Sealing. Select the Pressure Cook or Manual setting and set the cooking time for 20 minutes at high pressure. (The pot will take about 15 minutes to come up to pressure before the cooking program begins.) 4. To make the broccoli slaw: While the ribs are cooking, in a small bowl, stir together the yogurt, oil, lemon juice, salt, and pepper, mixing well. In a large bowl, combine the broccoli, radishes, bell pepper, apple, and onion. Drizzle with the yogurt mixture and toss until evenly coated. 5. When the ribs have about 10 minutes left in their cooking time, preheat the oven to 400°F.

Line a sheet pan with aluminum foil. 6. When the cooking program ends, perform a quick pressure release by moving the Pressure Release to Venting. Open the pot and, using tongs, transfer the ribs in a single layer to the prepared sheet pan. Brush the barbecue sauce onto both sides of the ribs, using 2 tablespoons of sauce per section of ribs. Bake, meaty-side up, for 15 to 20 minutes, until lightly browned. 7. Serve the ribs warm, with the slaw on the side.

Per Serving:

calories: 392 | fat: 15g | protein: 45g | carbs: 19g | sugars: 9g | fiber: 4g | sodium: 961mg

Kielbasa and Cabbage

Prep time: 10 minutes | Cook time: 20 to 25 minutes | Serves 4

1 pound (454 g) smoked kielbasa sausage, sliced into ½-inch pieces
1 head cabbage, very coarsely chopped
½ yellow onion, chopped

2 cloves garlic, chopped
2 tablespoons olive oil
½ teaspoon salt
½ teaspoon freshly ground black pepper
¼ cup water

1. Preheat the air fryer to 400°F (204°C). 2. In a large bowl, combine the sausage, cabbage, onion, garlic, olive oil, salt, and black pepper. Toss until thoroughly combined. 3. Transfer the mixture to the basket of the air fryer and pour the water over the top. Pausing two or three times during the cooking time to shake the basket, air fry for 20 to 25 minutes, until the sausage is browned and the vegetables are tender.

Per Serving:

calories: 368 | fat: 28g | protein: 18g | carbs: 11g | net carbs: 6g | fiber: 5g

Pork and Apple Skillet

Prep time: 10 minutes | Cook time: 20 minutes | Serves 4

1 pound ground pork
1 red onion, thinly sliced
2 apples, peeled, cored, and thinly sliced
2 cups shredded cabbage
1 teaspoon dried thyme

2 garlic cloves, minced
¼ cup apple cider vinegar
1 tablespoon Dijon mustard
½ teaspoon sea salt
⅛ teaspoon freshly ground black pepper

1. In a large skillet over medium-high heat, cook the ground pork, crumbling it with a spoon, until browned, about 5 minutes. Use a slotted spoon to transfer the pork to a plate. 2. Add the onion, apples, cabbage, and thyme to the fat in the pan. Cook, stirring occasionally, until the vegetables are soft, about 5 minutes. 3. Add the garlic and cook, stirring constantly, for 5 minutes. 4. Return the pork to the pan. 5. In a small bowl, whisk together the vinegar, mustard, salt, and pepper. Add to the pan. Bring to a simmer. Cook, stirring, until the sauce thickens, about 2 minutes.

Per Serving:

calorie: 218 | fat: 5g | protein: 25g | carbs: 20g | sugars: 12g | fiber: 4g | sodium: 425mg

Cheeseburger and Cauliflower Wraps

Prep time: 5 minutes | Cook time: 20 minutes | Serves 4

Avocado oil cooking spray
½ cup chopped white onion
1 cup chopped portobello mushrooms
1 pound 93% lean ground beef
½ teaspoon garlic powder

Pinch salt
1 (10-ounce) bag frozen cauliflower rice
12 iceberg lettuce leaves
¾ cup shredded Cheddar cheese

1. Heat a large skillet over medium heat. When hot, coat the cooking surface with cooking spray and add the onion and mushrooms. Cook for 5 minutes, stirring occasionally. 2. Add the beef, garlic powder, and salt, stirring and breaking apart the meat as needed. Cook for 5 minutes. 3. Stir in the frozen cauliflower rice and increase the heat to medium-high. Cook for 5 minutes more, or until the water evaporates. 4. For each portion, use three lettuce leaves. Spoon one-quarter of the filling onto the lettuce leaves, and top with one-quarter of the cheese. Then, working from the side closest to you, roll up the lettuce to close the wrap. Repeat with the remaining lettuce leaves and filling.

Per Serving:

calorie: 274 | fat: 13g | protein: 32g | carbs: 8g | sugars: 4g | fiber: 3g | sodium: 242mg

Salisbury Steaks with Seared Cauliflower

Prep time: 5 minutes | Cook time: 30 minutes | Serves 4

Salisbury Steaks
1 pound 95 percent lean ground beef
⅓ cup almond flour
1 large egg
½ teaspoon fine sea salt
¼ teaspoon freshly ground black pepper
2 tablespoons cold-pressed avocado oil
1 small yellow onion, sliced
1 garlic clove, chopped
8 ounces cremini or button mushrooms, sliced

½ teaspoon fine sea salt
2 tablespoons tomato paste
1½ teaspoons yellow mustard
1 cup low-sodium roasted beef bone broth
Seared Cauliflower
1 tablespoon olive oil
1 head cauliflower, cut into bite-size florets
2 tablespoons chopped fresh flat-leaf parsley
¼ teaspoon fine sea salt
2 teaspoons cornstarch
2 teaspoons water

1. To make the steaks: In a bowl, combine the beef, almond flour, egg, salt, and pepper and mix with your hands until all of the ingredients are evenly distributed. Divide the mixture into four equal portions, then shape each portion into an oval patty about ½ inch thick. 2. Select the Sauté setting on the Instant Pot and heat the oil for 2 minutes. Swirl the oil to coat the bottom of the pot, then add the patties and sear for 3 minutes, until browned on one side. Using a thin, flexible spatula, flip the patties and sear the second side for 2 to 3 minutes, until browned. Transfer the patties to a plate. 3. Add the onion, garlic, mushrooms, and salt to the pot and sauté for 4 minutes, until the onion is translucent and the mushrooms have begun to give up their liquid. Add the tomato paste, mustard, and broth and stir with a wooden spoon, using it

to nudge any browned bits from the bottom of the pot. Return the patties to the pot in a single layer and spoon a bit of the sauce over each one. 4. Secure the lid and set the Pressure Release to Sealing. Press the Cancel button to reset the cooking program, then select the Pressure Cook or Manual setting and set the cooking time for 10 minutes at high pressure. (The pot will take about 5 minutes to come up to pressure before the cooking program begins.) 5. When the cooking program ends, let the pressure release naturally for at least 10 minutes, then move the Pressure Release to Venting to release any remaining steam. 6. To make the cauliflower: While the pressure is releasing, in a large skillet over medium heat, warm the oil. Add the cauliflower and stir or toss to coat with the oil, then cook, stirring every minute or two, until lightly browned, about 8 minutes. Turn off the heat, sprinkle in the parsley and salt, and stir to combine. Leave in the skillet, uncovered, to keep warm. 7. Open the pot and, using a slotted spatula, transfer the patties to a serving plate. In a small bowl, stir together the cornstarch and water. Press the Cancel button to reset the cooking program, then select the Sauté setting. When the sauce comes to a simmer, stir in the cornstarch mixture and let the sauce boil for about 1 minute, until thickened. Press the Cancel button to turn off the Instant Pot. 8. Spoon the sauce over the patties. Serve right away, with the cauliflower.

Per Serving:

calorie: 362 | fat: 21g | protein: 33g | carbs: 21g | sugars: 4g | fiber: 6g | sodium: 846mg

Teriyaki Rib-Eye Steaks

Prep time: 10 minutes | Cook time: 15 minutes | Serves 2

2 tablespoons water
1 tablespoon reduced-sodium soy sauce
1½ teaspoons Worcestershire sauce
1¼ teaspoons distilled white vinegar
1 teaspoon extra-virgin olive oil
½ teaspoon granulated stevia
½ teaspoon onion powder

¼ teaspoon garlic powder
⅛ teaspoon ground
2 (6-ounce) lean beef rib-eye steaks
Extra-virgin olive oil cooking spray
2 cups sugar snap peas
1 cup sliced carrots
1 red bell pepper, sliced

1. In a large bowl, whisk together the water, soy sauce, Worcestershire sauce, white vinegar, olive oil, stevia, onion powder, garlic powder, and ginger. 2. With a fork, pierce the steaks several times. Add to the marinade. Let marinate in the refrigerator for at least 2 hours. 3. Spray a large skillet with cooking spray. Place it over medium heat. 4. Add the steaks. Cook for 7 minutes. Turn the steaks. Add the sugar snap peas, carrots, and bell pepper to the skillet. Cook for 7 minutes more, or until an instant-read thermometer inserted into the center of the steak reads 140°F. 5. Serve and savor!

Per Serving:

calorie: 630 | fat: 40g | protein: 40g | carbs: 29g | sugars: 12g | fiber: 9g | sodium: 271mg

Homey Pot Roast

Prep time: 15 minutes | Cook time: 2 hour 15 minutes | Serves 6

1 pound boneless beef chuck roast
2 tablespoons Creole seasoning
2 cups store-bought low-sodium chicken broth, divided
1 large portobello mushroom, cut into 2-inch pieces
1 small onion, roughly chopped
3 celery stalks, roughly chopped
4 medium tomatoes, chopped
2 garlic cloves, minced
1 medium green pepper, roughly chopped
8 ounces steamer potatoes, skin on, halved
6 small parsnips, peeled and halved
2 large carrots, peeled and cut into 2-inch pieces
3 bay leaves
Freshly ground black pepper
Pinch cayenne pepper
Pinch smoked paprika

1. Preheat the oven to 325°F. 2. Massage the roast all over with the Creole seasoning. 3. In a Dutch oven, bring ½ cup of broth to a simmer over medium heat. 4. Add the beef and cook on all sides, turning to avoid burning the meat, no more than about 2½ minutes per side, or until browned. Remove the beef from the pot and set aside. 5. Add the mushroom, onion, celery, tomatoes, garlic, and green pepper to pot, adding up to ½ cup of broth if needed to prevent blackening of the vegetables. 6. Reduce the heat to medium-low and cook, stirring continuously, for 5 to 7 minutes, or until the vegetables have softened. 7. Return the beef to the pot. Add the potatoes, parsnips, carrots, bay leaves, and remaining 1 cup of broth. 8. Season with the black pepper, cayenne, and paprika. 9. Cover the pot, transfer to the oven, and bake for 2 hours, or until the beef is juicy and falls apart easily. Discard the bay leaves. 10. Serve.

Per Serving:

calorie: 237 | fat: 5g | protein: 20g | carbs: 29g | sugars: 8g | fiber: 7g | sodium: 329mg

Red Wine Pot Roast with Winter Vegetables

Prep time: 10 minutes | Cook time: 1 hour 35 minutes | Serves 6

One 3-pound boneless beef chuck roast or bottom round roast (see Note)
2 teaspoons fine sea salt
1 teaspoon freshly ground black pepper
1 tablespoon cold-pressed avocado oil
4 large shallots, quartered
4 garlic cloves, minced
1 cup dry red wine
2 tablespoons Dijon mustard
2 teaspoons chopped fresh rosemary
1 pound parsnips or turnips, cut into ½-inch pieces
1 pound carrots, cut into ½-inch pieces
4 celery stalks, cut into ½-inch pieces

1. Put the beef onto a plate, pat it dry with paper towels, and then season all over with the salt and pepper. 2. Select the Sauté setting on the Instant Pot and heat the oil for 2 minutes. Using tongs, lower the roast into the pot and sear for about 4 minutes, until browned on the first side. Flip the roast and sear for about 4 minutes more, until browned on the second side. Return the roast to the plate. 3. Add the shallots to the pot and sauté for about 2 minutes, until they begin to soften. Add the garlic and sauté for about 1 minute more. Stir in the wine, mustard, and rosemary, using a wooden spoon to nudge any browned bits from the bottom of the pot. Return the roast to the pot, then spoon some of the cooking liquid over the top. 4. Secure the lid and set the Pressure Release to Sealing. Press the Cancel button to reset the cooking program, then select the Meat/Stew setting and set the cooking time for 1 hour 5 minutes at high pressure. (The pot will take about 5 minutes to come up to pressure before the cooking program begins.) 5. When the cooking program ends, let the pressure release naturally for at least 15 minutes, then move the Pressure Release to Venting to release any remaining steam. Open the pot and, using tongs, carefully transfer the pot roast to a cutting board. Tent with aluminum foil to keep warm. 6. Add the parsnips, carrots, and celery to the pot. 7. Secure the lid and set the Pressure Release to Sealing. Press the Cancel button to reset the cooking program, then select the Pressure Cook or Manual setting and set the cooking time for 3 minutes at low pressure. (The pot will take about 10 minutes to come up to pressure before the cooking program begins.) 8. When the cooking program ends, perform a quick pressure release by moving the Pressure Release to Venting. Open the pot and, using a slotted spoon, transfer the vegetables to a serving dish. Wearing heat-resistant mitts, lift out the inner pot and pour the cooking liquid into a gravy boat or other serving vessel with a spout. (If you like, use a fat separator to remove the fat from the liquid before serving.) 9. If the roast was tied, snip the string and discard. Carve the roast against the grain into ½-inch-thick slices and arrange them on the dish with the vegetables. Pour some cooking liquid over the roast and serve, passing the remaining cooking liquid on the side.

Per Serving:

calorie: 448 | fat: 25g | protein: 26g | carbs: 26g | sugars: 7g | fiber: 6g | sodium: 945mg

Asian Steak Salad

Prep time: 20 minutes | Cook time: 5 minutes | Serves 6

1 pound cut-up lean beef for stir-fry
1 package (3 ounces) Oriental-flavor ramen noodle soup mix
½ cup low-fat Asian marinade and dressing
1 bag (10 ounces) romaine and leaf lettuce mix
1 cup fresh snow pea pods
½ cup matchstick-cut carrots (from 10-ounce bag)
1 can (11 ounce) mandarin orange segments, drained

1 Spray 12-inch skillet with cooking spray; heat over medium-high heat. Place beef in skillet; sprinkle with 1 teaspoon seasoning mix from soup mix. (Discard remaining seasoning mix.) Cook beef 4 to 5 minutes, stirring occasionally, until brown. Stir in 1 tablespoon of the dressing. 2 Break block of noodles from soup mix into small pieces. Mix noodles, lettuce, pea pods, carrots, and orange segments in large bowl. Add remaining dressing; toss until well coated. Divide mixture among 6 serving plates. Top with beef.

Per Serving:

calories: 240 | fat: 7g | protein: 19g | carbs: 25g | sugars: 14g | fiber: 2g | sodium: 990mg

Pork Milanese

Prep time: 10 minutes | Cook time: 12 minutes | Serves 4

4 (1-inch) boneless pork chops
Fine sea salt and ground black pepper, to taste
2 large eggs
¾ cup powdered Parmesan

cheese
Chopped fresh parsley, for garnish
Lemon slices, for serving

1. Spray the air fryer basket with avocado oil. Preheat the air fryer to 400°F (204°C). 2. Place the pork chops between 2 sheets of plastic wrap and pound them with the flat side of a meat tenderizer until they're ¼ inch thick. Lightly season both sides of the chops with salt and pepper. 3. Lightly beat the eggs in a shallow bowl. Divide the Parmesan cheese evenly between 2 bowls and set the bowls in this order: Parmesan, eggs, Parmesan. Dredge a chop in the first bowl of Parmesan, then dip it in the eggs, and then dredge it again in the second bowl of Parmesan, making sure both sides and all edges are well coated. Repeat with the remaining chops. 4. Place the chops in the air fryer basket and air fry for 12 minutes, or until the internal temperature reaches 145°F (63°C), flipping halfway through. 5. Garnish with fresh parsley and serve immediately with lemon slices. Store leftovers in an airtight container in the refrigerator for up to 3 days. Reheat in a preheated 390°F (199°C) air fryer for 5 minutes, or until warmed through.

Per Serving:

calories: 349 | fat: 14g | protein: 50g | carbs: 3g | fiber: 0g | sodium: 464mg

Open-Faced Philly Cheesesteak Sandwiches

Prep time: 5 minutes | Cook time: 25 minutes | Serves 4

Avocado oil cooking spray
1 cup chopped yellow onion
1 green bell pepper, chopped
12 ounces 93% lean ground beef
Pinch salt

¾ teaspoon freshly ground black pepper
4 slices provolone or Swiss cheese
4 English muffins, 100% whole-wheat

1. Heat a large skillet over medium-low heat. When hot, coat the cooking surface with cooking spray, and arrange the onion and pepper in an even layer. Cook for 8 to 10 minutes, stirring every 3 to 4 minutes. 2. Push the vegetables to one side of the skillet and add the beef, breaking it into large chunks. Cook for 7 to 9 minutes, until a crisp crust forms on the bottom of the meat. 3. Season the beef with the salt and pepper, then flip the beef over and break it down into smaller chunks. 4. Stir the vegetables and the beef together, then top with the cheese and cook for 2 minutes. 5. Meanwhile, split each muffin in half, if necessary, then toast the muffins in a toaster. 6. Place one-eighth of the filling on each muffin half.

Per Serving:

calorie: 373 | fat: 13g | protein: 33g | carbs: 33g | sugars: 8g | fiber: 6g | sodium: 303mg

Loaded Cottage Pie

Prep time: 15 minutes | Cook time: 1 hour | Serves 6 to 8

4 large russet potatoes, peeled and halved
3 tablespoons extra-virgin olive oil, divided
1 small onion, chopped
1 bunch collard greens, stemmed and thinly sliced
2 carrots, peeled and chopped
2 medium tomatoes, chopped
1 garlic clove, minced

1 pound 90 percent lean ground beef
½ cup store-bought low-sodium chicken broth
1 teaspoon Worcestershire sauce
1 teaspoon celery seeds
1 teaspoon smoked paprika
½ teaspoon dried chives
½ teaspoon ground mustard
½ teaspoon cayenne pepper

1. Preheat the oven to 400°F. 2. Bring a large pot of water to a boil. 3. Add the potatoes, and boil for 15 to 20 minutes, or until fork-tender. 4. Transfer the potatoes to a large bowl and mash with 1 tablespoon of olive oil. 5. In a large cast iron skillet, heat the remaining 2 tablespoons of olive oil. 6. Add the onion, collard greens, carrots, tomatoes, and garlic and sauté, stirring often, for 7 to 10 minutes, or until the vegetables are softened. 7. Add the beef, broth, Worcestershire sauce, celery seeds, and smoked paprika. 8. Spread the meat and vegetable mixture evenly onto the bottom of a casserole dish. Sprinkle the chives, ground mustard, and cayenne on top of the mixture. Spread the mashed potatoes evenly over the top. 9. Transfer the casserole dish to the oven, and bake for 30 minutes, or until the top is light golden brown.

Per Serving:

calorie: 358 | fat: 10g | protein: 22g | carbs: 48g | sugars: 4g | fiber: 8g | sodium: 98mg

Air Fryer Chicken-Fried Steak

Prep time: 5 minutes | Cook time: 20 minutes | Serves 4

1 pound beef chuck sirloin steak
3 cups low-fat milk, divided
1 teaspoon dried thyme
1 teaspoon dried rosemary

2 medium egg whites
1 cup chickpea crumbs
½ cup coconut flour
1 tablespoon Creole seasoning

1. In a bowl, marinate the steak in 2 cups of milk for 30 to 45 minutes. 2. Remove the steak from milk, shake off the excess liquid, and season with the thyme and rosemary. Discard the milk. 3. In a shallow bowl, beat the egg whites with the remaining 1 cup of milk. 4. In a separate shallow bowl, combine the chickpea crumbs, coconut flour, and seasoning. 5. Dip the steak in the egg white mixture then dredge in the chickpea crumb mixture, coating well. 6. Place the steak in the basket of an air fryer. 7. Set the air fryer to 390°F, close, and cook for 10 minutes. 8. Open the air fryer, turn the steaks, close, and cook for 10 minutes. Let rest for 5 minutes.

Per Serving:

calorie: 423 | fat: 19g | protein: 37g | carbs: 25g | sugars: 12g | fiber: 4g | sodium: 180mg

Rosemary Lamb Chops

Prep time: 25 minutes | Cook time: 2 minutes | Serves 4

1½ pounds lamb chops (4 small chops)
1 teaspoon kosher salt
Leaves from 1 (6-inch) rosemary sprig

2 tablespoons avocado oil
1 shallot, peeled and cut in quarters
1 tablespoon tomato paste
1 cup beef broth

1. Place the lamb chops on a cutting board. Press the salt and rosemary leaves into both sides of the chops. Let rest at room temperature for 15 to 30 minutes. 2. Set the electric pressure cooker to Sauté/More setting. When hot, add the avocado oil. 3. Brown the lamb chops, about 2 minutes per side. (If they don't all fit in a single layer, brown them in batches.) 4. Transfer the chops to a plate. In the pot, combine the shallot, tomato paste, and broth. Cook for about a minute, scraping up the brown bits from the bottom. Hit Cancel. 5. Add the chops and any accumulated juices back to the pot. 6. Close and lock the lid of the pressure cooker. Set the valve to sealing. 7. Cook on high pressure for 2 minutes. 8. When the cooking is complete, hit Cancel and quick release the pressure. 9. Once the pin drops, unlock and remove the lid. 10. Place the lamb chops on plates and serve immediately.

Per Serving:

calorie: 352 | fat: 20g | protein: 37g | carbs: 7g | sugars: 1g | fiber: 0g | sodium: 440mg

Italian Sausages with Peppers and Onions

Prep time: 5 minutes | Cook time: 28 minutes | Serves 3

1 medium onion, thinly sliced
1 yellow or orange bell pepper, thinly sliced
1 red bell pepper, thinly sliced
¼ cup avocado oil or melted

coconut oil
1 teaspoon fine sea salt
6 Italian sausages
Dijon mustard, for serving (optional)

1. Preheat the air fryer to 400°F (204°C). 2. Place the onion and peppers in a large bowl. Drizzle with the oil and toss well to coat the veggies. Season with the salt. 3. Place the onion and peppers in a pie pan and cook in the air fryer for 8 minutes, stirring halfway through. Remove from the air fryer and set aside. 4. Spray the air fryer basket with avocado oil. Place the sausages in the air fryer basket and air fry for 20 minutes, or until crispy and golden brown. During the last minute or two of cooking, add the onion and peppers to the basket with the sausages to warm them through. 5. Place the onion and peppers on a serving platter and arrange the sausages on top. Serve Dijon mustard on the side, if desired. 6. Store leftovers in an airtight container in the fridge for up to 7 days or in the freezer for up to a month. Reheat in a preheated 390°F (199°C) air fryer for 3 minutes, or until heated through.

Per Serving:

calorie: 455 | fat: 33g | protein: 29g | carbs: 13g | sugars: 3g | fiber: 2g | sodium: 392mg

Steak Stroganoff

Prep time: 15 minutes | Cook time: 30 minutes | Serves 6

1 tablespoon olive oil
2 tablespoons flour
½ teaspoon garlic powder
½ teaspoon pepper
¼ teaspoon paprika
1¾-pound boneless beef round steak, trimmed of fat, cut into 1½ × ½-inch strips.
10¾-ounce can reduced-sodium, 98% fat-free cream of

mushroom soup
½ cup water
1 envelope sodium-free dried onion soup mix
9-ounce jar sliced mushrooms, drained
½ cup fat-free sour cream
1 tablespoon minced fresh parsley

1. Place the oil in the Instant Pot and press Sauté. 2. Combine flour, garlic powder, pepper, and paprika in a small bowl. Stir the steak pieces through the flour mixture until they are evenly coated. 3. Lightly brown the steak pieces in the oil in the Instant Pot, about 2 minutes each side. Press Cancel when done. 4. Stir the mushroom soup, water, and onion soup mix then pour over the steak. 5. Secure the lid and set the vent to sealing. Press the Manual button and set for 15 minutes. 6. When cook time is up, let the pressure release naturally for 15 minutes, then release the rest manually. 7. Remove the lid and press Cancel then Sauté. Stir in mushrooms, sour cream, and parsley. Let the sauce come to a boil and cook for about 10-15 minutes.

Per Serving:

calories: 248 | fat: 6g | protein: 33g | carbs: 12g | sugars: 2g | fiber: 2g | sodium: 563mg

Sirloin Steaks with Cilantro Chimichurri

Prep time: 25 minutes | Cook time: 7 to 10 minutes | Serves 4

1 cup loosely packed fresh cilantro
1 small onion, cut into quarters
2 cloves garlic, cut in half
1 jalapeño chile, cut in half, seeded
2 teaspoons lime juice

2 teaspoons canola oil
½ teaspoon salt
2 teaspoons ground cumin
½ teaspoon pepper
4 beef sirloin steaks, 1 inch thick (about 1½ pounds)

1. Heat gas or charcoal grill. In food processor, place cilantro, onion, garlic, chile, lime juice, oil and ¼ teaspoon of the salt. Cover; process until finely chopped. Blend in 2 to 3 teaspoons water to make sauce thinner, if desired. Transfer to small bowl; set aside until serving time. 2. In small bowl, mix cumin, pepper and remaining ¼ teaspoon salt; rub evenly over steaks. Place steaks on grill over medium heat. Cover grill; cook 7 to 10 minutes for medium-rare (145°F), turning once halfway through cooking. 3. Serve 2 tablespoons chimichurri over each steak.

Per Serving:

calorie: 266 | fat: 10g | protein: 38g | carbs: 3g | sugars: 1g | fiber: 1g | sodium: 392mg

Mediterranean Steak Sandwiches

Prep time: 10 minutes | Cook time: 10 minutes | Serves 4

2 tablespoons extra-virgin olive oil
2 tablespoons balsamic vinegar
2 teaspoons minced garlic
2 teaspoons freshly squeezed lemon juice
2 teaspoons chopped fresh oregano
1 teaspoon chopped fresh parsley
1 pound flank steak, trimmed of fat
4 whole-wheat pitas
2 cups shredded lettuce
1 red onion, thinly sliced
1 tomato, chopped
1 ounce low-sodium feta cheese

1. In a large bowl, whisk together the olive oil, balsamic vinegar, garlic, lemon juice, oregano, and parsley. 2. Add the steak to the bowl, turning to coat it completely. 3. Marinate the steak for 1 hour in the refrigerator, turning it over several times. 4. Preheat the broiler. Line a baking sheet with aluminum foil. 5. Take the steak out of the bowl and discard the marinade. 6. Place the steak on the baking sheet and broil until it is done to your liking, about 5 minutes per side for medium. 7. Let the steak rest for 10 minutes before slicing it thinly on a bias. 8. Stuff the pitas with the sliced steak, lettuce, onion, tomato, and feta.

Per Serving:
calorie: 331 | fat: 15g | protein: 30g | carbs: 20g | sugars: 3g | fiber: 3g | sodium: 191mg

Dry-Rubbed Sirloin

Prep time: 5 minutes | Cook time: 15 minutes | Serves 6

1⅛ pounds beef round sirloin tip
2 tablespoons Creole seasoning

1. Preheat the oven to 375°F. 2. Massage the beef all over with the Creole seasoning. 3. Put the beef in a Dutch oven, cover, and transfer to the oven. Cook for 15 minutes, or until the juices run clear when you pierce the beef. 4. Remove the beef from the oven, and let rest for 15 minutes. 5. Carve, and serve.

Per Serving:
calorie: 134 | fat: 4g | protein: 19g | carbs: 4g | sugars: 0g | fiber: 1g | sodium: 260mg

Chipotle Chili Pork Chops

Prep time: 5 minutes | Cook time: 20 minutes | Serves 4

Juice and zest of 1 lime
1 tablespoon extra-virgin olive oil
1 tablespoon chipotle chili powder
2 teaspoons minced garlic
1 teaspoon ground cinnamon
Pinch sea salt
4 (5-ounce) pork chops, about 1 inch thick
Lime wedges, for garnish

1. Combine the lime juice and zest, oil, chipotle chili powder, garlic, cinnamon, and salt in a resealable plastic bag. Add the pork chops. Remove as much air as possible and seal the bag. 2. Marinate the chops in the refrigerator for at least 4 hours, and up to 24 hours, turning them several times. 3. Preheat the oven to 400°F and set a rack on a baking sheet. Let the chops rest at room temperature for 15 minutes, then arrange them on the rack and discard the remaining marinade. 4. Roast the chops until cooked through, turning once, about 10 minutes per side. 5. Serve with lime wedges.

Per Serving:
calorie: 224 | fat: 9g | protein: 32g | carbs: 4g | sugars: 0g | fiber: 2g | sodium: 140mg

Roasted Pork Loin

Prep time: 5 minutes | Cook time: 40 minutes | Serves 4

1 pound pork loin
1 tablespoon extra-virgin olive oil, divided
2 teaspoons honey
¼ teaspoon freshly ground black pepper
½ teaspoon dried rosemary
2 small gold potatoes, chopped into 2-inch cubes
4 (6-inch) carrots, chopped into ½-inch rounds

1. Preheat the oven to 350°F. 2. Rub the pork loin with ½ tablespoon of oil and the honey. Season with the pepper and rosemary. 3. In a medium bowl, toss the potatoes and carrots in the remaining ½ tablespoon of oil. 4. Place the pork and the vegetables on a baking sheet in a single layer. Cook for 40 minutes. 5. Remove the baking sheet from the oven and let the pork rest for at least 10 minutes before slicing. Divide the pork and vegetables into four equal portions.

Per Serving:
calorie: 281 | fat: 8g | protein: 28g | carbs: 24g | sugars: 6g | fiber: 4g | sodium: 103mg

Garlic Balsamic London Broil

Prep time: 30 minutes | Cook time: 8 to 10 minutes | Serves 8

2 pounds (907 g) London broil
3 large garlic cloves, minced
3 tablespoons balsamic vinegar
3 tablespoons whole-grain mustard
2 tablespoons olive oil
Sea salt and ground black pepper, to taste
½ teaspoon dried hot red pepper flakes

1. Score both sides of the cleaned London broil. 2. Thoroughly combine the remaining ingredients; massage this mixture into the meat to coat it on all sides. Let it marinate for at least 3 hours. 3. Set the air fryer to 400°F (204°C); Then cook the London broil for 15 minutes. Flip it over and cook another 10 to 12 minutes. Bon appétit!

Per Serving:
calories: 240 | fat: 15g | protein: 23g | carbs: 2g | fiber: 0g | sodium: 141mg

Broccoli Beef Stir-Fry

Prep time: 10 minutes | Cook time: 15 minutes | Serves 4

2 tablespoons extra-virgin olive oil
1 pound sirloin steak, cut into ¼-inch-thick strips
2 cups broccoli florets
1 garlic clove, minced
1 teaspoon peeled and grated

fresh ginger
2 tablespoons reduced-sodium soy sauce
¼ cup beef broth
½ teaspoon Chinese hot mustard
Pinch red pepper flakes

1. In a large skillet over medium-high heat, heat the olive oil until it shimmers. Add the beef. Cook, stirring, until it browns, 3 to 5 minutes. With a slotted spoon, remove the beef from the oil and set it aside on a plate. 2. Add the broccoli to the oil. Cook, stirring, until it is crisp-tender, about 4 minutes. 3. Add the garlic and ginger and cook, stirring constantly, for 30 seconds. 4. Return the beef to the pan, along with any juices that have collected. 5. In a small bowl, whisk together the soy sauce, broth, mustard, and red pepper flakes. 6. Add the soy sauce mixture to the skillet and cook, stirring, until everything warms through, about 3 minutes.

Per Serving:

calorie: 305 | fat: 21g | protein: 25g | carbs: 3g | sugars: 2g | fiber: 1g | sodium: 234mg

Poblano Pepper Cheeseburgers

Prep time: 5 minutes | Cook time: 30 minutes | Serves 4

2 poblano chile peppers
1½ pounds (680 g) 85% lean ground beef
1 clove garlic, minced
1 teaspoon salt

½ teaspoon freshly ground black pepper
4 slices Cheddar cheese (about 3 ounces / 85 g)
4 large lettuce leaves

1. Preheat the air fryer to 400ºF (204ºC). 2. Arrange the poblano peppers in the basket of the air fryer. Pausing halfway through the cooking time to turn the peppers, air fry for 20 minutes, or until they are softened and beginning to char. Transfer the peppers to a large bowl and cover with a plate. When cool enough to handle, peel off the skin, remove the seeds and stems, and slice into strips. Set aside. 3. Meanwhile, in a large bowl, combine the ground beef with the garlic, salt, and pepper. Shape the beef into 4 patties. 4. Lower the heat on the air fryer to 360ºF (182ºC). Arrange the burgers in a single layer in the basket of the air fryer. Pausing halfway through the cooking time to turn the burgers, air fry for 10 minutes, or until a thermometer inserted into the thickest part registers 160ºF (71ºC). 5. Top the burgers with the cheese slices and continue baking for a minute or two, just until the cheese has melted. Serve the burgers on a lettuce leaf topped with the roasted poblano peppers.

Per Serving:

calories: 489 | fat: 35g | protein: 39g | carbs: 3g | fiber: 1g | sodium: 703mg

Easy Pot Roast and Vegetables

Prep time: 20 minutes | Cook time: 35 minutes | Serves 6

3-4 pound chuck roast, trimmed of fat and cut into serving-sized chunks
4 medium potatoes, cubed, unpeeled

4 medium carrots, sliced, or 1 pound baby carrots
2 celery ribs, sliced thin
1 envelope dry onion soup mix
3 cups water

1. Place the pot roast chunks and vegetables into the Instant Pot along with the potatoes, carrots and celery. 2. Mix together the onion soup mix and water and pour over the contents of the Instant Pot. 3. Secure the lid and make sure the vent is set to sealing. Set the Instant Pot to Manual mode for 35 minutes. Let pressure release naturally when cook time is up.

Per Serving:

calorie: 325 | fat: 8g | protein: 35g | carbs: 26g | sugars: 6g | fiber: 4g | sodium: 560mg

Steak with Bell Pepper

Prep time: 30 minutes | Cook time: 20 to 23 minutes | Serves 6

¼ cup avocado oil
¼ cup freshly squeezed lime juice
2 teaspoons minced garlic
1 tablespoon chili powder
½ teaspoon ground cumin
Sea salt and freshly ground black pepper, to taste
1 pound (454 g) top sirloin steak

or flank steak, thinly sliced against the grain
1 red bell pepper, cored, seeded, and cut into ½-inch slices
1 green bell pepper, cored, seeded, and cut into ½-inch slices
1 large onion, sliced

1. In a small bowl or blender, combine the avocado oil, lime juice, garlic, chili powder, cumin, and salt and pepper to taste. 2. Place the sliced steak in a zip-top bag or shallow dish. Place the bell peppers and onion in a separate zip-top bag or dish. Pour half the marinade over the steak and the other half over the vegetables. Seal both bags and let the steak and vegetables marinate in the refrigerator for at least 1 hour or up to 4 hours. 3. Line the air fryer basket with an air fryer liner or aluminum foil. Remove the vegetables from their bag or dish and shake off any excess marinade. Set the air fryer to 400ºF (204ºC). Place the vegetables in the air fryer basket and cook for 13 minutes. 4. Remove the steak from its bag or dish and shake off any excess marinade. Place the steak on top of the vegetables in the air fryer, and cook for 7 to 10 minutes or until an instant-read thermometer reads 120ºF (49ºC) for medium-rare (or cook to your desired doneness). 5. Serve with desired fixings, such as keto tortillas, lettuce, sour cream, avocado slices, shredded Cheddar cheese, and cilantro.

Per Serving:

calories: 252 | fat: 18g | protein: 17g | carbs: 6g | fiber: 2g | sodium: 81mg

Spice-Rubbed Pork Loin

Prep time: 5 minutes | Cook time: 20 minutes | Serves 6

1 teaspoon paprika
½ teaspoon ground cumin
½ teaspoon chili powder
½ teaspoon garlic powder
2 tablespoons coconut oil

1 (1½-pound / 680-g) boneless pork loin
½ teaspoon salt
¼ teaspoon ground black pepper

1. In a small bowl, mix paprika, cumin, chili powder, and garlic powder. 2. Drizzle coconut oil over pork. Sprinkle pork loin with salt and pepper, then rub spice mixture evenly on all sides. 3. Place pork loin into ungreased air fryer basket. Adjust the temperature to 400ºF (204ºC) and air fry for 20 minutes, turning pork halfway through cooking. Pork loin will be browned and have an internal temperature of at least 145ºF (63ºC) when done. Serve warm.

Per Serving:

calories: 192 | fat: 9g | protein: 26g | carbs: 1g | fiber: 0g | sodium: 257mg

Carnitas Burrito Bowls

Prep time: 10 minutes | Cook time: 1 hour | Serves 6

Carnitas
1 tablespoon chili powder
½ teaspoon garlic powder
1 teaspoon ground coriander
1 teaspoon fine sea salt
½ cup water
¼ cup fresh lime juice
One 2-pound boneless pork shoulder butt roast, cut into 2-inch cubes
Rice and Beans
1 cup Minute brand brown rice (see Note)
1½ cups drained cooked black beans, or one 15-ounce can black beans, rinsed and drained
Pico de Gallo
8 ounces tomatoes (see Note),

diced
½ small yellow onion, diced
1 jalapeño chile, seeded and finely diced
1 tablespoon chopped fresh cilantro
1 teaspoon fresh lime juice
Pinch of fine sea salt
¼ cup sliced green onions, white and green parts
2 tablespoons chopped fresh cilantro
3 hearts romaine lettuce, cut into ¼-inch-wide ribbons
2 large avocados, pitted, peeled, and sliced
Hot sauce (such as Cholula or Tapatío) for serving

1. To make the carnitas: In a small bowl, combine the chili powder, garlic powder, coriander, and salt and mix well. 2. Pour the water and lime juice into the Instant Pot. Add the pork, arranging the pieces in a single layer. Sprinkle the chili powder mixture evenly over the pork. 3. Secure the lid and set the Pressure Release to Sealing. Select the Meat/Stew setting and set the cooking time for 30 minutes at high pressure. (The pot will take about 10 minutes to come up to pressure before the cooking program begins.) 4. When the cooking program ends, let the pressure release naturally for at least 15 minutes, then move the Pressure Release to Venting to release any remaining steam. Open the pot and, using tongs, transfer the pork to a plate or cutting board. 5. While the pressure is releasing, preheat the oven to 400°F. 6. Wearing heat-resistant mitts, lift out the inner pot and pour the cooking liquid into a fat separator. Pour the defatted cooking liquid into a liquid measuring cup and discard the fat. (Alternatively, use a ladle or large spoon to skim the fat off the surface of the liquid.) Add water as needed to the cooking liquid to total 1 cup (you may have enough without adding water). 7. To make the rice and beans: Pour the 1 cup cooking liquid into the Instant Pot and add the rice, making sure it is in an even layer. Place a tall steam rack into the pot. Add the black beans to a 1½-quart stainless-steel bowl and place the bowl on top of the rack. (The bowl should not touch the lid once the pot is closed.) 8. Secure the lid and set the Pressure Release to Sealing. Press the Cancel button to reset the cooking program, then select the Pressure Cook or Manual setting and set the cooking time for 15 minutes at high pressure. (The pot will take about 5 minutes to come to pressure before the cooking program begins.) 9. While the rice and beans are cooking, using two forks, shred the meat into bite-size pieces. Transfer the pork to a sheet pan, spreading it out in an even layer. Place in the oven for 20 minutes, until crispy and browned. 10. To make the pico de gallo: While the carnitas, rice, and beans are cooking, in a medium bowl, combine the tomatoes, onion, jalapeño, cilantro, lime juice, and salt and mix well. Set aside. 11. When the cooking program ends, let the pressure release naturally for 5 minutes, then move the Pressure Release to Venting to release any remaining steam. Open the pot and, wearing heat-resistant mitts, remove the bowl of beans and then the steam rack from the pot. Then remove the inner pot. Add the green onions and cilantro to the rice and, using a fork, fluff the rice and mix in the green onions and cilantro. 12. Divide the rice, beans, carnitas, pico de gallo, lettuce, and avocados evenly among six bowls. Serve warm, with the hot sauce on the side.

Per Serving:

calories: 447 | fat: 20g | protein: 31g | carbs: 35g | sugars: 4g | fiber: 9g | sodium: 653mg

Bone-in Pork Chops

Prep time: 5 minutes | Cook time: 10 to 12 minutes | Serves 2

1 pound (454 g) bone-in pork chops
1 tablespoon avocado oil
1 teaspoon smoked paprika

½ teaspoon onion powder
¼ teaspoon cayenne pepper
Sea salt and freshly ground black pepper, to taste

1. Brush the pork chops with the avocado oil. In a small dish, mix together the smoked paprika, onion powder, cayenne pepper, and salt and black pepper to taste. Sprinkle the seasonings over both sides of the pork chops. 2. Set the air fryer to 400ºF (204ºC). Place the chops in the air fryer basket in a single layer, working in batches if necessary. Air fry for 10 to 12 minutes, until an instant-read thermometer reads 145ºF (63ºC) at the chops' thickest point. 3. Remove the chops from the air fryer and allow them to rest for 5 minutes before serving.

Per Serving:

calories: 356 | fat: 16g | protein: 50g | carbs: 1g | fiber: 1g | sodium: 133mg

Autumn Pork Chops with Red Cabbage and Apples

Prep time: 15 minutes | Cook time: 30 minutes | Serves 4

¼ cup apple cider vinegar
2 tablespoons granulated sweetener
4 (4-ounce) pork chops, about 1 inch thick
Sea salt
Freshly ground black pepper
1 tablespoon extra-virgin olive oil
½ red cabbage, finely shredded
1 sweet onion, thinly sliced
1 apple, peeled, cored, and sliced
1 teaspoon chopped fresh thyme

1. In a small bowl, whisk together the vinegar and sweetener. Set it aside. 2. Season the pork with salt and pepper. 3. Place a large skillet over medium-high heat and add the olive oil. 4. Cook the pork chops until no longer pink, turning once, about 8 minutes per side. 5. Transfer the chops to a plate and set aside. 6. Add the cabbage and onion to the skillet and sauté until the vegetables have softened, about 5 minutes. 7. Add the vinegar mixture and the apple slices to the skillet and bring the mixture to a boil. 8. Reduce the heat to low and simmer, covered, for 5 additional minutes. 9. Return the pork chops to the skillet, along with any accumulated juices and thyme, cover, and cook for 5 more minutes.

Per Serving:

calorie: 251 | fat: 8g | protein: 26g | carbs: 19g | sugars: 13g | fiber: 2g | sodium: 76mg

Chinese Spareribs

Prep time: 10 minutes | Cook time: 40 minutes | Serves 2

2 tablespoons hoisin sauce
2 tablespoons tomato paste
2 tablespoons water
1 tablespoon rice vinegar
2 teaspoons sesame oil
2 teaspoons low-sodium soy sauce
2 teaspoons Chinese five-spice
powder
2 garlic cloves, minced
1 teaspoon freshly squeezed lemon juice
1 teaspoon grated fresh ginger
½ teaspoon granulated stevia
1 pound pork spareribs

1. In a shallow glass dish, mix together the hoisin sauce, tomato paste, water, rice vinegar, sesame oil, soy sauce, Chinese five-spice powder, garlic, lemon juice, ginger, and stevia. 2. Add the ribs to the marinade. Turn to coat. Cover and refrigerate for 2 hours, or overnight. 3. Preheat the oven to 325°F. 4. Place a rack in the center of the oven. 5. Fill a broiler tray with enough water to cover the bottom. Place the grate over the tray. Arrange the ribs on the grate. Reserve the marinade. 6. Place the broiler pan in the preheated oven. Cook for 40 minutes, turning and brushing with the reserved marinade every 10 minutes. 7. Finish under the broiler for a crispier texture, if desired. Discard any remaining marinade. 8. Serve immediately with lots of napkins and enjoy!

Per Serving:

calorie: 594 | fat: 39g | protein: 45g | carbs: 13g | sugars: 8g | fiber: 1g | sodium: 557mg

Tenderloin with Crispy Shallots

Prep time: 30 minutes | Cook time: 18 to 20 minutes | Serves 6

1½ pounds (680 g) beef tenderloin steaks
Sea salt and freshly ground black pepper, to taste
4 medium shallots
1 teaspoon olive oil or avocado oil

1. Season both sides of the steaks with salt and pepper, and let them sit at room temperature for 45 minutes. 2. Set the air fryer to 400°F (204°C) and let it preheat for 5 minutes. 3. Working in batches if necessary, place the steaks in the air fryer basket in a single layer and air fry for 5 minutes. Flip and cook for 5 minutes longer, until an instant-read thermometer inserted in the center of the steaks registers 120°F (49°C) for medium-rare (or as desired). Remove the steaks and tent with aluminum foil to rest. 4. Set the air fryer to 300°F (149°C). In a medium bowl, toss the shallots with the oil. Place the shallots in the basket and air fry for 5 minutes, then give them a toss and cook for 3 to 5 minutes more, until crispy and golden brown. 5. Place the steaks on serving plates and arrange the shallots on top.

Per Serving:

calories: 166 | fat: 8g | protein: 24g | carbs: 1g | fiber: 0g | sodium: 72mg

Asian-Style Grilled Beef Salad

Prep time: 15 minutes | Cook time: 15 minutes | Serves 4

FOR THE DRESSING
¼ cup freshly squeezed lime juice
1 tablespoon low-sodium tamari or gluten-free soy sauce
1 tablespoon extra-virgin olive oil
1 garlic clove, minced
1 teaspoon honey
¼ teaspoon red pepper flakes
FOR THE SALAD
1 pound grass-fed flank steak
¼ teaspoon salt
Pinch freshly ground black pepper
6 cups chopped leaf lettuce
1 cucumber, halved lengthwise and thinly cut into half moons
½ small red onion, sliced
1 carrot, cut into ribbons
¼ cup chopped fresh cilantro

TO MAKE THE DRESSING In a small bowl, whisk together the lime juice, tamari, olive oil, garlic, honey, and red pepper flakes. Set aside. TO MAKE THE SALAD 1. Season the beef on both sides with the salt and pepper. 2. Heat a skillet over high heat until hot. Cook the beef for 3 to 6 minutes per side, depending on preferred doneness. Set aside, tented with aluminum foil, for 10 minutes. 3. In a large bowl, toss the lettuce, cucumber, onion, carrot, and cilantro. 4. Slice the beef thinly against the grain and transfer to the salad bowl. 5. Drizzle with the dressing and toss. Serve.

Per Serving:

calories: 231 | fat: 10g | protein: 26g | carbs: 10g | sugars: 4g | fiber: 2g | sodium: 349mg

Vegetable Beef Soup

Prep time: 10 minutes | Cook time: 15 minutes | Serves 4

1 pound ground beef
1 onion, chopped
2 celery stalks, chopped
1 carrot, chopped
1 teaspoon dried rosemary
6 cups low-sodium beef or

chicken broth
½ teaspoon sea salt
⅛ teaspoon freshly ground black pepper
2 cups peas

1. In a large pot over medium-high heat, cook the ground beef, crumbling with the side of a spoon, until browned, about 5 minutes. 2. Add the onion, celery, carrot, and rosemary. Cook, stirring occasionally, until the vegetables start to soften, about 5 minutes. 3. Add the broth, salt, pepper, and peas. Bring to a simmer. Reduce the heat and simmer, stirring, until warmed through, about 5 minutes more.

Per Serving:

calorie: 284 | fat: 8g | protein: 36g | carbs: 19g | sugars: 7g | fiber: 5g | sodium: 496mg

Pork Tenderloin Stir-Fry

Prep time: 5 minutes | Cook time: 20 minutes | Serves 6

1 tablespoon sesame oil
1-pound pork tenderloin, cut into thin strips
1 tablespoon oyster sauce (found in the Asian food section of the grocery store)
1 tablespoon cornstarch
½ cup low-sodium chicken

broth
1 tablespoon light soy sauce
1 cup fresh snow peas, trimmed
1 cup broccoli florets
½ cup sliced water chestnuts, drained
1 cup diced red pepper
¼ cup sliced scallions

1. In a large skillet or wok, heat the oil. Stir-fry the pork until the strips are no longer pink. 2. In a measuring cup, combine the oyster sauce, cornstarch, chicken broth, and soy sauce. Add the sauce to the pork, and cook until the sauce thickens. 3. Add the vegetables, cover, and steam for 5 minutes. Serve.

Per Serving:

calorie: 149 | fat: 5g | protein: 18g | carbs: 8g | sugars: 3g | fiber: g | sodium: 174mg

Spicy Beef Stew with Butternut Squash

Prep time: 15 minutes | Cook time: 30 minutes | Serves 8

1½ tablespoons smoked paprika
2 teaspoons ground cinnamon
1½ teaspoons kosher salt
1 teaspoon ground ginger
1 teaspoon red pepper flakes
½ teaspoon freshly ground black pepper

2 pounds beef shoulder roast, cut into 1-inch cubes
2 tablespoons avocado oil, divided
1 cup low-sodium beef or vegetable broth
1 medium red onion, cut into

wedges
8 garlic cloves, minced
1 (28-ounce) carton or can no-salt-added diced tomatoes
2 pounds butternut squash,

peeled and cut into 1-inch pieces
Chopped fresh cilantro or parsley, for serving

1. In a zip-top bag or medium bowl, combine the paprika, cinnamon, salt, ginger, red pepper, and black pepper. Add the beef and toss to coat. 2. Set the electric pressure cooker to the Sauté setting. When the pot is hot, pour in 1 tablespoon of avocado oil. 3. Add half of the beef to the pot and cook, stirring occasionally, for 3 to 5 minutes or until the beef is no longer pink. Transfer it to a plate, then add the remaining 1 tablespoon of avocado oil and brown the remaining beef. Transfer to the plate. Hit Cancel. 4. Stir in the broth and scrape up any brown bits from the bottom of the pot. Return the beef to the pot and add the onion, garlic, tomatoes and their juices, and squash. Stir well. 5. Close and lock lid of pressure cooker. Set the valve to sealing. 6. Cook on high pressure for 30 minutes. 7. When cooking is complete, hit Cancel. Allow the pressure to release naturally for 10 minutes, then quick release any remaining pressure. 8. Unlock and remove lid. 9. Spoon into serving bowls, sprinkle with cilantro or parsley, and serve.

Per Serving:

calorie: 275 | fat: 9g | protein: 28g | carbs: 24g | sugars: 7g | fiber: 6g | sodium: 512mg

Bavarian Beef

Prep time: 35 minutes | Cook time: 1 hour 15 minutes | Serves 8

1 tablespoon canola oil
3-pound boneless beef chuck roast, trimmed of fat
3 cups sliced carrots
3 cups sliced onions
2 large kosher dill pickles, chopped
1 cup sliced celery
½ cup dry red wine or beef

broth
⅓ cup German-style mustard
2 teaspoons coarsely ground black pepper
2 bay leaves
¼ teaspoon ground cloves
1 cup water
⅓ cup flour

1. Press Sauté on the Instant Pot and add in the oil. Brown roast on both sides for about 5 minutes. Press Cancel. 2. Add all of the remaining ingredients, except for the flour, to the Instant Pot. 3. Secure the lid and make sure the vent is set to sealing. Press Manual and set the time to 1 hour and 15 minutes. Let the pressure release naturally. 4. Remove meat and vegetables to large platter. Cover to keep warm. 5. Remove 1 cup of the liquid from the Instant Pot and mix with the flour. Press Sauté on the Instant Pot and add the flour/broth mixture back in, whisking. Cook until the broth is smooth and thickened. 6. Serve over noodles or spaetzle.

Per Serving:

calories: 251 | fat: 8g | protein: 26g | carbs: 17g | sugars: 7g | fiber: 4g | sodium: 525mg

Beef Burgundy

Prep time: 30 minutes | Cook time: 30 minutes | Serves 6

2 tablespoons olive oil	1 teaspoon salt
2 pounds stewing meat, cubed, trimmed of fat	¼ teaspoon dried marjoram
2½ tablespoons flour	¼ teaspoon dried thyme
5 medium onions, thinly sliced	⅛ teaspoon pepper
½ pound fresh mushrooms, sliced	¾ cup beef broth
	1½ cups burgundy

1. Press Sauté on the Instant pot and add in the olive oil. 2. Dredge meat in flour, then brown in batches in the Instant Pot. Set aside the meat. Sauté the onions and mushrooms in the remaining oil and drippings for about 3-4 minutes, then add the meat back in. Press Cancel. 3. Add the salt, marjoram, thyme, pepper, broth, and wine to the Instant Pot. 4. Secure the lid and make sure the vent is set to sealing. Press the Manual button and set to 30 minutes. 5. When cook time is up, let the pressure release naturally for 15 minutes, then perform a quick release. 6. Serve over cooked noodles.

Per Serving:

calories: 358 | fat: 11g | protein: 37g | carbs: 15g | sugars: 5g | fiber: 2g | sodium: 472mg

Pork Chops Pomodoro

Prep time: 0 minutes | Cook time: 30 minutes | Serves 6

2 pounds boneless pork loin chops, each about 5⅓ ounces and ½ inch thick	½ teaspoon Italian seasoning
¾ teaspoon fine sea salt	1 tablespoon capers, drained
½ teaspoon freshly ground black pepper	2 cups cherry tomatoes
2 tablespoons extra-virgin olive oil	2 tablespoons chopped fresh basil or flat-leaf parsley
2 garlic cloves, chopped	Spiralized zucchini noodles, cooked cauliflower "rice," or cooked whole-grain pasta for serving
½ cup low-sodium chicken broth or vegetable broth	Lemon wedges for serving

1. Pat the pork chops dry with paper towels, then season them all over with the salt and pepper. 2. Select the Sauté setting on the Instant Pot and heat 1 tablespoon of the oil for 2 minutes. Swirl the oil to coat the bottom of the pot. Using tongs, add half of the pork chops in a single layer and sear for about 3 minutes, until lightly browned on the first side. Flip the chops and sear for about 3 minutes more, until lightly browned on the second side. Transfer the chops to a plate. Repeat with the remaining 1 tablespoon oil and pork chops. 3. Add the garlic to the pot and sauté for about 1 minute, until bubbling but not browned. Stir in the broth, Italian seasoning, and capers, using a wooden spoon to nudge any browned bits from the bottom of the pot and working quickly so not too much liquid evaporates. Using the tongs, transfer the pork chops to the pot. Add the tomatoes in an even layer on top of the chops. 4. Secure the lid and set the Pressure Release to Sealing. Press the Cancel button to reset the cooking program, then select the Pressure Cook or Manual setting and set the cooking time for 10 minutes

at high pressure. (The pot will take about 5 minutes to come up to pressure before the cooking program begins.) 5. When the cooking program ends, let the pressure release naturally for at least 10 minutes, then move the Pressure Release to Venting to release any remaining steam. Open the pot and, using the tongs, transfer the pork chops to a serving dish. 6. Spoon the tomatoes and some of the cooking liquid on top of the pork chops. Sprinkle with the basil and serve right away, with zucchini noodles and lemon wedges on the side.

Per Serving:

calorie: 265 | fat: 13g | protein: 31g | carbs: 3g | sugars: 2g | fiber: 1g | sodium: 460mg

Pork Carnitas

Prep time: 10 minutes | Cook time: 20 minutes | Serves 8

1 teaspoon kosher salt	Juice and zest of 1 large orange
2 teaspoons chili powder	Juice and zest of 1 medium lime
2 teaspoons dried oregano	6-inch gluten-free corn tortillas, warmed, for serving (optional)
½ teaspoon freshly ground black pepper	Chopped avocado, for serving (optional)
1 (2½-pound) pork sirloin roast or boneless pork butt, cut into 1½-inch cubes	Roasted Tomatillo Salsa or salsa verde, for serving (optional)
2 tablespoons avocado oil, divided	Shredded cheddar cheese, for serving (optional)
3 garlic cloves, minced	

1. In a large bowl or gallon-size zip-top bag, combine the salt, chili powder, oregano, and pepper. Add the pork cubes and toss to coat. 2. Set the electric pressure cooker to the Sauté/More setting. When the pot is hot, pour in 1 tablespoon of avocado oil. 3. Add half of the pork to the pot and sear until the pork is browned on all sides, about 5 minutes. Transfer the pork to a plate, add the remaining 1 tablespoon of avocado oil to the pot, and sear the remaining pork. Hit Cancel. 4. Return all of the pork to the pot and add the garlic, orange zest and juice, and lime zest and juice to the pot. 5. Close and lock the lid of the pressure cooker. Set the valve to sealing. 6. Cook on high pressure for 20 minutes. 7. When the cooking is complete, hit Cancel. Allow the pressure to release naturally for 15 minutes then quick release any remaining pressure. 8. Once the pin drops, unlock and remove the lid. 9. Using two forks, shred the meat right in the pot. 10. (Optional) For more authentic carnitas, spread the shredded meat on a broiler-safe sheet pan. Preheat the broiler with the rack 6 inches from the heating element. Broil the pork for about 5 minutes or until it begins to crisp. (Watch carefully so you don't let the pork burn.) 11. Place the pork in a serving bowl. Top with some of the juices from the pot. Serve with tortillas, avocado, salsa, and Cheddar cheese (if using).

Per Serving:

calorie: 218 | fat: 7g | protein: 33g | carbs: 4g | sugars: 2g | fiber: 1g | sodium: 400mg

Chapter 5 Fish and Seafood

Shrimp Étouffée

Prep time: 20 minutes | Cook time: 30 minutes | Serves 4 to 6

2 cups store-bought low-sodium vegetable broth, divided
¼ cup whole-wheat flour
1 small onion, finely chopped
2 celery stalks including leaves, finely chopped
1 medium green bell pepper, finely chopped
1 medium poblano pepper, finely chopped
3 garlic cloves, minced
1 tablespoon Creole seasoning
2 pounds medium shrimp, shelled and deveined
⅓ cup finely chopped chives, for garnish

1. In a Dutch oven, bring ½ cup of broth to a simmer over medium heat. 2. Stir in the flour and reduce the heat to low. Cook, stirring often, for 5 minutes, or until a thick paste is formed. 3. Add ½ cup of broth, the onion, celery, bell pepper, poblano pepper, and garlic and cook for 2 to 5 minutes, or until the vegetables have softened. 4. Slowly add the seasoning and remaining 1 cup of broth, ¼ cup at a time. 5. Add the shrimp and cook for about 5 minutes, or until just opaque. 6. Serve with the vegetable of your choice. Garnish with the chives.

Per Serving:

calories: 164 | fat: 1g | protein: 32g | carbs: 8g | sugars: 2g | fiber: 1g | sodium: 500mg

Creamy Cod with Asparagus

Prep time: 5 minutes | Cook time: 15 minutes | Serves 4

½ cup uncooked brown rice or quinoa
4 (4-ounce) cod fillets
¼ teaspoon salt
¼ teaspoon freshly ground black pepper
½ teaspoon garlic powder, divided
24 asparagus spears
Avocado oil cooking spray
1 cup half-and-half

1. Cook the rice according to the package instructions. 2. Meanwhile, season both sides of the cod fillets with the salt, pepper, and ¼ teaspoon of garlic powder. 3. Cut the bottom 1½ inches from the asparagus. 4. Heat a large pan over medium-low heat. When hot, coat the cooking surface with cooking spray, and arrange the cod and asparagus in a single layer. 5. Cover and cook for 8 minutes. 6. Add the half-and-half and the remaining ¼ teaspoon of garlic powder and stir. Increase the heat to high and simmer for 2 minutes. 7. Divide the rice, cod, and asparagus into four equal portions.

Per Serving:

calories: 219 | fat: 2g | protein: 24g | carbs: 24g | sugars: 4g | fiber: 1g | sodium: 267mg

Scallops in Lemon-Butter Sauce

Prep time: 10 minutes | Cook time: 6 minutes | Serves 2

8 large dry sea scallops (about ¾ pound / 340 g)
Salt and freshly ground black pepper, to taste
2 tablespoons olive oil
2 tablespoons unsalted butter, melted
2 tablespoons chopped flat-leaf parsley
1 tablespoon fresh lemon juice
2 teaspoons capers, drained and chopped
1 teaspoon grated lemon zest
1 clove garlic, minced

1. Preheat the air fryer to 400°F (204°C). 2. Use a paper towel to pat the scallops dry. Sprinkle lightly with salt and pepper. Brush with the olive oil. Arrange the scallops in a single layer in the air fryer basket. Pausing halfway through the cooking time to turn the scallops, air fry for about 6 minutes until firm and opaque. 3. Meanwhile, in a small bowl, combine the oil, butter, parsley, lemon juice, capers, lemon zest, and garlic. Drizzle over the scallops just before serving.

Per Serving:

calories: 304 | fat: 22g | protein: 21g | carbs: 5g | net carbs: 4g | fiber: 1g

Whole Veggie-Stuffed Trout

Prep time: 10 minutes | Cook time: 25 minutes | Serves 2

Nonstick cooking spray
2 (8-ounce) whole trout fillets, dressed (cleaned but with bones and skin intact)
1 tablespoon extra-virgin olive oil
¼ teaspoon salt
⅛ teaspoon freshly ground black pepper
½ red bell pepper, seeded and thinly sliced
1 small onion, thinly sliced
2 or 3 shiitake mushrooms, sliced
1 poblano pepper, seeded and thinly sliced
1 lemon, sliced

1. Preheat the oven to 425°F. Spray a baking sheet with nonstick cooking spray. 2. Rub both trout, inside and out, with the olive oil, then season with the salt and pepper. 3. In a large bowl, combine the bell pepper, onion, mushrooms, and poblano pepper. Stuff half of this mixture into the cavity of each fish. Top the mixture with 2 or 3 lemon slices inside each fish. 4. Arrange the fish on the prepared baking sheet side by side and roast for 25 minutes until the fish is cooked through and the vegetables are tender.

Per Serving:

calories: 452 | fat: 22g | protein: 49g | carbs: 14g | sugars: 2g | fiber: 3g | sodium: 357mg

Lemon Pepper Tilapia with Broccoli and Carrots

Prep time: 0 minutes | Cook time: 15 minutes | Serves 4

1 pound tilapia fillets
1 teaspoon lemon pepper seasoning
¼ teaspoon fine sea salt
2 tablespoons extra-virgin olive oil
2 garlic cloves, minced
1 small yellow onion, sliced
½ cup low-sodium vegetable broth
2 tablespoons fresh lemon juice
1 pound broccoli crowns, cut into bite-size florets
8 ounces carrots, cut into ¼-inch thick rounds

1. Sprinkle the tilapia fillets all over with the lemon pepper seasoning and salt. 2. Select the Sauté setting on the Instant Pot and heat the oil and garlic for 2 minutes, until the garlic is bubbling but not browned. Add the onion and sauté for about 3 minutes more, until it begins to soften. 3. Pour in the broth and lemon juice, then use a wooden spoon to nudge any browned bits from the bottom of the pot. Using tongs, add the fish fillets to the pot in a single layer; it's fine if they overlap slightly. Place the broccoli and carrots on top. 4. Secure the lid and set the Pressure Release to Sealing. Press the Cancel button to reset the cooking program, then select the Pressure Cook or Manual setting and set the cooking time for 1 minute at low pressure. (The pot will take about 10 minutes to come up to pressure before the cooking program begins.) 5. When the cooking program ends, let the pressure release naturally for 10 minutes (don't open the pot before the 10 minutes are up, even if the float valve has gone down), then move the Pressure Release to Venting to release any remaining steam. Open the pot. Use a fish spatula to transfer the vegetables and fillets to plates. Serve right away.

Per Serving:

calories: 243 | fat: 9g | protein: 28g | carbs: 15g | sugars: 4g | fiber: 5g | sodium: 348mg

Almond Pesto Salmon

Prep time: 5 minutes | Cook time: 12 minutes | Serves 2

¼ cup pesto
¼ cup sliced almonds, roughly chopped
2 (1½-inch-thick) salmon fillets
(about 4 ounces / 113 g each)
2 tablespoons unsalted butter, melted

1. In a small bowl, mix pesto and almonds. Set aside. 2. Place fillets into a round baking dish. 3. Brush each fillet with butter and place half of the pesto mixture on the top of each fillet. Place dish into the air fryer basket. 4. Adjust the temperature to 390ºF (199ºC) and set the timer for 12 minutes. 5. Salmon will easily flake when fully cooked and reach an internal temperature of at least 145ºF (63ºC). Serve warm.

Per Serving:

calories: 478 | fat: 39g | protein: 29g | carbs: 4g | sugars: 1g | fiber: 2g | sodium: 366mg

Crab Cakes with Honeydew Melon Salsa

Prep time: 30 minutes | Cook time: 10 minutes | Serves 4

For the Salsa
1 cup finely chopped honeydew melon
1 scallion, white and green parts, finely chopped
1 red bell pepper, seeded, finely chopped
1 teaspoon chopped fresh thyme
Pinch sea salt
Pinch freshly ground black pepper

For the Crab Cakes
1 pound lump crabmeat, drained and picked over
¼ cup finely chopped red onion
¼ cup panko bread crumbs
1 tablespoon chopped fresh parsley
1 teaspoon lemon zest
1 egg
¼ cup whole-wheat flour
Nonstick cooking spray

To Make the Salsa 1. In a small bowl, stir together the melon, scallion, bell pepper, and thyme. 2. Season the salsa with salt and pepper and set aside. To Make the Crab Cakes 1. In a medium bowl, mix together the crab, onion, bread crumbs, parsley, lemon zest, and egg until very well combined. 2. Divide the crab mixture into 8 equal portions and form them into patties about ¾-inch thick. 3. Chill the crab cakes in the refrigerator for at least 1 hour to firm them up. 4. Dredge the chilled crab cakes in the flour until lightly coated, shaking off any excess flour. 5. Place a large skillet over medium heat and lightly coat it with cooking spray. 6. Cook the crab cakes until they are golden brown, turning once, about 5 minutes per side. 7. Serve warm with the salsa.

Per Serving:

calories: 222 | fat: 3g | protein: 29g | carbs: 18g | sugars: 6g | fiber: 2g | sodium: 504mg

Orange-Infused Scallops

Prep time: 10 minutes | Cook time: 10 minutes | Serves 4

2 pounds sea scallops
Sea salt
Freshly ground black pepper
2 tablespoons extra-virgin olive oil
1 tablespoon minced garlic
¼ cup freshly squeezed orange juice
1 teaspoon orange zest
2 teaspoons chopped fresh thyme, for garnish

1. Clean the scallops and pat them dry with paper towels, then season them lightly with salt and pepper. 2. Place a large skillet over medium-high heat and add the olive oil. 3. Sauté the garlic until it is softened and translucent, about 3 minutes. 4. Add the scallops to the skillet and cook until they are lightly seared and just cooked through, turning once, about 4 minutes per side. 5. Transfer the scallops to a plate, cover to keep warm, and set them aside. 6. Add the orange juice and zest to the skillet and stir to scrape up any cooked bits. 7. Spoon the sauce over the scallops and serve, garnished with the thyme.

Per Serving:

calories: 227 | fat: 8g | protein: 28g | carbs: 10g | sugars: 1g | fiber: 0g | sodium: 690mg

Cobia with Lemon-Caper Sauce

Prep time: 25 minutes | Cook time: 10 minutes | Serves 4

⅓ cup all-purpose flour
¼ teaspoon salt
¼ teaspoon pepper
1¼ pounds cobia or sea bass fillets, cut into 4 pieces
2 tablespoons olive oil
⅓ cup dry white wine

½ cup reduced-sodium chicken broth
2 tablespoons lemon juice
1 tablespoon capers, rinsed, drained
1 tablespoon chopped fresh parsley

1 In shallow dish, stir flour, salt and pepper. Coat cobia pieces in flour mixture (reserve remaining flour mixture). In 12-inch nonstick skillet, heat oil over medium-high heat. Place coated cobia in oil. Cook 8 to 10 minutes, turning halfway through cooking, until fish flakes easily with fork; remove from heat. Lift fish from skillet to serving platter with slotted spatula (do not discard drippings); keep warm. 2 Heat skillet (with drippings) over medium heat. Stir in 1 tablespoon reserved flour mixture; cook and stir 30 seconds. Stir in wine; cook about 30 seconds or until thickened and slightly reduced. Stir in chicken broth and lemon juice; cook and stir 1 to 2 minutes until sauce is smooth and slightly thickened. Stir in capers. 3 Serve sauce over cobia; sprinkle with parsley.

Per Serving:

calories: 230 | fat: 9g | protein: 28g | carbs: 9g | sugars: 0g | fiber: 0g | sodium: 400mg

Scallops and Asparagus Skillet

Prep time: 10 minutes | Cook time: 15 minutes | Serves 4

3 teaspoons extra-virgin olive oil, divided
1 pound asparagus, trimmed and cut into 2-inch segments
1 tablespoon butter
1 pound sea scallops

¼ cup dry white wine
Juice of 1 lemon
2 garlic cloves, minced
¼ teaspoon freshly ground black pepper

1. In a large skillet, heat 1½ teaspoons of oil over medium heat. 2. Add the asparagus and sauté for 5 to 6 minutes until just tender, stirring regularly. Remove from the skillet and cover with aluminum foil to keep warm. 3. Add the remaining 1½ teaspoons of oil and the butter to the skillet. When the butter is melted and sizzling, place the scallops in a single layer in the skillet. Cook for about 3 minutes on one side until nicely browned. Use tongs to gently loosen and flip the scallops, and cook on the other side for another 3 minutes until browned and cooked through. Remove and cover with foil to keep warm. 4. In the same skillet, combine the wine, lemon juice, garlic, and pepper. Bring to a simmer for 1 to 2 minutes, stirring to mix in any browned pieces left in the pan. 5. Return the asparagus and the cooked scallops to the skillet to coat with the sauce. Serve warm.

Per Serving:

calories: 252 | fat: 7g | protein: 26g | carbs: 15g | sugars: 3g | fiber: 2g | sodium: 493mg

Roasted Tilapia and Vegetables

Prep time: 15 minutes | Cook time: 20 minutes | Serves 4

½ pound fresh asparagus spears, trimmed, halved
2 small zucchini, halved lengthwise, cut into ½-inch pieces
1 red bell pepper, cut into ½-inch strips
1 large onion, cut into ½-inch wedges

1 tablespoon olive oil
2 teaspoons Montreal steak seasoning
4 tilapia fillets (about 1½ pounds)
2 teaspoons butter or margarine, melted
½ teaspoon paprika

1 Heat oven to 450°F. In large bowl, toss asparagus, zucchini, bell pepper, onion and oil. Sprinkle with 1 teaspoon of the steak seasoning; toss to coat. Spread vegetables in ungreased 15x10x1-inch pan. Place on lower oven rack; roast 5 minutes. 2 Meanwhile, spray 13x9-inch (3-quart) glass baking dish with cooking spray. Pat tilapia fillets dry with paper towels. Brush with butter; sprinkle with remaining 1 teaspoon steak seasoning and the paprika. Place in baking dish. 3 Place baking dish on middle oven rack. Roast fish and vegetables 17 to 18 minutes longer or until fish flakes easily with fork and vegetables are tender.

Per Serving:

calories: 250 | fat: 8g | protein: 35g | carbs: 10g | sugars: 5g | fiber: 3g | sodium: 160mg

Cucumber and Salmon Salad

Prep time: 10 minutes | Cook time: 8 to 10 minutes | Serves 2

1 pound (454 g) salmon fillet
1½ tablespoons olive oil, divided
1 tablespoon sherry vinegar
1 tablespoon capers, rinsed and drained
1 seedless cucumber, thinly

sliced
¼ Vidalia onion, thinly sliced
2 tablespoons chopped fresh parsley
Salt and freshly ground black pepper, to taste

1. Preheat the air fryer to 400ºF (204ºC). 2. Lightly coat the salmon with ½ tablespoon of the olive oil. Place skin-side down in the air fryer basket and air fry for 8 to 10 minutes until the fish is opaque and flakes easily with a fork. Transfer the salmon to a plate and let cool to room temperature. Remove the skin and carefully flake the fish into bite-size chunks. 3. In a small bowl, whisk the remaining 1 tablespoon olive oil and the vinegar until thoroughly combined. Add the flaked fish, capers, cucumber, onion, and parsley. Season to taste with salt and freshly ground black pepper. Toss gently to coat. Serve immediately or cover and refrigerate for up to 4 hours.

Per Serving:

calories: 399 | fat: 20g | protein: 47g | carbs: 4g | fiber: 1g | sodium: 276mg

Charcuterie Dinner For One

Prep time: 5 minutes | Cook time: 10 to 12 minutes | Serves 1

1 (6-ounce/170-g) salmon fillet
Cooking oil spray, as needed
1 ounce (28 g) fresh mozzarella cheese slices or balls
½ cup (60 g) thinly sliced

cucumbers
¼ cup (50 g) plain nonfat Greek yogurt
1 ounce (28 g) grain-free or whole-grain crackers

1. Preheat the oven to 400°F (204°C). Line a medium baking sheet with parchment paper. 2. Lightly spray the salmon fillet with the cooking oil spray and place the salmon on the prepared baking sheet. Bake the salmon for 10 to 12 minutes, or until it has browned slightly on top. 3. Meanwhile, assemble the mozzarella cheese, cucumbers, yogurt, and crackers on a plate. 4. Transfer the salmon to the plate and serve.

Per Serving:
calorie: 517 | fat: 29g | protein: 47g | carbs: 16g | sugars: 5g | fiber: 1g | sodium: 418mg

Lemony Salmon

Prep time: 30 minutes | Cook time: 10 minutes | Serves 4

1½ pounds (680 g) salmon steak
½ teaspoon grated lemon zest
Freshly cracked mixed peppercorns, to taste
⅓ cup lemon juice
Fresh chopped chives, for

garnish
½ cup dry white wine
½ teaspoon fresh cilantro, chopped
Fine sea salt, to taste

1. To prepare the marinade, place all ingredients, except for salmon steak and chives, in a deep pan. Bring to a boil over medium-high flame until it has reduced by half. Allow it to cool down. 2. After that, allow salmon steak to marinate in the refrigerator approximately 40 minutes. Discard the marinade and transfer the fish steak to the preheated air fryer. 3. Air fry at 400ºF (204ºC) for 9 to 10 minutes. To finish, brush hot fish steaks with the reserved marinade, garnish with fresh chopped chives, and serve right away!

Per Serving:
calories: 244 | fat: 8g | protein: 35g | carbs: 3g | fiber: 0g | sodium: 128mg

Tuna Steaks with Olive Tapenade

Prep time: 10 minutes | Cook time: 10 minutes | Serves 4

4 (6-ounce / 170-g) ahi tuna steaks
1 tablespoon olive oil
Salt and freshly ground black pepper, to taste
½ lemon, sliced into 4 wedges
Olive Tapenade:

½ cup pitted kalamata olives
1 tablespoon olive oil
1 tablespoon chopped fresh parsley
1 clove garlic
2 teaspoons red wine vinegar
1 teaspoon capers, drained

1. Preheat the air fryer to 400°F (204°C). 2. Drizzle the tuna steaks with the olive oil and sprinkle with salt and black pepper. Arrange the tuna steaks in a single layer in the air fryer basket. Pausing to turn the steaks halfway through the cooking time, air fry for 10 minutes until the fish is firm. 3. To make the tapenade: In a food processor fitted with a metal blade, combine the olives, olive oil, parsley, garlic, vinegar, and capers. Pulse until the mixture is finely chopped, pausing to scrape down the sides of the bowl if necessary. Spoon the tapenade over the top of the tuna steaks and serve with lemon wedges.

Per Serving:
calories: 269 | fat: 9g | protein: 42g | carbs: 2g | fiber: 1g | sodium: 252mg

Herb-Crusted Halibut

Prep time: 10 minutes | Cook time: 20 minutes | Serves 4

4 (5-ounce) halibut fillets
Extra-virgin olive oil, for brushing
½ cup coarsely ground unsalted pistachios
1 tablespoon chopped fresh

parsley
1 teaspoon chopped fresh thyme
1 teaspoon chopped fresh basil
Pinch sea salt
Pinch freshly ground black pepper

1. Preheat the oven to 350°F. 2. Line a baking sheet with parchment paper. 3. Pat the halibut fillets dry with a paper towel and place them on the baking sheet. 4. Brush the halibut generously with olive oil. 5. In a small bowl, stir together the pistachios, parsley, thyme, basil, salt, and pepper. 6. Spoon the nut and herb mixture evenly on the fish, spreading it out so the tops of the fillets are covered. 7. Bake the halibut until it flakes when pressed with a fork, about 20 minutes. 8. Serve immediately.

Per Serving:
calories: 351 | fat: 27g | protein: 24g | carbs: 4g | sugars: 1g | fiber: 2g | sodium: 214mg

Ahi Tuna Steaks

Prep time: 5 minutes | Cook time: 14 minutes | Serves 2

2 (6-ounce / 170-g) ahi tuna steaks
2 tablespoons olive oil

3 tablespoons everything bagel seasoning

1. Drizzle both sides of each steak with olive oil. Place seasoning on a medium plate and press each side of tuna steaks into seasoning to form a thick layer. 2. Place steaks into ungreased air fryer basket. Adjust the temperature to 400ºF (204ºC) and air fry for 14 minutes, turning steaks halfway through cooking. Steaks will be done when internal temperature is at least 145ºF (63ºC) for well-done. Serve warm.

Per Serving:
calories: 305 | fat: 14g | protein: 42g | carbs: 0g | fiber: 0g | sodium: 377mg

Marinated Swordfish Skewers

Prep time: 30 minutes | Cook time: 6 to 8 minutes | Serves 4

1 pound (454 g) filleted swordfish
¼ cup avocado oil
2 tablespoons freshly squeezed lemon juice
1 tablespoon minced fresh parsley
2 teaspoons Dijon mustard
Sea salt and freshly ground black pepper, to taste
3 ounces (85 g) cherry tomatoes

1. Cut the fish into 1½-inch chunks, picking out any remaining bones. 2. In a large bowl, whisk together the oil, lemon juice, parsley, and Dijon mustard. Season to taste with salt and pepper. Add the fish and toss to coat the pieces. Cover and marinate the fish chunks in the refrigerator for 30 minutes. 3. Remove the fish from the marinade. Thread the fish and cherry tomatoes on 4 skewers, alternating as you go. 4. Set the air fryer to 400ºF (204ºC). Place the skewers in the air fryer basket and air fry for 3 minutes. Flip the skewers and cook for 3 to 5 minutes longer, until the fish is cooked through and an instant-read thermometer reads 140ºF (60ºC).

Per Serving:

calories: 291 | fat: 21g | protein: 23g | carbs: 2g | fiber: 0g | sodium: 121mg

Citrus-Glazed Salmon

Prep time: 10 minutes | Cook time: 13 to 17 minutes | Serves 4

2 medium limes
1 small orange
⅓ cup agave syrup
1 teaspoon salt
1 teaspoon pepper
4 cloves garlic, finely chopped
1¼ pounds salmon fillet, cut
into 4 pieces
2 tablespoons sliced green onions
1 lime slice, cut into 4 wedges
1 orange slice, cut into 4 wedges
Hot cooked orzo pasta or rice, if desired

1 Heat oven to 400°F. Line 15x10x1-inch pan with cooking parchment paper or foil. In small bowl, grate lime peel from limes. Squeeze enough lime juice to equal 2 tablespoons; add to peel in bowl. Grate orange peel from oranges into bowl. Squeeze enough orange juice to equal 2 tablespoons; add to peel mixture. Stir in agave syrup, salt, pepper and garlic. In small cup, measure ¼ cup citrus mixture for salmon (reserve remaining citrus mixture). 2 Place salmon fillets in pan, skin side down. Using ¼ cup citrus mixture, brush tops and sides of salmon. Bake 13 to 17 minutes or until fish flakes easily with fork. Lift salmon pieces from skin with metal spatula onto serving plate. Sprinkle with green onions. Top each fish fillet with lime and orange wedges. Serve each fillet with 3 tablespoons reserved sauce and rice.

Per Serving:

calories: 320 | fat: 8g | protein: 31g | carbs: 30g | sugars: 23g | fiber: 3g | sodium: 680mg

Five-Spice Tilapia

Prep time: 15 minutes | Cook time: 5 minutes | Serves 2

8 ounces tilapia fillets
½ teaspoon Chinese five-spice powder
2 tablespoons reduced-sodium soy sauce
1 tablespoon granulated stevia
2 teaspoons extra-virgin olive oil
2 cups sugar snap peas
2 scallions, thinly sliced

1. Sprinkle both sides of the fillets with the Chinese five-spice powder. 2. In a small bowl, stir together the soy sauce and stevia. Set aside. 3. In a large nonstick skillet set over medium-high heat, heat the olive oil. 4. Add the tilapia. Cook for about 2 minutes, or until the outer edges are opaque. Reduce the heat to medium. Turn the fish over. Stir the soy mixture and pour into the skillet. 5. Add the sugar snap peas. Bring the sauce to a boil. Cook for about 2 minutes, or until the fish is cooked through, the sauce thickens, and the peas are bright green. 6. Add scallions. Remove from the heat. 7. Serve the fish and the sugar snap peas drizzled with the pan sauce.

Per Serving:

calories: 260 | fat: 10g | protein: 27g | carbs: 18g | sugars: 13g | fiber: 3g | sodium: 304mg

Roasted Red Snapper and Shrimp in Parchment

Prep time: 10 minutes | Cook time:45 minutes | Serves 8

One 3-pound whole red snapper or bass, cleaned
1 medium garlic clove, minced
¼ cup extra-virgin olive oil
⅛ teaspoon freshly ground black pepper
½ teaspoon finely chopped fresh thyme
1 teaspoon flour
½ pound large shrimp, shelled and deveined
½ pound sliced mushrooms
3 tablespoons lemon juice, divided
½ cup dry white wine, divided
¼ cup minced fresh parsley
Zest of 1 lemon

1 Preheat oven to 375 degrees. Wash the fish, inside and out, under cold running water, and pat dry with paper towels. 2 In a small bowl, combine the garlic, olive oil, pepper, thyme, and flour. Mix well. 3 Place the fish on a double thickness of parchment paper. In the cavity of the fish, place 1 tablespoon of the garlic mixture, 4 shrimp, and ½ cup sliced mushrooms. Sprinkle with 1 tablespoon of the lemon juice and 2 tablespoons of the wine. 4 Dot the top of the fish with the remaining garlic mixture, and arrange the remaining shrimp and mushrooms on top. Sprinkle with the remaining lemon juice and wine, and the parsley. 5 Bring the long sides of the parchment together over the fish, and secure with a double fold. Fold both ends of the parchment upward several times. 6 Place the fish on a baking sheet; bake for 30-35 minutes at 375 degrees. Transfer to a serving platter, garnish with lemon zest, and serve.

Per Serving:

calories: 272 | fat: 9g | protein: 40g | carbs: 3g | sugars: 1g | fiber: 1g | sodium: 273mg

Caribbean Haddock in a Packet

Prep time: 10 minutes | Cook time: 20 minutes | Serves 2

1 tablespoon extra-virgin olive oil, divided
1 cup angel hair coleslaw, divided
1 (8-ounce) haddock fillet, halved and rinsed
1 small tomato, thinly sliced
1 small red bell pepper, thinly sliced
½ cup chopped fresh chives
2 tablespoons chopped fresh cilantro
Juice of 1 lime
4 dashes hot pepper sauce
Dash salt
Dash freshly ground black pepper

1. Preheat the oven to 450°F. 2. Fold 2 (12-by-24-inch) aluminum foil sheets in half widthwise into 2 (12-by-12-inch) squares. 3. In the center of each foil square, brush ½ teaspoon of olive oil. 4. Place ½ cup of coleslaw in each square. 5. Top each with 1 piece of haddock. 6. Add half of the tomato slices and half of the red bell pepper slices atop each fillet. 7. Sprinkle each with 1 of the remaining 2 teaspoons of olive oil, ¼ cup of chives, 1 tablespoon of cilantro, half of the lime juice, and 2 dashes of hot pepper sauce. Season with salt and pepper. 8. Fold and seal the foil into airtight packets. Place the packets in a baking dish and into the preheated oven. Bake for 20 minutes. 9. Carefully avoiding the steam that will be released, open a packet and check that the fish is cooked. It should be opaque and flake easily. To test for doneness, poke the tines of a fork into the thickest portion of the fish at a 45-degree angle. Gently twist the fork and pull up some of the fish. If the fish resists flaking, return it to the oven for another 2 minutes then test again. Fish cooks very quickly, so be careful not to overcook it. 10. Divide the fish, vegetables, and juices between 2 serving plates.
Per Serving:
calories: 310 | fat: 16g | protein: 21g | carbs: 21g | sugars: 16g | fiber: 4g | sodium: 536mg

Tuna Poke with Riced Broccoli

Prep time: 15 minutes | Cook time: 5 minutes | Serves 2

For the tuna poke
½ pound sushi-grade tuna (see tip), cut into ½-inch cubes
2 tablespoons soy sauce or tamari
1 tablespoon rice vinegar
1 teaspoon sesame oil
For the bowl
½ tablespoon extra-virgin olive oil
1 small head broccoli, grated
1 cup thawed (if frozen) edamame
1 medium carrot, julienned
1 cucumber, diced
2 scallions, both white and green parts, thinly sliced
Optional toppings
Avocado slices
Shaved radish
Toasted sesame seeds
Pickled ginger

To make the tuna poke 1. In a medium bowl, toss together the tuna, soy sauce, rice vinegar, and sesame oil. 2. Set aside. To make the bowl 3. Heat the oil in a large skillet over medium heat and sauté the broccoli until tender, 2 to 3 minutes. Remove the skillet from the heat and allow the broccoli to cool. 4. Assemble two bowls by placing riced broccoli as the base. Top each bowl with the tuna poke, edamame, carrot, and cucumber. Drizzle the remaining juices from the tuna marinade over the bowls and garnish with sliced scallions. 5. Store any leftovers in an airtight container in the refrigerator for up to 2 days.

Per Serving:
calories: 454 | fat: 18g | protein: 43g | carbs: 34g | sugars: 13g | fiber: 13g | sodium: 412mg

Grilled Rosemary Swordfish

Prep time: 5 minutes | Cook time: 15 minutes | Serves 4

2 scallions, thinly sliced
2 tablespoons extra-virgin olive oil
2 tablespoons white wine vinegar
1 teaspoon fresh rosemary, finely chopped
4 swordfish steaks (1 pound total)

1. In a small bowl, combine the scallions, olive oil, vinegar, and rosemary. Pour over the swordfish steaks. Let the steaks marinate for 30 minutes. 2. Remove the steaks from the marinade, and grill for 5-7 minutes per side, brushing with marinade. Transfer to a serving platter, and serve.

Per Serving:
calories: 225 | fat: 14g | protein: 22g | carbs: 0g | sugars: 0g | fiber: 0g | sodium: 92mg

Grilled Scallop Kabobs

Prep time: 15 minutes | Cook time: 20 minutes | Serves 6

15 ounces pineapple chunks, packed in their own juice, undrained
¼ cup dry white wine
¼ cup light soy sauce
2 tablespoons minced fresh parsley
4 garlic cloves, minced
⅛ teaspoon freshly ground black pepper
1 pound scallops
18 large cherry tomatoes
1 large green bell pepper, cut into 1-inch squares
18 medium mushroom caps

1. Drain the pineapple, reserving the juice. In a shallow baking dish, combine the pineapple juice, wine, soy sauce, parsley, garlic, and pepper. Mix well. 2. Add the pineapple, scallops, tomatoes, green pepper, and mushrooms to the marinade. Marinate 30 minutes at room temperature, stirring occasionally. 3. Alternate pineapple, scallops, and vegetables on metal or wooden skewers (remember to soak wooden skewers in water before using). 4. Grill the kabobs over medium-hot coals about 4-5 inches from the heat, turning frequently, for 5-7 minutes.

Per Serving:
calories: 132 | fat: 1g | protein: 13g | carbs: 18g | sugars: 10g | fiber: 3g | sodium: 587mg

Mediterranean-Style Cod

Prep time: 5 minutes | Cook time: 12 minutes | Serves 4

4 (6-ounce / 170-g) cod fillets
3 tablespoons fresh lemon juice
1 tablespoon olive oil
¼ teaspoon salt

6 cherry tomatoes, halved
¼ cup pitted and sliced kalamata olives

1. Place cod into an ungreased round nonstick baking dish. Pour lemon juice into dish and drizzle cod with olive oil. Sprinkle with salt. Place tomatoes and olives around baking dish in between fillets. 2. Place dish into air fryer basket. Adjust the temperature to 350°F (177°C) and bake for 12 minutes, carefully turning cod halfway through cooking. Fillets will be lightly browned, easily flake, and have an internal temperature of at least 145°F (63°C) when done. Serve warm.

Per Serving:
calories: 186 | fat: 5g | protein: 31g | carbs: 2g | fiber: 1g | sodium: 300mg

Crab-Stuffed Avocado Boats

Prep time: 5 minutes | Cook time: 7 minutes | Serves 4

2 medium avocados, halved and pitted
8 ounces (227 g) cooked crab meat

¼ teaspoon Old Bay seasoning
2 tablespoons peeled and diced yellow onion
2 tablespoons mayonnaise

1. Scoop out avocado flesh in each avocado half, leaving ½ inch around edges to form a shell. Chop scooped-out avocado. 2. In a medium bowl, combine crab meat, Old Bay seasoning, onion, mayonnaise, and chopped avocado. Place ¼ mixture into each avocado shell. 3. Place avocado boats into ungreased air fryer basket. Adjust the temperature to 350°F (177°C) and air fry for 7 minutes. Avocado will be browned on the top and mixture will be bubbling when done. Serve warm.

Per Serving:
calories: 226 | fat: 17g | protein: 12g | carbs: 10g | sugars: 1g | fiber: 7g | sodium: 239mg

Tomato Tuna Melts

Prep time: 5 minutes | Cook time: 5 minutes | Serves 2

1 (5-ounce) can chunk light tuna packed in water, drained
2 tablespoons plain nonfat Greek yogurt
2 teaspoons freshly squeezed lemon juice
2 tablespoons finely chopped

celery
1 tablespoon finely chopped red onion
Pinch cayenne pepper
1 large tomato, cut into ¾-inch-thick rounds
½ cup shredded cheddar cheese

1. Preheat the broiler to high. 2. In a medium bowl, combine the tuna, yogurt, lemon juice, celery, red onion, and cayenne pepper. Stir well. 3. Arrange the tomato slices on a baking sheet. Top each with some tuna salad and cheddar cheese. 4. Broil for 3 to 4 minutes until the cheese is melted and bubbly. Serve.

Per Serving:
calories: 243 | fat: 10g | protein: 30g | carbs: 7g | sugars: 2g | fiber: 1g | sodium: 444mg

Lime Lobster Tails

Prep time: 10 minutes | Cook time: 6 minutes | Serves 4

4 lobster tails, peeled
2 tablespoons lime juice

½ teaspoon dried basil
½ teaspoon coconut oil, melted

1. Mix lobster tails with lime juice, dried basil, and coconut oil. 2. Put the lobster tails in the air fryer and cook at 380°F (193°C) for 6 minutes.

Per Serving:
calories: 123 | fat: 2g | protein: 25g | carbs: 1g | fiber: 0g | sodium: 635mg

Parmesan Mackerel with Coriander

Prep time: 10 minutes | Cook time: 7 minutes | Serves 2

12 ounces (340 g) mackerel fillet
2 ounces (57 g) Parmesan,

grated
1 teaspoon ground coriander
1 tablespoon olive oil

1. Sprinkle the mackerel fillet with olive oil and put it in the air fryer basket. 2. Top the fish with ground coriander and Parmesan. 3. Cook the fish at 390°F (199°C) for 7 minutes.

Per Serving:
calories: 522 | fat: 39g | protein: 42g | carbs: 1g | fiber: 0g | sodium: 544mg

Tuna Cakes

Prep time: 10 minutes | Cook time: 10 minutes | Serves 4

4 (3-ounce / 85-g) pouches tuna, drained
1 large egg, whisked

2 tablespoons peeled and chopped white onion
½ teaspoon Old Bay seasoning

1. In a large bowl, mix all ingredients together and form into four patties. 2. Place patties into ungreased air fryer basket. Adjust the temperature to 400°F (204°C) and air fry for 10 minutes. Patties will be browned and crispy when done. Let cool 5 minutes before serving.

Per Serving:
calories: 113 | fat: 2g | protein: 22g | carbs: 1g | fiber: 0g | sodium: 56mg

Salmon Florentine

Prep time: 10 minutes | Cook time: 30 minutes | Serves 4

1 teaspoon extra-virgin olive oil
½ sweet onion, finely chopped
1 teaspoon minced garlic
3 cups baby spinach
1 cup kale, tough stems

removed, torn into 3-inch pieces
Sea salt
Freshly ground black pepper
4 (5-ounce) salmon fillets
Lemon wedges, for serving

1. Preheat the oven to 350°F. 2. Place a large skillet over medium-high heat and add the oil. 3. Sauté the onion and garlic until softened and translucent, about 3 minutes. 4. Add the spinach and kale and sauté until the greens wilt, about 5 minutes. 5. Remove the skillet from the heat and season the greens with salt and pepper. 6. Place the salmon fillets so they are nestled in the greens and partially covered by them. Bake the salmon until it is opaque, about 20 minutes. 7. Serve immediately with a squeeze of fresh lemon.

Per Serving:

calories: 211 | fat: 8g | protein: 30g | carbs: 5g | sugars: 2g | fiber: 1g | sodium: 129mg

Stuffed Flounder Florentine

Prep time: 10 minutes | Cook time: 25 minutes | Serves 4

¼ cup pine nuts
2 tablespoons olive oil
½ cup chopped tomatoes
1 (6-ounce / 170-g) bag spinach, coarsely chopped
2 cloves garlic, chopped
Salt and freshly ground black

pepper, to taste
2 tablespoons unsalted butter, divided
4 flounder fillets (about 1½ pounds / 680 g)
Dash of paprika
½ lemon, sliced into 4 wedges

1. Place the pine nuts in a baking dish that fits in your air fryer. Set the air fryer to 400°F (204°C) and air fry for 4 minutes until the nuts are lightly browned and fragrant. Remove the baking dish from the air fryer, tip the nuts onto a plate to cool, and continue preheating the air fryer. When the nuts are cool enough to handle, chop them into fine pieces. 2. In the baking dish, combine the oil, tomatoes, spinach, and garlic. Use tongs to toss until thoroughly combined. Air fry for 5 minutes until the tomatoes are softened and the spinach is wilted. 3. Transfer the vegetables to a bowl and stir in the toasted pine nuts. Season to taste with salt and freshly ground black pepper. 4. Place 1 tablespoon of the butter in the bottom of the baking dish. Lower the heat on the air fryer to 350°F (177°C). 5. Place the flounder on a clean work surface. Sprinkle both sides with salt and black pepper. Divide the vegetable mixture among the flounder fillets and carefully roll up, securing with toothpicks. 6. Working in batches if necessary, arrange the fillets seam-side down in the baking dish along with 1 tablespoon of water. Top the fillets with remaining 1 tablespoon butter and sprinkle with a dash of paprika. 7.Cover loosely with foil and air fry for 10 to 15 minutes until the fish is opaque and flakes easily with a fork. Remove the toothpicks before serving with the lemon wedges.

Per Serving:

calories: 287 | fat: 21g | protein: 21g | carbs: 5g | sugars: 1g | fiber: 2g | sodium: 692mg

Baked Salmon with Lemon Sauce

Prep time: 10 minutes | Cook time: 15 minutes | Serves 4

4 (5-ounce) salmon fillets
Sea salt
Freshly ground black pepper
1 tablespoon extra-virgin olive oil
½ cup low-sodium vegetable broth

Juice and zest of 1 lemon
1 teaspoon chopped fresh thyme
½ cup fat-free sour cream
1 teaspoon honey
1 tablespoon chopped fresh chives

1. Preheat the oven to 400°F. 2. Season the salmon lightly on both sides with salt and pepper. 3. Place a large ovenproof skillet over medium-high heat and add the olive oil. 4. Sear the salmon fillets on both sides until golden, about 3 minutes per side. 5. Transfer the salmon to a baking dish and bake until it is just cooked through, about 10 minutes. 6. While the salmon is baking, whisk together the vegetable broth, lemon juice, zest, and thyme in a small saucepan over medium-high heat until the liquid reduces by about one-quarter, about 5 minutes. 7. Whisk in the sour cream and honey. 8. Stir in the chives and serve the sauce over the salmon.

Per Serving:

calories: 243 | fat: 10g | protein: 30g | carbs: 8g | sugars: 2g | fiber: 1g | sodium: 216mg

Baked Oysters

Prep time: 30 minutes | Cook time: 15 minutes | Serves 2

2 cups coarse salt, for holding the oysters
1 dozen fresh oysters, scrubbed
1 tablespoon butter
½ cup finely chopped artichoke hearts
¼ cup finely chopped scallions, both white and green parts

¼ cup finely chopped red bell pepper
1 garlic clove, minced
1 tablespoon finely chopped fresh parsley
Zest and juice of ½ lemon
Pinch salt
Freshly ground black pepper

1. Pour the coarse salt into an 8-by-8-inch baking dish and spread to evenly fill the bottom of the dish. 2. Prepare a clean surface to shuck the oysters. Using a shucking knife, insert the blade at the joint of the shell, where it hinges open and shut. Firmly apply pressure to pop the blade in, and work the knife around the shell to open. Discard the empty half of the shell. Use the knife to gently loosen the oyster, and remove any shell particles. Set the oysters in their shells on the salt, being careful not to spill the juices. 3. Preheat the oven to 425°F. 4. In a large skillet, melt the butter over medium heat. Add the artichoke hearts, scallions, and bell pepper, and cook for 5 to 7 minutes. Add the garlic and cook an additional minute. Remove from the heat and mix in the parsley, lemon zest and juice, and season with salt and pepper. 5. Divide the vegetable mixture evenly among the oysters and bake for 10 to 12 minutes until the vegetables are lightly browned.

Per Serving:

calories: 134 | fat: 7g | protein: 6g | carbs: 11g | sugars: 7g | fiber: 2g | sodium: 281mg

Baked Monkfish

Prep time: 20 minutes | Cook time: 12 minutes | Serves 2

2 teaspoons olive oil
1 cup celery, sliced
2 bell peppers, sliced
1 teaspoon dried thyme
½ teaspoon dried marjoram
½ teaspoon dried rosemary
2 monkfish fillets

1 tablespoon coconut aminos
2 tablespoons lime juice
Coarse salt and ground black pepper, to taste
1 teaspoon cayenne pepper
½ cup Kalamata olives, pitted and sliced

1. In a nonstick skillet, heat the olive oil for 1 minute. Once hot, sauté the celery and peppers until tender, about 4 minutes. Sprinkle with thyme, marjoram, and rosemary and set aside. 2. Toss the fish fillets with the coconut aminos, lime juice, salt, black pepper, and cayenne pepper. Place the fish fillets in the lightly greased air fryer basket and bake at 390°F (199°C) for 8 minutes. 3. Turn them over, add the olives, and cook an additional 4 minutes. Serve with the sautéed vegetables on the side. Bon appétit!

Per Serving:

calories: 263 | fat: 11g | protein: 27g | carbs: 13g | fiber: 5g | sodium: 332mg

Asian Cod with Brown Rice, Asparagus, and Mushrooms

Prep time: 5 minutes | Cook time: 25 minutes | Serves 2

¾ cup Minute brand brown rice
½ cup water
Two 5-ounce skinless cod fillets
1 tablespoon soy sauce or tamari
1 tablespoon fresh lemon juice
½ teaspoon peeled and grated fresh ginger
1 tablespoon extra-virgin olive oil or 1 tablespoon unsalted butter, cut into 8 pieces

2 green onions, white and green parts, thinly sliced
12 ounces asparagus, trimmed
4 ounces shiitake mushrooms, stems removed and sliced
⅛ teaspoon fine sea salt
⅛ teaspoon freshly ground black pepper
Lemon wedges for serving

1. Pour 1 cup water into the Instant Pot. Have ready two-tier stackable stainless-steel containers. 2. In one of the containers, combine the rice and ½ cup water, then gently shake the container to spread the rice into an even layer, making sure all of the grains are submerged. Place the fish fillets on top of the rice. In a small bowl, stir together the soy sauce, lemon juice, and ginger. Pour the soy sauce mixture over the fillets. Drizzle 1 teaspoon olive oil on each fillet (or top with two pieces of the butter), and sprinkle the green onions on and around the fish. 3. In the second container, arrange the asparagus in the center in as even a layer as possible. Place the mushrooms on either side of the asparagus. Drizzle with the remaining 2 teaspoons olive oil (or put the remaining six pieces butter on top of the asparagus, spacing them evenly). Sprinkle the salt and pepper evenly over the vegetables. 4. Place the container with the rice and fish on the bottom and the vegetable container on top. Cover the top container with its lid and then latch the containers together. Grasping the handle, lower the containers into the Instant Pot. 5. Secure the lid and set the Pressure Release to Sealing. Select the Pressure Cook or Manual setting and set the cooking time for 15 minutes at high pressure. (The pot will take about 10 minutes to come up to pressure before the cooking program begins.) 6. When the cooking program ends, let the pressure release naturally for 5 minutes, then move the Pressure Release to Venting to release any remaining steam. Open the pot and, wearing heat-resistant mitts, lift out the stacked containers. Unlatch, unstack, and open the containers, taking care not to get burned by the steam. 7. Transfer the vegetables, rice, and fish to plates and serve right away, with the lemon wedges on the side.

Per Serving:

calories: 344 | fat: 11g | protein: 27g | carbs: 46g | sugars: 6g | fiber: 7g | sodium: 637mg

Faux Conch Fritters

Prep time: 15 minutes | Cook time: 20 minutes | Serves 4

4 medium egg whites
½ cup fat-free milk
1 cup chickpea crumbs
¼ teaspoon freshly ground black pepper
½ teaspoon ground cumin
3 cups frozen chopped scallops,

thawed
1 small onion, finely chopped
1 small green bell pepper, finely chopped
2 celery stalks, finely chopped
2 garlic cloves, minced
Juice of 2 limes

1. Preheat the oven to 350°F. 2. In a large bowl, combine the egg whites, milk, and chickpea crumbs. 3. Add the black pepper and cumin and mix well. 4. Add the scallops, onion, bell pepper, celery, and garlic. 5. Form golf ball-size patties and place on a rimmed baking sheet 1 inch apart. 6. Transfer the baking sheet to the oven and cook for 5 to 7 minutes, or until golden brown. 7. Flip the patties, return to the oven, and bake for 5 to 7 minutes, or until golden brown. 8. Top with the lime juice, and serve.

Per Serving:

calories: 280 | fat: 4g | protein: 23g | carbs: 40g | sugars: 9g | fiber: 7g | sodium: 327mg

Coconut Chicken Curry

Prep time: 15 minutes | Cook time: 35 minutes | Serves 4

2 teaspoons extra-virgin olive oil
3 (5-ounce) boneless, skinless chicken breasts, cut into 1-inch chunks
1 tablespoon grated fresh ginger
1 tablespoon minced garlic
2 tablespoons curry powder
2 cups low-sodium chicken broth
1 cup canned coconut milk
1 carrot, peeled and diced
1 sweet potato, diced
2 tablespoons chopped fresh cilantro

1. Place a large saucepan over medium-high heat and add the oil. 2. Sauté the chicken until lightly browned and almost cooked through, about 10 minutes. 3. Add the ginger, garlic, and curry powder, and sauté until fragrant, about 3 minutes. 4. Stir in the chicken broth, coconut milk, carrot, and sweet potato and bring the mixture to a boil. 5. Reduce the heat to low and simmer, stirring occasionally, until the vegetables and chicken are tender, about 20 minutes. 6. Stir in the cilantro and serve.

Per Serving:

calorie: 327 | fat: 18g | protein: 29g | carbs: 14g | sugars: 2g | fiber: 3g | sodium: 122mg

Grilled Herb Chicken with Wine and Roasted Garlic

Prep time: 5 minutes | Cook time: 45 minutes | Serves 4

Four 3-ounce boneless, skinless chicken breast halves
2 tablespoons extra-virgin olive oil, divided
1 cup red wine
3 sprigs fresh thyme
5 garlic cloves, minced
5 garlic cloves, whole and unpeeled
⅛ teaspoon freshly ground black pepper

1. In a plastic zippered bag, place chicken, 1 tablespoon of the oil, wine, thyme, and minced garlic. Marinate for 2-3 hours in the refrigerator. 2. Preheat the oven to 375 degrees. 3. Spread the whole garlic cloves on a cookie sheet, drizzle with the remaining oil, and sprinkle with pepper. Bake for 30 minutes, stirring occasionally, until soft. 4. When cool, squeeze the garlic paste from the cloves, and mash in a small bowl with a fork. 5. Remove the chicken from the marinade, and grill for 12-15 minutes, turning frequently and brushing with garlic paste. Transfer to a platter, and serve hot.

Per Serving:

calorie: 222 | fat: 9g | protein: 20g | carbs: 4g | sugars: 0g | fiber: 0g | sodium: 40mg

Turkey and Quinoa Caprese Casserole

Prep time: 10 minutes | Cook time: 35 minutes | Serves 8

⅔ cup quinoa
1⅓ cups water
Nonstick cooking spray
2 teaspoons extra-virgin olive oil
1 pound lean ground turkey
¼ cup chopped red onion
½ teaspoon salt
1 (15-ounce can) fire-roasted tomatoes, drained
4 cups spinach leaves, finely sliced
3 garlic cloves, minced
¼ cup sliced fresh basil
¼ cup chicken or vegetable broth
2 large ripe tomatoes, sliced
4 ounces mozzarella cheese, thinly sliced

1. In a small pot, combine the quinoa and water. Bring to a boil, reduce the heat, cover, and simmer for 10 minutes. Turn off the heat, and let the quinoa sit for 5 minutes to absorb any remaining water. 2. Preheat the oven to 400°F. Spray a baking dish with nonstick cooking spray. 3. In a large skillet, heat the oil over medium heat. Add the turkey, onion, and salt. Cook until the turkey is cooked through and crumbled. 4. Add the tomatoes, spinach, garlic, and basil. Stir in the broth and cooked quinoa. Transfer the mixture to the prepared baking dish. Arrange the tomato and cheese slices on top. 5. Bake for 15 minutes until the cheese is melted and the tomatoes are softened. Serve.

Per Serving:

calories: 218 | fat: 9g | protein: 18g | carbs: 17g | sugars: 3g | fiber: 3g | sodium: 340mg

Chicken in Wine

Prep time: 10 minutes | Cook time: 12 minutes | Serves 6

2 pounds chicken breasts, trimmed of skin and fat
10¾-ounce can 98% fat-free, reduced-sodium cream of mushroom soup
10¾-ounce can French onion soup
1 cup dry white wine or chicken broth

1. Place the chicken into the Instant Pot. 2. Combine soups and wine. Pour over chicken. 3. Secure the lid and make sure vent is set to sealing. Cook on Manual mode for 12 minutes. 4. When cook time is up, let the pressure release naturally for 5 minutes and then release the rest manually.

Per Serving:

calories: 225 | fat: 5g | protein: 35g | carbs: 7g | sugars: 3g | fiber: 1g | sodium: 645mg

Roast Chicken with Pine Nuts and Fennel

Prep time: 20 minutes | Cook time: 30 minutes | Serves 2

For the herb paste
2 tablespoons fresh rosemary leaves
1 tablespoon freshly grated lemon zest
2 garlic cloves, quartered
½ teaspoon freshly ground black pepper
¼ teaspoon salt
1 teaspoon extra-virgin olive oil
For the chicken
4 (6-ounce) skinless chicken drumsticks
2 teaspoons extra-virgin olive oil
For the vegetables
1 large fennel bulb, cored and chopped (about 3 cups)
1 cup sliced fresh mushrooms
½ cup sliced carrots
¼ cup chopped sweet onion
2 teaspoons extra-virgin olive oil
2 tablespoons pine nuts
2 teaspoons white wine vinegar

To make the vegetables 1. Preheat the oven to 450°F. 2. In a 9-by-13-inch baking dish, toss together the fennel, mushrooms, carrots, onion, and olive oil. Place the dish in the preheated oven. Bake for 10 minutes. 3. Stir in the pine nuts. 4. Top with the browned drumsticks. Return the dish to the oven. Bake for 15 to 20 minutes more, or until the fennel is golden and an instant-read thermometer inserted into the thickest part of a drumstick without touching the bone registers 165°F. 5. Remove the chicken from the pan. 6. Stir the white wine vinegar into the pan. Toss the vegetables to coat, scraping up any browned bits. 7. Serve the chicken with the vegetables and enjoy!

Per Serving:

calorie: 316 | fat: 15g | protein: 35g | carbs: 10g | sugars: 4g | fiber: 3g | sodium: 384mg

Saffron-Spiced Chicken Breasts

Prep time: 10 minutes | Cook time: 10 minutes | Serves 4

Pinch saffron (3 or 4 threads)
½ cup plain nonfat yogurt
2 tablespoons water
½ onion, chopped
3 garlic cloves, minced
2 tablespoons chopped fresh cilantro
Juice of ½ lemon
½ teaspoon salt
1 pound boneless, skinless chicken breasts, cut into 2-inch strips
1 tablespoon extra-virgin olive oil

1. In a blender jar, combine the saffron, yogurt, water, onion, garlic, cilantro, lemon juice, and salt. Pulse to blend. 2. In a large mixing bowl, combine the chicken and the yogurt sauce, and stir to coat. Cover and refrigerate for at least 1 hour or up to overnight. 3. In a large skillet, heat the oil over medium heat. Add the chicken pieces, shaking off any excess marinade. Discard the marinade. Cook the chicken pieces on each side for 5 minutes, flipping once, until cooked through and golden brown.

Per Serving:

calories: 155 | fat: 5g | protein: 26g | carbs: 3g | sugars: 1g | fiber: 0g | sodium: 501mg

Jerk Chicken Kebabs

Prep time: 10 minutes | Cook time: 14 minutes | Serves 4

8 ounces (227 g) boneless, skinless chicken thighs, cut into 1-inch cubes
2 tablespoons jerk seasoning
2 tablespoons coconut oil
½ medium red bell pepper,
seeded and cut into 1-inch pieces
¼ medium red onion, peeled and cut into 1-inch pieces
½ teaspoon salt

1. Place chicken in a medium bowl and sprinkle with jerk seasoning and coconut oil. Toss to coat on all sides. 2. Using eight (6-inch) skewers, build skewers by alternating chicken, pepper, and onion pieces, about three repetitions per skewer. 3. Sprinkle salt over skewers and place into ungreased air fryer basket. Adjust the temperature to 370ºF (188ºC) and air fry for 14 minutes, turning skewers halfway through cooking. Chicken will be golden and have an internal temperature of at least 165ºF (74ºC) when done. Serve warm.

Per Serving:

calories: 142 | fat: 9g | protein: 12g | carbs: 4g | fiber: 1g | sodium: 348mg

Garlic Galore Rotisserie Chicken

Prep time: 5 minutes | Cook time: 3 minutes | Serves 4

3-pound whole chicken
2 tablespoons olive oil, divided
Salt to taste
Pepper to taste
20-30 cloves fresh garlic, peeled and left whole
1 cup low-sodium chicken
stock, broth, or water
2 tablespoons garlic powder
2 teaspoons onion powder
½ teaspoon basil
½ teaspoon cumin
½ teaspoon chili powder

1. Rub chicken with one tablespoon of the olive oil and sprinkle with salt and pepper. 2. Place the garlic cloves inside the chicken. Use butcher's twine to secure the legs. 3. Press the Sauté button on the Instant Pot, then add the rest of the olive oil to the inner pot. 4. When the pot is hot, place the chicken inside. You are just trying to sear it, so leave it for about 4 minutes on each side. 5. Remove the chicken and set aside. Place the trivet at the bottom of the inner pot and pour in the chicken stock. 6. Mix together the remaining seasonings and rub them all over the entire chicken. 7. Place the chicken back inside the inner pot, breast-side up, on top of the trivet and secure the lid to the sealing position. 8. Press the Manual button and use the +/- to set it for 25 minutes. 9. When the timer beeps, allow the pressure to release naturally for 15 minutes. If the lid will not open at this point, quick release the remaining pressure and remove the chicken. 10. Let the chicken rest for 5-10 minutes before serving.

Per Serving:

calories: 333 | fat: 23g | protein: 24g | carbs: 9g | sugars: 0g | fiber: 1g | sodium: 110mg

Pizza in a Pot

Prep time: 25 minutes | Cook time: 15 minutes | Serves 8

1 pound bulk lean sweet Italian turkey sausage, browned and drained
28-ounce can crushed tomatoes
15½-ounce can chili beans
2¼-ounce can sliced black olives, drained
1 medium onion, chopped
1 small green bell pepper, chopped
2 garlic cloves, minced
¼ cup grated Parmesan cheese
1 tablespoon quick-cooking tapioca
1 tablespoon dried basil
1 bay leaf

1. Set the Instant Pot to Sauté, then add the turkey sausage. Sauté until browned. 2. Add the remaining ingredients into the Instant Pot and stir. 3. Secure the lid and make sure the vent is set to sealing. Cook on Manual for 15 minutes. 4. When cook time is up, let the pressure release naturally for 5 minutes then perform a quick release. Discard bay leaf.

Per Serving:

calorie: 251 | fat: 10g | protein: 18g | carbs: 23g | sugars: 8g | fiber: 3g | sodium: 936mg

Spicy Chicken Cacciatore

Prep time: 20 minutes | Cook time: 1 hour | Serves 6

1 (2-pound) chicken
¼ cup all-purpose flour
Sea salt
Freshly ground black pepper
2 tablespoons extra-virgin olive oil
3 slices bacon, chopped
1 sweet onion, chopped
2 teaspoons minced garlic
4 ounces button mushrooms, halved
1 (28-ounce) can low-sodium stewed tomatoes
½ cup red wine
2 teaspoons chopped fresh oregano
Pinch red pepper flakes

1. Cut the chicken into pieces: 2 drumsticks, 2 thighs, 2 wings, and 4 breast pieces. 2. Dredge the chicken pieces in the flour and season each piece with salt and pepper. 3. Place a large skillet over medium-high heat and add the olive oil. 4. Brown the chicken pieces on all sides, about 20 minutes in total. Transfer the chicken to a plate. 5. Add the chopped bacon to the skillet and cook until crispy, about 5 minutes. With a slotted spoon, transfer the cooked bacon to the same plate as the chicken. 6. Pour off most of the oil from the skillet, leaving just a light coating. Sauté the onion, garlic, and mushrooms in the skillet until tender, about 4 minutes. 7. Stir in the tomatoes, wine, oregano, and red pepper flakes. 8. Bring the sauce to a boil. Return the chicken and bacon, plus any accumulated juices from the plate, to the skillet. 9. Reduce the heat to low and simmer until the chicken is tender, about 30 minutes.

Per Serving:

calorie: 330 | fat: 14g | protein: 35g | carbs: 14g | sugars: 7g | fiber: 4g | sodium: 196mg

Herbed Buttermilk Chicken

Prep time: 5 minutes | Cook time: 25 minutes | Serves 4

1½ pounds boneless, skinless chicken breasts
4 cups buttermilk
Pinch kosher salt
Pinch freshly ground black pepper
1 cup thinly sliced yellow onion
2 tablespoons canola oil
¼ cup Italian seasoning
1 lemon, cut into wedges

1. In a large bowl or sealable plastic bag, combine the chicken, buttermilk, salt, and pepper. Cover or seal and refrigerate for at least 1 hour and up to 24 hours. 2. When the chicken is ready to cook, preheat the oven to 425°F. Line a baking sheet with parchment paper. 3. Remove the chicken from the buttermilk brine and pat it dry. Place the chicken on the prepared baking sheet along with the onion, and drizzle everything with the canola oil. Toss together on the baking sheet (this will save you a bowl) to coat the chicken and onion evenly. 4. Bake for 25 minutes or until the chicken is cooked through. (If the chicken is thick, you can cut the breasts in half lengthwise. It will cut down on your cook time by half or less. Check the chicken after it's cooked for 8 minutes if the breasts are thin.) 5. Allow the chicken to rest and sprinkle it and the onions with the Italian seasoning. 6. Serve with a squeeze of lemon juice.

Per Serving:

calorie: 380 | fat: 14g | protein: 47g | carbs: 16g | sugars: 13g | fiber: 1g | sodium: 543mg

Smoky Chicken Leg Quarters

Prep time: 30 minutes | Cook time: 23 to 27 minutes | Serves 6

½ cup avocado oil
2 teaspoons smoked paprika
1 teaspoon sea salt
1 teaspoon garlic powder
½ teaspoon dried rosemary
½ teaspoon dried thyme
½ teaspoon freshly ground black pepper
2 pounds (907 g) bone-in, skin-on chicken leg quarters

1. In a blender or small bowl, combine the avocado oil, smoked paprika, salt, garlic powder, rosemary, thyme, and black pepper. 2. Place the chicken in a shallow dish or large zip-top bag. Pour the marinade over the chicken, making sure all the legs are coated. Cover and marinate for at least 2 hours or overnight. 3. Place the chicken in a single layer in the air fryer basket, working in batches if necessary. Set the air fryer to 400°F (204°C) and air fry for 15 minutes. Flip the chicken legs, then reduce the temperature to 350°F (177°C). Cook for 8 to 12 minutes more, until an instant-read thermometer reads 160°F (71°C) when inserted into the thickest piece of chicken. 4. Allow to rest for 5 to 10 minutes before serving.

Per Serving:

calories: 347 | fat: 25g | protein: 29g | carbs: 1g | fiber: 0g | sodium: 534mg

Mediterranean-Style Chicken Scaloppine

Prep time: 15 minutes | Cook time: 1 hour | Serves

Six 3-ounce boneless, skinless chicken breast halves
2 cups fat-free Greek yogurt
¼ cup lemon juice
Zest of 1 lemon
¼ cup freshly chopped baby dill
2 teaspoons paprika
2 garlic cloves, minced
 teaspoon salt
¼ teaspoon freshly ground black

pepper
1 cup dried whole-wheat bread crumbs
2½ cups frozen artichoke hearts, thawed
2 tablespoons extra-virgin olive oil
¼ cup finely chopped fresh parsley
1 lemon, sliced

1. Wash chicken breasts under cold running water, and pat dry. 2. In a medium bowl, combine the yogurt, lemon juice, lemon zest, baby dill, paprika, garlic, salt, and pepper. Measure out ½ cup of this marinade, and reserve the rest in the refrigerator. 3. Add the chicken to the ½ cup of marinade, and coat each piece well. Refrigerate overnight. 4. Preheat the oven to 350 degrees. 5. Remove the chicken from the marinade, discard the marinade, and roll the chicken in bread crumbs, coating evenly. 6. Arrange the chicken in a single layer in a large baking pan. Add the artichoke hearts in with the chicken. Drizzle the olive oil over the chicken and artichokes. Bake at 350 degrees, uncovered, for 45 minutes, or until the chicken is no longer pink. 7. Transfer to a serving platter, and serve with the remaining marinade as a sauce and parsley and lemon slices as a garnish.

Per Serving:

calorie: 344 | fat: 11g | protein: 40g | carbs: 23g | sugars: 11g | fiber: 6g | sodium: 502mg

Turkey Cabbage Soup

Prep time: 15 minutes | Cook time: 30 minutes | Serves 4

1 tablespoon extra-virgin olive oil
1 sweet onion, chopped
2 celery stalks, chopped
2 teaspoons minced fresh garlic
4 cups finely shredded green cabbage
1 sweet potato, peeled, diced

8 cups chicken or turkey broth
2 bay leaves
1 cup chopped cooked turkey
2 teaspoons chopped fresh thyme
Sea salt
Freshly ground black pepper

1. Place a large saucepan over medium-high heat and add the olive oil. 2. Sauté the onion, celery, and garlic until softened and translucent, about 3 minutes. 3. Add the cabbage and sweet potato and sauté for 3 minutes. 4. Stir in the chicken broth and bay leaves and bring the soup to a boil. 5. Reduce the heat to low and simmer until the vegetables are tender, about 20 minutes. 6. Add the turkey and thyme and simmer until the turkey is heated through, about 4 minutes. 7. Remove the bay leaves and season the soup with salt and pepper.

Per Serving:

calorie: 444 | fat: 14g | protein: 38g | carbs: 46g | sugars: 17g | fiber: 7g | sodium: 427mg

Lemon Chicken

Prep time: 5 minutes | Cook time: 20 to 25 minutes | Serves 4

8 bone-in chicken thighs, skin on
1 tablespoon olive oil
1½ teaspoons lemon-pepper seasoning

½ teaspoon paprika
½ teaspoon garlic powder
¼ teaspoon freshly ground black pepper
Juice of ½ lemon

1. Preheat the air fryer to 360ºF (182ºC). 2. Place the chicken in a large bowl and drizzle with the olive oil. Top with the lemon-pepper seasoning, paprika, garlic powder, and freshly ground black pepper. Toss until thoroughly coated. 3. Working in batches if necessary, arrange the chicken in a single layer in the basket of the air fryer. Pausing halfway through the cooking time to turn the chicken, air fry for 20 to 25 minutes, until a thermometer inserted into the thickest piece registers 165ºF (74ºC). 4. Transfer the chicken to a serving platter and squeeze the lemon juice over the top.

Per Serving:

calories: 399 | fat: 19g | protein: 56g | carbs: 1g | fiber: 0g | sodium: 367mg

Broccoli Cheese Chicken

Prep time: 10 minutes | Cook time: 19 to 24 minutes | Serves 6

1 tablespoon avocado oil
¼ cup chopped onion
½ cup finely chopped broccoli
4 ounces (113 g) cream cheese, at room temperature
2 ounces (57 g) Cheddar cheese, shredded
1 teaspoon garlic powder

½ teaspoon sea salt, plus additional for seasoning, divided
¼ freshly ground black pepper, plus additional for seasoning, divided
2 pounds (907 g) boneless, skinless chicken breasts
1 teaspoon smoked paprika

1. Heat a medium skillet over medium-high heat and pour in the avocado oil. Add the onion and broccoli and cook, stirring occasionally, for 5 to 8 minutes, until the onion is tender. 2. Transfer to a large bowl and stir in the cream cheese, Cheddar cheese, and garlic powder, and season to taste with salt and pepper. 3. Hold a sharp knife parallel to the chicken breast and cut a long pocket into one side. Stuff the chicken pockets with the broccoli mixture, using toothpicks to secure the pockets around the filling. 4. In a small dish, combine the paprika, ½ teaspoon salt, and ¼ teaspoon pepper. Sprinkle this over the outside of the chicken. 5. Set the air fryer to 400ºF (204ºC). Place the chicken in a single layer in the air fryer basket, cooking in batches if necessary, and cook for 14 to 16 minutes, until an instant-read thermometer reads 160ºF (71ºC). Place the chicken on a plate and tent a piece of aluminum foil over the chicken. Allow to rest for 5 to 10 minutes before serving.

Per Serving:

calorie: 287 | fat: 16g | protein: 32g | carbs: 1g | sugars: 0g | fiber: 0g | sodium: 291mg

Fiber-Full Chicken Tostadas

Prep time: 15 minutes | Cook time: 10 minutes | Serves 4

1 tablespoon (9 g) chili powder
½ tablespoon (5 g) onion powder
1 tablespoon (9 g) paprika
1 teaspoon garlic powder
1 teaspoon ground cumin
1 teaspoon dried oregano
¼ teaspoon black pepper
¼ teaspoon sea salt
2 tablespoons (30 ml) cooking oil of choice
1 pound (454 g) boneless, skinless chicken breast, cut into 1 to 1½-inch (2.5 to 3.8-cm) strips
8 corn tostada shells
1 (15.5-ounce/439-g) can low-sodium pinto beans, undrained
1 cup (30 g) baby arugula leaves, coarsely chopped
1 large avocado, peeled and sliced to the desired thickness
4 tablespoons (32 g) crumbled queso fresco cheese
Jalapeño slices (optional)
Chopped onion (optional)
Diced tomatoes (optional)

1. In a small bowl, mix together the chili powder, onion powder, paprika, garlic powder, cumin, oregano, black pepper, and sea salt. Add the cooking oil and mix it with the seasonings to make a marinade. 2. Place the chicken strips in a large ziptop plastic bag, then add the marinade. Seal the bag and shake it to coat the chicken with the marinade. (If time permits, marinate the chicken for 30 to 60 minutes.) 3. Heat a large skillet over medium-high heat. Add the chicken strips and cook them for 4 to 5 minutes. Flip the chicken strips and cook them for 3 to 4 minutes, until they are cooked through and no longer pink. Set the skillet aside. 4. Line up the tostada shells on a serving tray. Place the pinto beans in a medium bowl and mash them to the desired consistency. Spread the beans on top of each tostada. Top each tostada with an equal amount of arugula, avocado slices, cheese, chicken and any desired additional toppings, then serve.

Per Serving:

calorie: 547 | fat: 27g | protein: 40g | carbs: 12g | sugars: 1g | fiber: 12g | sodium: 738mg

Spicy Chicken Drumsticks

Prep time: 5 minutes | Cook time: 50 minutes | Serves 2

¼ cup plain low-fat yogurt
2 tablespoons hot pepper sauce
Crushed red pepper flakes, to taste
4 chicken drumsticks, skinned (about 1 pound)
¼ cup dried bread crumbs

1. In a shallow dish, combine the yogurt, hot pepper sauce, and crushed red pepper flakes, mixing well. Add the drumsticks, turning to coat. Cover, and marinate in the refrigerator for 2-4 hours. 2. Preheat the oven to 350 degrees. 3. Remove the drumsticks from the marinade, dredge in the bread crumbs, and place in a baking dish. Bake at 350 degrees for 40-50 minutes. Transfer to a serving platter, and serve.

Per Serving:

calorie: 337 | fat: 10g | protein: 48g | carbs: 12g | sugars: 3g | fiber: 1g | sodium: 501mg

Chicken with Lemon Caper Pan Sauce

Prep time: 10 minutes | Cook time: 15 minutes | Serves 4

3 tablespoons extra-virgin olive oil
4 chicken breast halves or thighs, pounded slightly to even thickness
½ teaspoon sea salt
⅛ teaspoon freshly ground black pepper
¼ cup freshly squeezed lemon juice
¼ cup dry white wine
2 tablespoons capers, rinsed
2 tablespoons salted butter, very cold, cut into pieces

1. In a large skillet over medium-high heat, heat the olive oil until it shimmers. 2. Season the chicken with the salt and pepper. Add it to the hot oil and cook until opaque with an internal temperature of 165°F, about 5 minutes per side. Transfer the chicken to a plate and tent loosely with foil to keep warm. Keep the pan on the heat. 3. Add the lemon juice and wine to the pan, using the side of a spoon to scrape any browned bits from the bottom of the pan. Add the capers. Simmer until the liquid is reduced by half, about 3 minutes. Reduce the heat to low. 4. Whisk in the butter, one piece at a time, until incorporated. 5. Return the chicken to the pan, turning once to coat with the sauce. Serve with additional sauce spooned over the top.

Per Serving:

calorie: 367 | fat: 23g | protein: 37g | carbs: 2g | sugars: 1g | fiber: 0g | sodium: 591mg

Creamy Garlic Chicken with Broccoli

Prep time: 5 minutes | Cook time: 15 minutes | Serves 4

½ cup uncooked brown rice or quinoa
4 (4-ounce) boneless, skinless chicken breasts
¼ teaspoon salt
¼ teaspoon freshly ground black pepper
1 teaspoon garlic powder, divided
Avocado oil cooking spray
3 cups fresh or frozen broccoli florets
1 cup half-and-half

1. Cook the rice according to the package instructions. 2. Meanwhile, season both sides of the chicken breasts with the salt, pepper, and ½ teaspoon of garlic powder. 3. Heat a large skillet over medium-low heat. When hot, coat the cooking surface with cooking spray and add the chicken and broccoli in a single layer. 4. Cook for 4 minutes, then flip the chicken breasts over and cover. Cook for 5 minutes more. 5. Add the half-and-half and remaining ½ teaspoon of garlic powder to the skillet and stir. Increase the heat to high and simmer for 2 minutes. 6. Divide the rice into four equal portions. Top each portion with 1 chicken breast and one-quarter of the broccoli and cream sauce.

Per Serving:

calorie: 274 | fat: 5g | protein: 31g | carbs: 27g | sugars: 3g | fiber: 1g | sodium: 271mg

One-Pan Chicken Dinner

Prep time: 5 minutes | Cook time: 35 minutes | Serves 4

3 tablespoons extra-virgin olive oil
1 tablespoon red wine vinegar or apple cider vinegar
¼ teaspoon garlic powder
3 tablespoons Italian seasoning

4 (4-ounce) boneless, skinless chicken breasts
2 cups cubed sweet potatoes
20 Brussels sprouts, halved lengthwise

1. Preheat the oven to 400°F. 2. In a large bowl, whisk together the oil, vinegar, garlic powder, and Italian seasoning. 3. Add the chicken, sweet potatoes, and Brussels sprouts, and coat thoroughly with the marinade. 4. Remove the ingredients from the marinade and arrange them on a baking sheet in a single layer. Roast for 15 minutes. 5. Remove the baking sheet from the oven, flip the chicken over, and bake for another 15 to 20 minutes.

Per Serving:

calorie: 346 | fat: 13g | protein: 30g | carbs: 26g | sugars: 6g | fiber: 7g | sodium: 575mg

Thai Yellow Curry with Chicken Meatballs

Prep time: 5 minutes | Cook time: 30 minutes | Serves 4

1 pound 95 percent lean ground chicken
⅓ cup gluten-free panko (Japanese bread crumbs)
1 egg white
1 tablespoon coconut oil
1 yellow onion, cut into 1-inch pieces
One 14-ounce can light coconut milk
3 tablespoons yellow curry paste
¾ cup water
8 ounces carrots, halved lengthwise, then cut crosswise

into 1-inch lengths (or quartered if very large)
8 ounces zucchini, quartered lengthwise, then cut crosswise into 1-inch lengths (or cut into halves, then thirds if large)
8 ounces cremini mushrooms, quartered
Fresh Thai basil leaves for serving (optional)
Fresno or jalapeño chile, thinly sliced, for serving (optional)
1 lime, cut into wedges
Cooked cauliflower "rice" for serving

1. In a medium bowl, combine the chicken, panko, and egg white and mix until evenly combined. Set aside. 2. Select the Sauté setting on the Instant Pot and heat the oil for 2 minutes. Add the onion and sauté for 5 minutes, until it begins to soften and brown. Add ½ cup of the coconut milk and the curry paste and sauté for 1 minute more, until bubbling and fragrant. Press the Cancel button to turn off the pot, then stir in the water. 3. Using a 1½-tablespoon cookie scoop, shape and drop meatballs into the pot in a single layer. 4. Secure the lid and set the Pressure Release to Sealing. Select the Pressure Cook or Manual setting and set the cooking time for 5 minutes at high pressure. (The pot will take about 5 minutes to come up to pressure before the cooking program begins.) 5. When the cooking program ends, perform a quick pressure release by moving the Pressure Release to Venting, or let the pressure release naturally. Open the pot and stir in the carrots, zucchini, mushrooms, and remaining 1¼ cups coconut milk. 6. Press the Cancel button to

reset the cooking program, then select the Sauté setting. Bring the curry to a simmer (this will take about 2 minutes), then let cook, uncovered, for about 8 minutes, until the carrots are fork-tender. Press the Cancel button to turn off the pot. 7. Ladle the curry into bowls. Serve piping hot, topped with basil leaves and chile slices, if desired, and the lime wedges and cauliflower "rice" on the side.

Per Serving:
calories: 349 | fat: 15g | protein: 30g | carbs: 34g | sugars: 8g | fiber: 5g | sodium: 529mg

Spice-Rubbed Chicken Thighs

Prep time: 10 minutes | Cook time: 25 minutes | Serves 4

4 (4-ounce / 113-g) bone-in, skin-on chicken thighs
½ teaspoon salt
½ teaspoon garlic powder

2 teaspoons chili powder
1 teaspoon paprika
1 teaspoon ground cumin
1 small lime, halved

1. Pat chicken thighs dry and sprinkle with salt, garlic powder, chili powder, paprika, and cumin. 2. Squeeze juice from ½ lime over thighs. Place thighs into ungreased air fryer basket. Adjust the temperature to 380°F (193°C) and roast for 25 minutes, turning thighs halfway through cooking. Thighs will be crispy and browned with an internal temperature of at least 165°F (74°C) when done. 3. Transfer thighs to a large serving plate and drizzle with remaining lime juice. Serve warm.

Per Serving:

calories: 151 | fat: 5g | protein: 23g | carbs: 3g | fiber: 1g | sodium: 439mg

One-Pot Roast Chicken Dinner

Prep time: 10 minutes | Cook time: 40 minutes | Serves 6

½ head cabbage, cut into 2-inch chunks
1 sweet onion, peeled and cut into eighths
1 sweet potato, peeled and cut into 1-inch chunks
4 garlic cloves, peeled and lightly crushed

2 tablespoons extra-virgin olive oil, divided
2 teaspoons minced fresh thyme
Sea salt
Freshly ground black pepper
2½ pounds bone-in chicken thighs and drumsticks

1. Preheat the oven to 450°F. 2. Lightly grease a large roasting pan and arrange the cabbage, onion, sweet potato, and garlic in the bottom. Drizzle with 1 tablespoon of oil, sprinkle with the thyme, and season the vegetables lightly with salt and pepper. 3. Season the chicken with salt and pepper. 4. Place a large skillet over medium-high heat and brown the chicken on both sides in the remaining 1 tablespoon of oil, about 10 minutes in total. 5. Place the browned chicken on top of the vegetables in the roasting pan. Roast until the chicken is cooked through, about 30 minutes.

Per Serving:

calorie: 328 | fat: 13g | protein: 38g | carbs: 14g | sugars: 6g | fiber: 3g | sodium: 217mg

Jerk Chicken Casserole

Prep time: 15 minutes | Cook time: 45 minutes | Serves 6

1¼ teaspoons salt
½ teaspoon pumpkin pie spice
¾ teaspoon ground allspice
¾ teaspoon dried thyme leaves
¼ teaspoon ground red pepper (cayenne)
6 boneless skinless chicken thighs
1 tablespoon vegetable oil

1 can (15 ounces) black beans, drained, rinsed
1 large sweet potato (1 pound), peeled, cubed (3 cups)
¼ cup honey
¼ cup lime juice
2 teaspoons cornstarch
2 tablespoons sliced green onions (2 medium)

1 Heat oven to 375°F. Spray 8-inch square (2-quart) glass baking dish with cooking spray. In small bowl, mix salt, pumpkin pie spice, allspice, thyme and red pepper. Rub mixture on all sides of chicken. In 12-inch nonstick skillet, heat oil over medium-high heat. Cook chicken in oil 2 to 3 minutes per side, until brown. 2 In baking dish, layer beans and sweet potato. Top with browned chicken. In small bowl, mix honey, lime juice and cornstarch; add to skillet. Heat to boiling, stirring constantly. Pour over chicken in baking dish. 3 Bake 35 to 45 minutes or until juice of chicken is clear when center of thickest part is cut (165°F) and sweet potatoes are fork-tender. Sprinkle with green onions.

Per Serving:

calories: 330 | fat: 8g | protein: 21g | carbs: 43g | sugars: 16g | fiber: 9g | sodium: 550mg

Kung Pao Chicken and Zucchini Noodles

Prep time: 15 minutes | Cook time: 15 minutes | Serves 2

For the noodles
2 medium zucchini, ends trimmed
For the sauce
1½ tablespoons low-sodium soy sauce
1 tablespoon balsamic vinegar
1 teaspoon hoisin sauce
2½ tablespoons water
1½ teaspoons red chili paste
2 teaspoons granulated stevia
2 teaspoons cornstarch
For the chicken
6 ounces boneless skinless chicken breast, cut into ½-inch pieces
Salt, to season

Freshly ground black pepper, to season
1 teaspoon extra-virgin olive oil
1 teaspoon sesame oil
2 garlic cloves, minced
1 tablespoon chopped fresh ginger
½ red bell pepper, cut into ½-inch pieces
½ (8-ounce) can water chestnuts, drained and sliced
1 celery stalk, cut into ¾-inch dice
2 tablespoons crushed dry-roasted peanuts, divided
2 tablespoons scallions, divided

To make the noodles With a spiralizer or julienne peeler, cut the zucchini lengthwise into spaghetti-like strips. Set aside. To make the sauce In a small bowl, whisk together the soy sauce, balsamic vinegar, hoisin sauce, water, red chili paste, stevia, and cornstarch. Set aside. To make the chicken 1. Season the chicken with salt and pepper. 2. In a large, deep nonstick pan or wok set over medium-high heat, heat the olive oil. 3. Add the chicken. Cook for 4 to 5 minutes, stirring, or until browned and cooked through. Transfer the chicken to a plate. Set aside. 4. Return the pan to the stove. Reduce the heat to medium. 5. Add the sesame oil, garlic, and ginger. Cook for about 30 seconds, or until fragrant. 6. Add the red bell pepper, water chestnuts, and celery. 7. Stir in the sauce. Bring to a boil. Reduce the heat to low. Simmer for 1 to 2 minutes, until thick and bubbling. 8. Stir in the zucchini noodles. Cook for about 2 minutes, tossing, until just tender and mixed with the sauce. 9. Add the chicken and any accumulated juices. Stir to combine. Cook for about 2 minutes, or until heated through. 10. Divide the mixture between 2 bowls. Top each serving with 1 tablespoon of peanuts and 1 tablespoon of scallions. Enjoy!

Per Serving:

calorie: 322 | fat: 13g | protein: 29g | carbs: 28g | sugars: 12g | fiber: 8g | sodium: 553mg

Unstuffed Peppers with Ground Turkey and Quinoa

Prep time: 0 minutes | Cook time: 35 minutes | Serves 8

2 tablespoons extra-virgin olive oil
1 yellow onion, diced
2 celery stalks, diced
2 garlic cloves, chopped
2 pounds 93 percent lean ground turkey
2 teaspoons Cajun seasoning blend (plus 1 teaspoon fine sea salt if using a salt-free blend)
½ teaspoon freshly ground black pepper
¼ teaspoon cayenne pepper

1 cup quinoa, rinsed
1 cup low-sodium chicken broth
One 14½-ounce can fire-roasted diced tomatoes and their liquid
3 red, orange, and/or yellow bell peppers, seeded and cut into 1-inch squares
1 green onion, white and green parts, thinly sliced
1½ tablespoons chopped fresh flat-leaf parsley
Hot sauce (such as Crystal or Frank's RedHot) for serving

1. Select the Sauté setting on the Instant Pot and heat the oil for 2 minutes. Add the onion, celery, and garlic and sauté for about 4 minutes, until the onion begins to soften. Add the turkey, Cajun seasoning, black pepper, and cayenne and sauté, using a wooden spoon or spatula to break up the meat as it cooks, for about 6 minutes, until cooked through and no streaks of pink remain. 2. Sprinkle the quinoa over the turkey in an even layer. Pour the broth and the diced tomatoes and their liquid over the quinoa, spreading the tomatoes on top. Sprinkle the bell peppers over the top in an even layer. 3. Secure the lid and set the Pressure Release to Sealing. Press the Cancel button to reset the cooking program, then select the Pressure Cook or Manual setting and set the cooking time for 8 minutes at high pressure. (The pot will take about 15 minutes to come up to pressure before the cooking program begins.) 4. When the cooking program ends, let the pressure release naturally for at least 15 minutes, then move the Pressure Release to Venting to release any remaining steam. Open the pot and sprinkle the green onion and parsley over the top in an even layer. 5. Spoon the unstuffed peppers into bowls, making sure to dig down to the bottom of the pot so each person gets an equal amount of peppers, quinoa, and meat. Serve hot, with hot sauce on the side.

Per Serving:

calories: 320 | fat: 14g | protein: 27g | carbs: 23g | sugars: 3g | fiber: 3g | sodium: 739mg

Juicy Turkey Burgers

Prep time: 10 minutes | Cook time: 20 minutes | Serves 4

1½ pounds lean ground turkey
½ cup bread crumbs
½ sweet onion, chopped
1 carrot, peeled, grated
1 teaspoon minced garlic

1 teaspoon chopped fresh thyme
Sea salt
Freshly ground black pepper
Nonstick cooking spray

1. In a large bowl, mix together the turkey, bread crumbs, onion, carrot, garlic, and thyme until very well mixed. 2. Season the mixture lightly with salt and pepper. 3. Shape the turkey mixture into 4 equal patties. 4. Place a large skillet over medium-high heat and coat it lightly with cooking spray. 5. Cook the turkey patties until golden and completely cooked through, about 10 minutes per side. 6. Serve the burgers plain or with your favorite toppings on a whole-wheat bun.

Per Serving:

calorie: 330 | fat: 15g | protein: 34g | carbs: 15g | sugars: 4g | fiber: 1g | sodium: 230mg

Grain-Free Parmesan Chicken

Prep time: 5 minutes | Cook time: 20 minutes | Serves 4

1½ cups (144 g) almond flour
½ cup (50 g) grated Parmesan cheese
1 tablespoon (3 g) Italian seasoning
1 teaspoon garlic powder
½ teaspoon black pepper
2 large eggs
4 (6-ounce/170-g, ½-inch

[13-mm]-thick) boneless, skinless chicken breasts
½ cup (120 ml) no-added-sugar marinara sauce
½ cup (56 g) shredded mozzarella cheese
2 tablespoons (8 g) minced fresh herbs of choice (optional)

1. Preheat the oven to 375°F (191°C). Line a large, rimmed baking sheet with parchment paper. 2. In a shallow dish, mix together the almond flour, Parmesan cheese, Italian seasoning, garlic powder, and black pepper. In another shallow dish, whisk the eggs. Dip a chicken breast into the egg wash, then gently shake off any extra egg. Dip the chicken breast into the almond flour mixture, coating it well. Place the chicken breast on the prepared baking sheet. Repeat this process with the remaining chicken breasts. 3. Bake the chicken for 15 to 20 minutes, or until the meat is no longer pink in the center. 4. Remove the chicken from the oven and flip each breast. Top each breast with 2 tablespoons (30 ml) of marinara sauce and 2 tablespoons (14 g) of mozzarella cheese. 5. Increase the oven temperature to broil and place the chicken back in the oven. Broil it until the cheese is melted and just starting to brown. Carefully remove the chicken from the oven, top it with the herbs (if using), and let it rest for about 10 minutes before serving.

Per Serving:

calorie: 572 | fat: 32g | protein: 60g | carbs: 13g | sugars: 4g | fiber:5g | sodium: 560mg

Chicken Provençal

Prep time: 5 minutes | Cook time: 25 minutes | Serves 4

2 tablespoons extra-virgin olive oil
Two 8-ounce boneless, skinless chicken breasts, halved
1 medium garlic clove, minced
¼ cup minced onion
¼ cup minced green bell pepper

½ cup dry white wine
1 cup canned diced tomatoes
¼ cup pitted Kalamata olives
¼ cup finely chopped fresh basil
⅛ teaspoon freshly ground black pepper

1. Heat the oil in a skillet over medium heat. Add the chicken, and brown about 3-5 minutes. 2. Add the remaining ingredients, and cook uncovered over medium heat for 20 minutes or until the chicken is no longer pink. Transfer to a serving platter and season with additional pepper to taste, if desired, before serving.

Per Serving:

calorie: 245 | fat: 11g | protein: 26g | carbs: 5g | sugars: 2g | fiber: 2g | sodium: 121mg

Cheesy Stuffed Cabbage

Prep time: 30 minutes | Cook time: 18 minutes | Serves 6 to 8

1-2 heads savoy cabbage
1 pound ground turkey
1 egg
1 cup reduced-fat shredded cheddar cheese
2 tablespoons evaporated skim milk
¼ cup reduced-fat shredded Parmesan cheese
¼ cup reduced-fat shredded mozzarella cheese
¼ cup finely diced onion

¼ cup finely diced bell pepper
¼ cup finely diced mushrooms
1 teaspoon salt
½ teaspoon black pepper
1 teaspoon garlic powder
6 basil leaves, fresh and cut chiffonade
1 tablespoon fresh parsley, chopped
1 quart of your favorite pasta sauce

1. Remove the core from the cabbages. 2. Boil pot of water and place 1 head at a time into the water for approximately 10 minutes. 3. Allow cabbage to cool slightly. Once cooled, remove the leaves carefully and set aside. You'll need about 15 or 16. 4. Mix together the meat and all remaining ingredients except the pasta sauce. 5. One leaf at a time, put a heaping tablespoon of meat mixture in the center. 6. Tuck the sides in and then roll tightly. 7. Add ½ cup sauce to the bottom of the inner pot of the Instant Pot. 8. Place the rolls, fold-side down, into the pot and layer them, putting a touch of sauce between each layer and finally on top. (You may want to cook the rolls in two batches.) 9. Lock lid and make sure vent is at sealing. Set timer on 18 minutes on Manual at high pressure, then manually release the pressure when cook time is over.

Per Serving:

calories: 199| fat: 8g | protein: 2mg | carbs: 14g | sugars: 7g | fiber: 3g | sodium: 678mg

BBQ Turkey Meat Loaf

Prep time: 5 minutes | Cook time: 40 minutes | Serves 6

1 pound 93 percent lean ground turkey	½ small yellow onion, finely diced
⅓ cup low-sugar or unsweetened barbecue sauce, plus 2 tablespoons	1 garlic clove, minced
⅓ cup gluten-free panko (Japanese bread crumbs)	½ teaspoon fine sea salt
1 large egg	½ teaspoon freshly ground black pepper
	Cooked cauliflower "rice" or brown rice for serving

1. Pour 1 cup water into the Instant Pot. Lightly grease a 7 by 3-inch round cake pan or a 5½ by 3-inch loaf pan with olive oil or coat with nonstick cooking spray. 2. In a medium bowl, combine the turkey, ⅓ cup barbecue sauce, panko, egg, onion, garlic, salt, and pepper and mix well with your hands until all of the ingredients are evenly distributed. Transfer the mixture to the prepared pan, pressing it into an even layer. Cover the pan tightly with aluminum foil. Place the pan on a long-handled silicone steam rack, then, holding the handles of the steam rack, lower it into the pot. (If you don't have the long-handled rack, use the wire metal steam rack and a homemade sling) 3. Secure the lid and set the Pressure Release to Sealing. Select the Pressure Cook or Manual setting and set the cooking time for 25 minutes at high pressure if using a 7-inch round cake pan, or for 35 minutes at high pressure if using a 5½ by 3-inch loaf pan. (The pot will take about 10 minutes to come up to pressure before the cooking program begins.) 4. Preheat a toaster oven or position an oven rack 4 to 6 inches below the heat source and preheat the broiler. 5. When the cooking program ends, perform a quick pressure release by moving the Pressure Release to Venting. Open the pot and, wearing heat-resistant mitts, grasp the handles of the steam rack and lift it out of the pot. Uncover the pan, taking care not to get burned by the steam or to drip condensation onto the meat loaf. Brush the remaining 2 tablespoons barbecue sauce on top of the meat loaf. 6. Broil the meat loaf for a few minutes, just until the glaze becomes bubbly and browned. Cut the meat loaf into slices and serve hot, with the cauliflower "rice" alongside.

Per Serving:

calories: 236 | fat: 11g | protein: 25g | carbs: 10g | sugars: 2g | fiber: 3g | sodium: 800mg

Herbed Cornish Hens

Prep time: 5 minutes | Cook time: 30 minutes | Serves 8

4 Cornish hens, giblets removed (about 1¼ pound each)	½ teaspoon poultry seasoning
2 cups white wine, divided	½ teaspoon paprika
2 garlic cloves, minced	½ teaspoon dried oregano
1 small onion, minced	¼ teaspoon freshly ground black pepper
½ teaspoon celery seeds	

1. Using a long, sharp knife, split each hen lengthwise. You may also buy precut hens. 2. Place the hens, cavity side up, on a rack in a shallow roasting pan. Pour 1½ cups of the wine over the hens; set aside. 3. In a shallow bowl, combine the garlic, onion, celery seeds, poultry seasoning, paprika, oregano, and pepper. Sprinkle half of the combined seasonings over the cavity of each split half. Cover, and refrigerate. Allow the hens to marinate for 2-3 hours. 4. Preheat the oven to 350 degrees. Bake the hens uncovered for 1 hour. Remove from the oven, turn breast side up, and remove the skin. Pour the remaining ½ cup of wine over the top, and sprinkle with the remaining seasonings. 5. Continue to bake for an additional 25-30 minutes, basting every 10 minutes until the hens are done. Transfer to a serving platter, and serve hot.

Per Serving:

calorie: 383 | fat: 10g | protein: 57g | carbs: 3g | sugars: 1g | fiber: 0g | sodium: 197mg

Grilled Lemon Mustard Chicken

Prep time: 5 minutes | Cook time: 15 minutes | Serves 6

Juice of 6 medium lemons	4 garlic cloves, minced
½ cup mustard seeds	2 tablespoons extra-virgin olive oil
1 tablespoon minced fresh tarragon	Three 8-ounce boneless, skinless chicken breasts, halved
2 tablespoons freshly ground black pepper	

1. In a small mixing bowl, combine the lemon juice, mustard seeds, tarragon, pepper, garlic, and oil; mix well. 2. Place the chicken in a baking dish, and pour the marinade on top. Cover, and refrigerate overnight. 3. Grill the chicken over medium heat for 10-15 minutes, basting with the marinade. Serve hot.

Per Serving:

calorie: 239 | fat: 11g | protein: 28g | carbs: 8g | sugars: 2g | fiber: 2g | sodium: 54mg

Chicken Reuben Bake

Prep time: 10 minutes | Cook time: 6 to 8 hours | Serves 6

4 boneless, skinless chicken-breast halves	cheese
¼ cup water	¾ cup fat-free Thousand Island salad dressing
1-pound bag sauerkraut, drained and rinsed	2 tablespoons chopped fresh parsley
4-5 (1 ounce each) slices Swiss	

1. Place chicken and water in inner pot of the Instant Pot along with ¼ cup water. Layer sauerkraut over chicken. Add cheese. Top with salad dressing. Sprinkle with parsley. 2. Secure the lid and cook on the Slow Cook setting on low 6-8 hours.

Per Serving:

calories: 217 | fat: 5g | protein: 28g | carbs: 13g | sugars: 6g | fiber: 2g | sodium: 693mg

Sesame-Ginger Chicken Soba

Prep time: 10 minutes | Cook time: 15 minutes | Serves 6

8 ounces soba noodles
2 boneless, skinless chicken breasts, halved lengthwise
¼ cup tahini
2 tablespoons rice vinegar
1 tablespoon reduced-sodium gluten-free soy sauce or tamari
1 teaspoon toasted sesame oil
1 (1-inch) piece fresh ginger, finely grated
⅓ cup water
1 large cucumber, seeded and diced
1 scallions bunch, green parts only, cut into 1-inch segments
1 tablespoon sesame seeds

1. Preheat the broiler to high. 2. Bring a large pot of water to a boil. Add the noodles and cook until tender, according to the package directions. Drain and rinse the noodles in cool water. 3. On a baking sheet, arrange the chicken in a single layer. Broil for 5 to 7 minutes on each side, depending on the thickness, until the chicken is cooked through and its juices run clear. Use two forks to shred the chicken. 4. In a small bowl, combine the tahini, rice vinegar, soy sauce, sesame oil, ginger, and water. Whisk to combine. 5. In a large bowl, toss the shredded chicken, noodles, cucumber, and scallions. Pour the tahini sauce over the noodles and toss to combine. Served sprinkled with the sesame seeds.

Per Serving:

calories: 251 | fat: 8g | protein: 16g | carbs: 35g | sugars: 2g | fiber: 2g | sodium: 482mg

Mild Chicken Curry with Coconut Milk

Prep time: 10 minutes | Cook time: 14 minutes | Serves 4 to 6

1 large onion, diced
6 cloves garlic, crushed
¼ cup coconut oil
½ teaspoon black pepper
½ teaspoon turmeric
½ teaspoon paprika
¼ teaspoon cinnamon
¼ teaspoon cloves
¼ teaspoon cumin
¼ teaspoon ginger
½ teaspoon salt
1 tablespoon curry powder (more if you like more flavor)
½ teaspoon chili powder
24-ounce can of low-sodium diced or crushed tomatoes
13½-ounce can of light coconut milk (I prefer a brand that has no unwanted ingredients, like guar gum or sugar)
4 pounds boneless skinless chicken breasts, cut into chunks

1. Sauté onion and garlic in the coconut oil, either with Sauté setting in the inner pot of the Instant Pot or on stove top, then add to pot. 2. Combine spices in a small bowl, then add to the inner pot. 3. Add tomatoes and coconut milk and stir. 4. Add chicken, and stir to coat the pieces with the sauce. 5. Secure the lid and make sure vent is at sealing. Set to Manual mode (or Pressure Cook on newer models) for 14 minutes. 6. Let pressure release naturally (if you're crunched for time, you can do a quick release). 7. Serve with your favorite sides, and enjoy!

Per Serving:

calorie: 535 | fat: 21g | protein: 71g | carbs: 10g | sugars: 5g | fiber: 2g | sodium: 315mg

Chicken Legs with Leeks

Prep time: 30 minutes | Cook time: 18 minutes | Serves 6

2 leeks, sliced
2 large-sized tomatoes, chopped
3 cloves garlic, minced
½ teaspoon dried oregano
6 chicken legs, boneless and
skinless
½ teaspoon smoked cayenne pepper
2 tablespoons olive oil
A freshly ground nutmeg

1. In a mixing dish, thoroughly combine all ingredients, minus the leeks. Place in the refrigerator and let it marinate overnight. 2. Lay the leeks onto the bottom of the air fryer basket. Top with the chicken legs. 3. Roast chicken legs at 375°F (191°C) for 18 minutes, turning halfway through. Serve with hoisin sauce.

Per Serving:

calories: 390 | fat: 16g | protein: 52g | carbs: 7g | fiber: 1g | sodium: 264mg

Wine-Poached Chicken with Herbs and Vegetables

Prep time: 5 minutes | Cook time: 1 hour | Serves 8

4 quarts low-sodium chicken broth
2 cups dry white wine
4 large bay leaves
4 sprigs fresh thyme
¼ teaspoon freshly ground black pepper
4-pound chicken, giblets removed, washed and patted dry
½ pound carrots, peeled and julienned
½ pound turnips, peeled and julienned
½ pound parsnips, peeled and julienned
4 small leeks, washed and trimmed

1. In a large stockpot, combine the broth, wine, bay leaves, thyme, dash salt (optional), and pepper. Let simmer over medium heat while you prepare the chicken. 2. Stuff the cavity with ⅓ each of the carrots, turnips, and parsnips; then truss. Add the stuffed chicken to the stockpot, and poach, covered, over low heat for 30 minutes. 3. Add the remaining vegetables with the leeks, and continue to simmer for 25-30 minutes, or until juices run clear when the chicken is pierced with a fork. 4. Remove the chicken and vegetables to a serving platter. Carve the chicken, remove the skin, and surround the sliced meat with poached vegetables to serve.

Per Serving:

calorie: 476 | fat: 13g | protein: 57g | carbs: 24g | sugars: 6g | fiber: 4g | sodium: 387mg

Chicken Nuggets

Prep time: 10 minutes | Cook time: 15 minutes | Serves 4

1 pound (454 g) ground chicken thighs
½ cup shredded Mozzarella cheese
1 large egg, whisked

½ teaspoon salt
¼ teaspoon dried oregano
¼ teaspoon garlic powder

1. In a large bowl, combine all ingredients. Form mixture into twenty nugget shapes, about 2 tablespoons each. 2. Place nuggets into ungreased air fryer basket, working in batches if needed. Adjust the temperature to 375°F (191°C) and air fry for 15 minutes, turning nuggets halfway through cooking. Let cool 5 minutes before serving.

Per Serving:

calories: 195 | fat: 8g | protein: 28g | carbs: 1g | fiber: 0g | sodium: 419mg

Chapter 7 Salads

Roasted Asparagus-Berry Salad

Prep time: 10 minutes | Cook time: 18 minutes | Serves 4

1 pound fresh asparagus spears
Cooking spray
2 tablespoons chopped pecans
1 cup sliced fresh strawberries
4 cups mixed salad greens
¼ cup fat-free balsamic vinaigrette dressing
Cracked pepper, if desired

1 Heat oven to 400°F. Line 15x10x1-inch pan with foil; spray with cooking spray. Break off tough ends of asparagus as far down as stalks snap easily. Cut into 1-inch pieces. 2 Place asparagus in single layer in pan; spray with cooking spray. Place pecans in another shallow pan. 3 Bake pecans 5 to 6 minutes or until golden brown, stirring occasionally. Bake asparagus 10 to 12 minutes or until crisp-tender. Cool pecans and asparagus 8 to 10 minutes or until room temperature. 4 In medium bowl, mix asparagus, pecans, strawberries, greens and dressing. Sprinkle with pepper.

Per Serving:
calorie: 90 | fat: 3g | protein: 4g | carbs: 11g | sugars: 6g | fiber: 4g | sodium: 180mg

Lobster Salad

Prep time: 10 minutes | Cook time: 45 minutes | Serves 6

2 pounds lobster in the shell or 1 pound lobster meat
¾ pound small red potatoes
½ cup light mayonnaise
3 tablespoons plain low-fat yogurt
1 tablespoon chopped tarragon
¼ cup chopped scallions
¼ teaspoon freshly ground black pepper
1 small head romaine lettuce, washed and leaves separated

1. To prepare lobster in the shell, place the lobster in boiling water, and boil until the meat is tender, about 20 minutes. Cool the lobster, remove the meat from the shell, and cut into 1-inch cubes. Or buy lobster meat from the seafood department at the supermarket. 2. Wash, but do not peel, the potatoes. Boil the potatoes in water until just tender, about 15-20 minutes. Drain, cool, and quarter. 3. In a bowl, combine mayonnaise, yogurt, tarragon, scallions, and pepper for the dressing. 4. In a separate bowl, combine the lobster and potatoes. 5. Add the dressing to the lobster and potatoes, and mix well. To serve, line plates with lettuce. Spoon lobster salad over the lettuce.

Per Serving:
calorie: 245 | fat: 8g | protein: 29g | carbs: 14g | sugars: 3g | fiber: 4g | sodium: 564mg

Pasta Salad-Stuffed Tomatoes

Prep time: 10 minutes | Cook time: 0 minutes | Serves 4

1 cup uncooked whole-wheat fusilli
2 small carrots, sliced
2 scallions, chopped
¼ cup chopped pimiento
1 cup cooked kidney beans
½ cup sliced celery
¼ cup cooked peas
2 tablespoons chopped fresh
parsley
¼ cup calorie-free, fat-free Italian salad dressing
2 tablespoons low-fat mayonnaise
¼ teaspoon dried marjoram
¼ teaspoon freshly ground black pepper
4 medium tomatoes

1. Cook the fusilli in boiling water until cooked, about 7-8 minutes; drain. 2. In a large bowl, combine the macaroni with the remaining salad ingredients (except the tomatoes), and toss well. Cover, and chill in the refrigerator 1 hour or more. 3. With the stem end down, cut each tomato into 6 wedges, cutting to, but not through, the base of the tomato. Spread the wedges slightly apart, and spoon the pasta mixture into the tomatoes. Chill until ready to serve.

Per Serving:
calorie: 214 | fat: 3g | protein: 10g | carbs: 40g | sugars: 6g | fiber: 8g | sodium: 164mg

Greek Island Potato Salad

Prep time: 5 minutes | Cook time: 35 minutes | Serves 10

⅓ cup extra-virgin olive oil
4 garlic cloves, minced
2 pounds red potatoes, cut into 1½-inch pieces (leave the skin on if you wish)
6 medium carrots, peeled, halved lengthwise, and cut into 1½-inch pieces
1 onion, chopped
16 ounces artichoke hearts packed in water, drained and cut in half
½ cup Kalamata olives, pitted and halved
¼ cup lemon juice

1. In a large skillet, heat the olive oil. Add the garlic, and sauté for 30 seconds. Add the potatoes, carrots, and onion; cook over medium heat for 25-30 minutes until vegetables are just tender. 2. Add the artichoke hearts, and cook for 3-5 minutes more. Remove from the heat, and stir in the olives and lemon juice. Season with a dash of salt and pepper. Transfer to a serving bowl, and serve warm.

Per Serving:
calorie: 178 | fat: 8g | protein: 4g | carbs: 25g | sugars: 4g | fiber: 6g | sodium: 134mg

Cheeseburger Wedge Salad

Prep time: 15 minutes | Cook time: 10 minutes | Serves 4

salad
1 pound (454 g) lean ground beef
2 medium heads romaine lettuce, rinsed, dried, and sliced in half lengthwise
½ cup (60 g) shredded Cheddar cheese
½ cup (80 g) coarsely chopped tomatoes
⅓ cup (50 g) finely chopped red onion

1 small dill pickle, finely chopped (optional)
dressing
2 ounces (57 g) no-salt-added tomato paste
2 tablespoons (30 ml) apple cider vinegar
2 tablespoons (30 ml) water
1 tablespoon (15 ml) honey
¼ teaspoon sea salt
½ teaspoon onion powder
¼ teaspoon garlic powder

1. To make the salad, heat a large skillet over medium-high heat. Once the skillet is hot, add the beef and cook it for 9 to 10 minutes, until it is brown and cooked though. 2. Meanwhile, place a ½ head of romaine lettuce on each of four plates. Divide the beef evenly on top of each of the romaine halves. Then top each with the Cheddar cheese, tomatoes, onion, and pickle (if using). 3. To make the dressing, combine the tomato paste, vinegar, water, honey, sea salt, onion powder, and garlic powder in a small mason jar, secure the lid on top, and shake the jar thoroughly until everything is combined. Drizzle the dressing evenly over each salad and serve.

Per Serving:

calorie: 320 | fat: 14g | protein: 32g | carbs: 19g | sugars: 11g | fiber: 8g | sodium: 341mg

Romaine Lettuce Salad with Cranberry, Feta, and Beans

Prep time: 10 minutes | Cook time: 0 minutes | Serves 2

1 cup chopped fresh green beans
6 cups washed and chopped romaine lettuce
1 cup sliced radishes
2 scallions, sliced
¼ cup chopped fresh oregano
1 cup canned kidney beans, drained and rinsed
½ cup cranberries, fresh or

frozen
¼ cup crumbled fat-free feta cheese
1 tablespoon extra-virgin olive oil
Salt, to season
Freshly ground black pepper, to season

1. In a microwave-safe dish, add the green beans and a small amount of water. Microwave on high for about 2 minutes, or until tender. 2. In a large bowl, toss together the romaine lettuce, radishes, scallions, and oregano. 3. Add the green beans, kidney beans, cranberries, feta cheese, and olive oil. Season with salt and pepper. Toss to coat. 4. Evenly divide between 2 plates and enjoy immediately.

Per Serving:

calorie: 271 | fat: 9g | protein: 16g | carbs: 36g | sugars: 10g | fiber: 13g | sodium: 573mg

Winter Fruit Salad

Prep time: 10 minutes | Cook time: 0 minutes | Serves 4

3 cups cored, chopped apples (peels optional)
3 cups cored, chopped pears (peels optional)
2 cups peeled, cubed oranges,

mandarins, or grapefruit
1 cup ripe sliced bananas
1½ tablespoons freshly squeezed orange juice
⅛ teaspoon cinnamon

1. In a large bowl, combine the apples, pears, citrus, bananas, orange juice, and cinnamon. Toss gently to combine.
Per Serving:
calorie: 196 | fat: 1g | protein: 2g | carbs: 51g | sugars: 35g | fiber: 9g | sodium: 3mg

Shaved Brussels Sprouts and Kale with Poppy Seed Dressing

Prep time: 20 minutes | Cook time: 0 minutes | Serves 4 to 6

1 pound Brussels sprouts, shaved
1 bunch kale, thinly shredded
4 scallions, both white and green parts, thinly sliced

4 ounces shredded Romano cheese
Poppy seed dressing
Kosher salt
Freshly ground black pepper

1. In a large bowl, toss together the Brussels sprouts, kale, scallions, and Romano cheese. Add the dressing to the greens and toss to combine. Season with salt and pepper to taste.

Per Serving:

calorie: 139 | fat: 7g | protein: 11g | carbs: 11g | sugars: 3g | fiber: 4g | sodium: 357mg

Herbed Spring Peas

Prep time: 10 minutes | Cook time: 15 minutes | Serves 6

1 tablespoon unsalted non-hydrogenated plant-based butter
½ Vidalia onion, thinly sliced
1 cup store-bought low-sodium

vegetable broth
3 cups fresh shelled peas
1 tablespoon minced fresh tarragon

1. In a skillet, melt the butter over medium heat. 2. Add the onion and sauté for 2 to 3 minutes, or until the onion is translucent. 3. Add the broth, and reduce the heat to low. 4. Add the peas and tarragon, cover, and cook for 7 to 10 minutes, or until the peas soften. 5. Serve.

Per Serving:

calorie: 43 | fat: 2g | protein: 2g | carbs: 6g | sugars: 3g | fiber: 2g | sodium: 159mg

Italian Bean Salad

Prep time: 15 minutes | Cook time: 0 minutes | Serves 4

2 tablespoons lemon juice
1 tablespoon red wine vinegar
1 tablespoon pure maple syrup
1½ teaspoons Dijon mustard
Rounded ¼ teaspoon sea salt
½ teaspoon dried oregano
¼ teaspoon garlic powder
Freshly ground black pepper to taste (optional)
1 can (15 ounces) chickpeas, rinsed
1 can (15 ounces) white beans, rinsed
1 cup chopped red, yellow, or orange bell pepper
½ cup chopped fresh tomatoes
1-1½ cups quartered or roughly chopped artichoke hearts (frozen or canned, not marinated in oil)
¼ cup chopped or sliced dry-pack sun-dried tomatoes
¼ cup sliced green portion of green onion or chives
⅓ cup sliced kalamata olives
¼ cup chopped fresh basil leaves
3 tablespoons raisins or ¼ cup sliced grapes (optional)

1. In a large bowl, combine the lemon juice, vinegar, syrup, mustard, salt, oregano, garlic powder, and black pepper (if using). Whisk to thoroughly combine. Add the chickpeas, beans, bell pepper, fresh tomatoes, artichoke hearts, sun-dried tomatoes, green onion or chives, olives, basil, and raisins or grapes (if using). Mix well to fully coat with the dressing. Taste, and season with extra salt and black pepper, if desired. Serve, or refrigerate for up to 4 days.

Per Serving:

calorie: 275 | fat: 4g | protein: 15g | carbs: 49g | sugars: 10g | fiber: 15g | sodium: 801mg

Thai Broccoli Slaw

Prep time: 20 minutes | Cook time: 0 minutes | Serves 8

Dressing
2 tablespoons reduced-fat creamy peanut butter
1 tablespoon grated gingerroot
1 tablespoon rice vinegar
1 tablespoon orange marmalade
1½ teaspoons reduced-sodium soy sauce
¼ to ½ teaspoon chili garlic sauce

Slaw
3 cups broccoli slaw mix (from 10-ounce bag)
½ cup bite-size thin strips red bell pepper
½ cup julienne (matchstick-cut) carrots
½ cup shredded red cabbage
2 tablespoons chopped fresh cilantro

1 In small bowl, combine all dressing ingredients. Beat with whisk, until blended. 2 In large bowl, toss all slaw ingredients. Pour dressing over slaw mixture; toss until coated. Cover and refrigerate at least 1 hour to blend flavors but no longer than 6 hours, tossing occasionally to blend dressing from bottom of bowl back into slaw mixture.

Per Serving:

calorie: 50 | fat: 1.5g | protein: 2g | carbs: 7g | sugars: 3g | fiber: 1g | sodium: 75mg

Roasted Carrot and Quinoa with Goat Cheese

Prep time: 10 minutes | Cook time: 20 minutes | Serves 4

4 large carrots, cut into ⅛-inch-thick rounds
4 tablespoons oil (olive, safflower, or grapeseed), divided
2 teaspoons paprika
1 teaspoon turmeric
2 teaspoons ground cumin
2 cups water
1 cup quinoa, rinsed
½ cup shelled pistachios, toasted
4 ounces goat cheese
12 ounces salad greens

1. Preheat the oven to 400°F. Line a baking sheet with parchment paper. 2. In a large bowl, toss together the carrots, 2 tablespoons of oil, the paprika, turmeric, and cumin until the carrots are well coated. Spread them evenly on the prepared baking sheet and roast until tender, 15 to 17 minutes. 3. In a medium saucepan, combine the water and quinoa over high heat. Bring to a boil, reduce the heat to low and simmer until tender, about 15 minutes. 4. Transfer the roasted carrots to a large bowl and add the cooked quinoa, remaining 2 tablespoons of oil, the pistachios, and goat cheese and toss to combine. 5. Evenly divide the greens among four plates and top with the carrot mixture. Serve. 6. Store any leftovers in an airtight container in the refrigerator for up to 2 days.

Per Serving:

calorie: 544 | fat: 33g | protein: 21g | carbs: 43g | sugars: 6g | fiber: 9g | sodium: 202mg

Haricot Verts, Walnut, and Feta Salad

Prep time: 10 minutes | Cook time: 15 minutes | Serves 12

½ cup walnuts, toasted
1½ pounds fresh haricot verts, trimmed and halved
½ cup cooked green lentils
1 medium red onion, sliced into rings
½ cup peeled, seeded, and diced cucumber
⅓ cup crumbled fat-free feta cheese
¼ cup extra-virgin olive oil
¼ cup white wine vinegar
¼ cup chopped fresh mint leaves
1 garlic clove, minced

1. Place the walnuts in a small baking dish in a 350-degree oven for 5-10 minutes until lightly browned. Remove from the oven, and set aside. 2. Steam the haricot verts about 4-5 minutes, or until desired degree of crispness. 3. In a salad bowl, combine the haricot verts with the walnuts, lentils, red onion rings, cucumber, and feta cheese. 4. Combine all the dressing ingredients together, and toss with the vegetables. Chill in the refrigerator for 2-3 hours before serving.

Per Serving:

calorie: 119 | fat: 7g | protein: 5g | carbs: 11g | sugars: 3g | fiber: 4g | sodium: 61mg

Three Bean and Basil Salad

Prep time: 10 minutes | Cook time: 0 minutes | Serves 8

1 (15-ounce) can low-sodium chickpeas, drained and rinsed
1 (15-ounce) can low-sodium kidney beans, drained and rinsed
1 (15-ounce) can low-sodium white beans, drained and rinsed
1 red bell pepper, seeded and finely chopped
¼ cup chopped scallions, both white and green parts
¼ cup finely chopped fresh basil
3 garlic cloves, minced
2 tablespoons extra-virgin olive oil
1 tablespoon red wine vinegar
1 teaspoon Dijon mustard
¼ teaspoon freshly ground black pepper

1. In a large mixing bowl, combine the chickpeas, kidney beans, white beans, bell pepper, scallions, basil, and garlic. Toss gently to combine. 2. In a small bowl, combine the olive oil, vinegar, mustard, and pepper. Toss with the salad. 3. Cover and refrigerate for an hour before serving, to allow the flavors to mix.

Per Serving:
Calorie: 193 | fat: 5g | protein: 10g | carbs: 29g | sugars: 3g | fiber: 8g | sodium: 246mg

Carrot and Cashew Chicken Salad

Prep time: 20 minutes | Cook time: 25 minutes | Serves 2

Extra-virgin olive oil cooking spray
1 cup carrots rounds
1 red bell pepper, thinly sliced
1½ teaspoons granulated stevia
1 tablespoon extra-virgin olive oil, divided
¼ teaspoon salt, divided
⅜ teaspoon freshly ground black pepper, divided
1 (6-ounce) boneless skinless chicken breast, thinly sliced across the grain
2 tablespoons chopped scallions
1 tablespoon apple cider vinegar
1 cup sugar snap peas
4 cups baby spinach
4 tablespoons chopped cashews, divided

1. Preheat the oven to 425°F. 2. Coat an 8-by-8-inch baking pan and a rimmed baking sheet with cooking spray. 3. In the prepared baking pan, add the carrots and red bell pepper. Sprinkle with the stevia, 1 teaspoon of olive oil, ⅛ teaspoon of salt, and ⅛ teaspoon of pepper. Toss to coat. 4. Place the pan in the preheated oven. Roast for about 25 minutes, stirring several times, or until tender. 5. About 5 minutes before the vegetables are done, place the sliced chicken in a medium bowl and drizzle with 1 teaspoon of olive oil. Sprinkle with the scallions. Season with the remaining ⅛ teaspoon of salt and ⅛ teaspoon of pepper. Toss to mix. Arrange in a single layer on the prepared baking sheet. 6. Place the sheet in the preheated oven. Roast for 5 to 7 minutes, turning once, or until cooked through. 7. Remove the pan with the vegetables and the baking sheet from the oven. Cool for about 3 minutes. 8. In a large salad bowl, mix together the apple cider vinegar, the remaining 1 teaspoon of olive oil, the sugar snap peas, and remaining ⅛ teaspoon of pepper. Let stand 5 minutes to blend the flavors. 9. To finish, add the spinach to the bowl with the dressing and peas. Toss to mix well. 10. Evenly divide between 2 serving plates. Top each with half of the roasted carrots, half of the roasted red bell peppers, and half of the cooked chicken. 11. Sprinkle each with about 2 tablespoons of cashews. Serve warm.

Per Serving:
calorie: 335 | fat: 17g | protein: 26g | carbs: 21g | sugars: 8g | fiber: 6g | sodium: 422mg

Chicken Salad with Apricots

Prep time: 10 minutes | Cook time: 0 minutes | Makes 4 cups

1 cup plain Greek yogurt
2 tablespoons minced shallots
1 teaspoon ground coriander
1 teaspoon Dijon mustard (optional)
1 tablespoon freshly squeezed lemon juice
¼ teaspoon cayenne pepper
12 ounces cooked rotisserie chicken, shredded
2 cups chopped celery with the leaves
¼ cup slivered almonds, toasted
¼ cup thinly sliced dried apricots
1 bunch fresh parsley, chopped

1. In a medium bowl, mix together the Greek yogurt, shallots, coriander, mustard (if using), lemon juice, and cayenne until well combined. 2. Add the chicken, celery, almonds, apricots, and parsley. 3. Serve on your food of choice (lettuce, crackers, jicama slices, radish slices—you name it). 4. Store any leftovers in an airtight container in the refrigerator for up to 3 days.
Per Serving:
calorie: 232 | fat: 7g | protein: 31g | carbs: 11g | sugars: 7g | fiber: 3g | sodium: 152mg

Sweet Beet Grain Bowl

Prep time: 10 minutes | Cook time: 20 minutes | Serves 2

3 cups water
1 cup farro, rinsed
2 tablespoons extra-virgin olive oil
1 tablespoon honey
3 tablespoons cider vinegar
Pinch freshly ground black pepper
4 small cooked beets, sliced
1 pear, cored and diced
6 cups mixed greens
⅓ cup pumpkin seeds, roasted
¼ cup ricotta cheese

1. In a medium saucepan, stir together the water and farro over high heat and bring to a boil. Reduce the heat to medium and simmer until the farro is tender, 15 to 20 minutes. Drain and rinse the farro under cold running water until cool. Set aside. 2. Meanwhile, in a small bowl, whisk together the extra-virgin olive oil, honey, and vinegar. Season with black pepper. 3. Evenly divide the farro between two bowls. Top each with the beets, pear, greens, pumpkin seeds, and ricotta. Drizzle the bowls with the dressing before serving and adjust the seasonings as desired.

Per Serving:
calorie: 750 | fat: 28g | protein: 21g | carbs: 104g | sugars: 18g | fiber: 12g | sodium: 174mg

Chickpea "Tuna" Salad

Prep time: 15 minutes | Cook time: 0 minutes | Serves 2

2 cups canned chickpeas, drained and rinsed
½ cup plain nonfat Greek yogurt
2 small celery stalks, chopped
1 small cucumber, chopped
½ cup chopped red onion
2 tablespoons freshly squeezed lemon juice

1 tablespoon chia seeds
1 garlic clove, chopped
1 teaspoon minced fresh parsley
Salt, to season
Freshly ground black pepper, to season
2 large romaine lettuce leaves

1. In a medium bowl, roughly mash the chickpeas with the back of a fork. 2. Add the yogurt, celery, cucumber, red onion, lemon juice, chia seeds, garlic, and parsley. Mix well. Season with salt and pepper. 3. Place half of the chickpea mixture on each romaine lettuce leaf. Wrap and serve chilled or at room temperature.

Per Serving:
calorie: 293 | fat: 6g | protein: 17g | carbs: 46g | sugars: 14g | fiber: 13g | sodium: 401mg

Quinoa, Beet, and Greens Salad

Prep time: 15 minutes | Cook time: 25 minutes | Serves 2

For the vinaigrette
1 tablespoon extra-virgin olive oil
2 tablespoons red wine vinegar
1 garlic clove, chopped
Freshly ground black pepper, to season
For the salad
2 medium beets

1 small bunch fresh kale leaves, thoroughly washed, deveined, and dried
Extra-virgin olive oil cooking spray
⅓ cup dry quinoa
⅔ cup water
¼ cup chopped scallions
½ cup unsalted soy nuts

To make the vinaigrette In a large bowl, whisk together the olive oil, red wine vinegar, and garlic. Season with pepper. Set aside. To make the salad 1. Into a medium saucepan set over high heat, insert a steamer basket. Fill the pan with water to just below the bottom of the steamer. Cover and bring to a boil. 2. Add the beets. Cover and steam for 7 to 10 minutes, or until just tender. Remove from the steamer. Let sit until cool enough to handle. Peel and slice. Set aside. 3. Spray the kale leaves with cooking spray. Massage the leaves, breaking down the fibers so they're easier to chew. Chop finely. You should have 1 cup. 4. In a small saucepan set over high heat, mix together the quinoa and water. Bring to a boil. Reduce the heat to medium-low. Cover and simmer for about 15 minutes, or until the quinoa is tender and the liquid has been absorbed. Remove from the heat. 5. Immediately add half of the vinaigrette to the saucepan while fluffing the quinoa with a fork. Cover and refrigerate for at least 1 hour, or until completely cooled. Set aside the remaining vinaigrette. 6. Into the cooled quinoa, stir the chopped kale, scallions, soy nuts, sliced beets, and remaining vinaigrette. Toss lightly before serving.

Per Serving:
calorie: 461 | fat: 29g | protein: 14g | carbs: 41g | sugars: 7g | fiber: 9g | sodium: 100mg

Mediterranean Pasta Salad with Goat Cheese

Prep time: 25 minutes | Cook time: 0 minutes | Serves 4

½ cup (75 g) grape tomatoes, sliced in half lengthwise
1 medium red bell pepper, coarsely chopped
½ medium red onion, sliced into thin strips
1 medium zucchini, coarsely chopped
1 cup (175 g) broccoli florets
½ cup (110 g) oil-packed artichoke hearts, drained
¼ cup (60 ml) olive oil

½ teaspoon sea salt
½ teaspoon black pepper
1 tablespoon (3 g) dried oregano
½ teaspoon garlic powder
4 ounces (113 g) crumbled goat cheese
½ cup (50 g) shaved Parmesan cheese
8 ounces (227 g) lentil or chickpea penne pasta, cooked, rinsed, and drained

1. In a large bowl, combine the tomatoes, bell pepper, onion, zucchini, broccoli, artichoke hearts, oil, sea salt, black pepper, oregano, garlic powder, goat cheese, and Parmesan cheese. Gently mix everything together to combine and coat all of the ingredients with the oil. 2. Add the pasta to the bowl and stir to combine. 3. Let the pasta salad rest for 1 to 2 hours in the refrigerator to marinate it, or serve the pasta salad immediately if desired.

Per Serving:
calorie: 477 | fat: 24g | protein: 23g | carbs: 41g | sugars: 6g | fiber: 6g | sodium: 706mg

Zucchini, Carrot, and Fennel Salad

Prep time: 10 minutes | Cook time: 8 minutes | Serves ½ cup

2 medium carrots, peeled and julienned
1 medium zucchini, julienned
½ medium fennel bulb, core removed and julienned
1 tablespoon fresh orange juice
2 tablespoons Dijon mustard
3 tablespoons extra-virgin olive oil
1 teaspoon white wine vinegar

½ teaspoon dried thyme
1 tablespoon finely minced parsley
 teaspoon salt
¼ teaspoon freshly ground black pepper
¼ cup chopped walnuts
1 medium head romaine lettuce, washed and leaves separated

1. Place the carrots, zucchini, and fennel in a medium bowl; set aside. 2. In a medium bowl, combine the orange juice, mustard, olive oil, vinegar, thyme, parsley, salt, and pepper; mix well. 3. Pour the dressing over the vegetables and toss. Add the walnuts, and mix again. Refrigerate until ready to serve. 4. To serve, line a bowl or plates with lettuce leaves, and spoon ½ cup of salad on top.

Per Serving:
calorie: 201 | fat: 16g | protein: 5g | carbs: 14g | sugars: 6g | fiber: 6g | sodium: 285mg

Chickpea Salad

Prep time: 15 minutes | Cook time: 0 minutes | Serves 4

½ cup bottled balsamic vinaigrette
1 (15-ounce) can chickpeas, rinsed and drained
1 cup cherry tomatoes
1 small red onion, quartered and sliced
2 large cucumbers, peeled and cut into bite-size pieces
1 large zucchini, cut into bite-size pieces
1 (10-ounce) package frozen shelled edamame, steamed or microwaved
Chopped fresh parsley, for garnish

1. Pour the vinaigrette into a large bowl. Add the chickpeas, tomatoes, onion, cucumbers, zucchini, and edamame and toss until all the ingredients are coated. 2. Garnish with chopped parsley.

Per Serving:
calorie: 188 | fat: 4g | protein: 10g | carbs: 29g | sugars: 11g | fiber: 8g | sodium: 171mg

First-of-the-Season Tomato, Peach, and Strawberry Salad

Prep time: 15 minutes | Cook time: 0 minutes | Serves 6

6 cups mixed spring greens
4 large ripe plum tomatoes, thinly sliced
4 large ripe peaches, pitted and thinly sliced
12 ripe strawberries, thinly sliced
½ Vidalia onion, thinly sliced
2 tablespoons white balsamic vinegar
2 tablespoons extra-virgin olive oil
Freshly ground black pepper

1. Put the greens in a large salad bowl, and layer the tomatoes, peaches, strawberries, and onion on top. 2. Dress with the vinegar and oil, toss together, and season with pepper.

Per Serving:
calorie: 122 | fat: 5g | protein: 3g | carbs: 19g | sugars: 14g | fiber: 4g | sodium: 20mg

Salmon and Baby Greens with Edamame

Prep time: 15 minutes | Cook time: 10 minutes | Serves 2

3 teaspoons extra-virgin olive oil, divided
4 cups mixed baby greens, divided
¼ cup edamame
1 teaspoon balsamic vinegar
¼ teaspoon salt
1 (6-ounce) salmon fillet
Extra-virgin olive oil cooking spray
2 tablespoons chopped fresh dill

1. In a large skillet set over medium heat, heat 1½ teaspoons of olive oil. 2. Add 2 cups of baby greens. Cook for 1 minute. Transfer to a medium salad bowl. Repeat with the remaining 1½ teaspoons of olive oil and 2 cups of baby greens. 3. Add the edamame, balsamic vinegar, and salt to the greens. Toss to combine. 4. Place an oven rack about 8 inches from the broiler. 5. Preheat the broiler to high. 6. To a small ovenproof dish, add the salmon. Coat the salmon with cooking spray. 7. Put the dish under the preheated broiler. Broil for 8 to 10 minutes, depending on its thickness, or until the fish is just cooked. 8. Cut the fish in half. Place it on top of the greens. 9. Top with the fresh dill. 10. Serve immediately.

Per Serving:
calorie: 225 | fat: 12g | protein: 22g | carbs: 9g | sugars: 2g | fiber: 4g | sodium: 389mg

Shrimp and Radicchio Salad

Prep time: 10 minutes | Cook time: 0 minutes | Serves 4

¼ cup olive oil
2 tablespoons red wine vinegar
3 medium garlic cloves, minced
1 medium shallot, minced
2 teaspoons Dijon mustard
1 teaspoon prepared horseradish
¼ teaspoon freshly ground black
pepper
½ pound fresh (never frozen) cooked bay shrimp
1 medium head Boston lettuce, shredded
1 medium head radicchio lettuce, shredded

1. In a medium bowl, combine the olive oil, vinegar, garlic, shallots, mustard, horseradish, and pepper. Add the shrimp, and toss well. Chill in the refrigerator for 30 minutes. 2. Just before serving, combine the lettuce and radicchio in a serving bowl. Place the shrimp mixture on top, toss, and serve.

Per Serving:
calorie: 220 | fat: 15g | protein: 15g | carbs: 7g | sugars: 3g | fiber: 2g | sodium: 587mg

Five-Layer Salad

Prep time: 10 minutes | Cook time: 6 minutes | Serves 6

1 cup frozen sweet peas
1 tablespoon water
⅓ cup plain fat-free yogurt
¼ cup reduced-fat mayonnaise (do not use salad dressing)
1 tablespoon cider vinegar
2 teaspoons sugar
½ teaspoon salt
3 cups coleslaw mix (shredded cabbage and carrots; from 16-ounce bag)
1 cup shredded carrots (2 medium)
1 cup halved cherry tomatoes

1 In small microwavable bowl, place peas and water. Cover with microwavable plastic wrap, folding back one edge ¼ inch to vent steam. Microwave on High 4 to 6 minutes, stirring after 2 minutes, until tender; drain. Let stand until cool. 2 Meanwhile, in small bowl, mix yogurt, mayonnaise, vinegar, sugar and salt. 3 In 1½- or 2-quart glass bowl, layer coleslaw mix, carrots, tomatoes and peas. Spread mayonnaise mixture over top. Refrigerate 15 minutes. Toss gently before serving.

Per Serving:
calorie: 100 | fat: 3.5g | protein: 3g | carbs: 13g | sugars: 7g | fiber: 3g | sodium: 330mg

Garden-Fresh Greek Salad

Prep time: 20 minutes | Cook time: 0 minutes | Serves 6

Dressing
3 tablespoons fresh lemon juice
1 tablespoon chopped fresh or 1 teaspoon dried oregano leaves
½ teaspoon salt
½ teaspoon sugar
½ teaspoon Dijon mustard
¼ teaspoon pepper
1 clove garlic, finely chopped
Salad

1 bag (10 ounces) ready-to-eat romaine lettuce
¾ cup chopped seeded peeled cucumber
½ cup sliced red onion
¼ cup sliced kalamata olives
2 medium tomatoes, seeded, chopped (1½ cups)
¼ cup reduced-fat feta cheese

1 In small bowl, beat all dressing ingredients with whisk. 2 In large bowl, toss all salad ingredients except cheese. Stir in dressing until salad is well coated. Sprinkle with cheese.

Per Serving:
calorie: 45 | fat: 1.5g | protein: 3g | carbs: 6g | sugars: 3g | fiber: 2g | sodium: 340mg

Strawberry-Spinach Salad

Prep time: 15 minutes | Cook time: 0 minutes | Serves 4

½ cup extra-virgin olive oil
¼ cup balsamic vinegar
1 tablespoon Worcestershire sauce
1 (10-ounce) package baby spinach
1 medium red onion, quartered

and sliced
1 cup strawberries, sliced
1 (6-ounce) container feta cheese, crumbled
4 tablespoons bacon bits, divided
1 cup slivered almonds, divided

1. In a large bowl, whisk together the olive oil, balsamic vinegar, and Worcestershire sauce. 2. Add the spinach, onion, strawberries, and feta cheese and mix until all the ingredients are coated. 3. Portion into 4 servings and top each with 1 tablespoon of bacon bits and ¼ cup of slivered almonds.

Per Serving:
calorie: 417 | fat: 29g | protein: 24g | carbs: 19g | sugars: 7g | fiber: 7g | sodium: 542mg

Tu-No Salad

Prep time: 10 minutes | Cook time: 0 minutes | Serves 2

1 can (15 ounces) chickpeas, rinsed and drained
1 tablespoon tahini
2 tablespoons water
1 tablespoon red wine vinegar (can substitute apple cider vinegar)
1 tablespoon chickpea miso (or

other mild-flavored miso)
1 teaspoon vegan Worcestershire sauce (optional)
½ teaspoon Dijon mustard
½ teaspoon coconut nectar
2 tablespoons minced celery
2 tablespoons minced cucumber
2 tablespoons minced apple

⅛ teaspoon sea salt   taste
Freshly ground black pepper to

1. In a small food processor, pulse the chickpeas until fairly crumbly but not finely ground. (Alternatively, you can mash by hand.) In a large bowl, combine the chickpeas, tahini, water, vinegar, miso, Worcestershire sauce, mustard, nectar, celery, cucumber, apple, and salt. Mix together well. Season with additional salt and pepper to taste, and serve!

Per Serving:
calorie: 264 | fat: 8g | protein: 12g | carbs: 37g | sugars: 8g | fiber: 10g | sodium: 800mg

Crumbles

Prep time: 15 minutes | Cook time: 0 minutes | Serves 4

½ cup bottled Italian dressing
2 cups frozen black bean crumbles, microwaved per package instructions
1 cup cherry tomatoes, halved
1 (16-ounce) can or jar three-

bean salad mix, drained
1 medium onion, quartered and thinly sliced
4 cups romaine salad greens
1 cup shredded reduced-fat cheddar cheese, divided

1. Pour the Italian dressing into a large bowl. Add the black bean crumbles, cherry tomatoes, three-bean salad, and onion and mix until everything is well coated. 2. Divide the greens into 4 bowls and top each with the bean mixture. 3. Sprinkle ¼ cup of shredded cheddar cheese on each portion.

Per Serving:
calorie: 357 | fat: 10g | protein: 22g | carbs: 48g | sugars: 6g | fiber: 9g | sodium: 478mg

Apple-Bulgur Salad

Prep time: 10 minutes | Cook time: 15 minutes | Serves 2

2 cups water
1 cup bulgur
1 teaspoon dried thyme
2 tablespoons extra-virgin olive oil
2 teaspoons cider vinegar

Kosher salt
Freshly ground black pepper
6 kale leaves, shredded
1 small apple, cored and diced
3 tablespoons sliced, toasted almonds

1. In a large saucepan, bring the water to a boil over high heat and remove it from the heat. Add the bulgur and thyme, cover, and allow the grain to rest for 7 to 15 minutes or until cooked through. 2. Meanwhile, in a large bowl, whisk together the extra-virgin olive oil and cider vinegar with a pinch of salt and pepper. Add the cooked bulgur, kale, apple, and almonds to the dressing and toss to combine. Adjust the seasonings as desired. 3. Store any leftovers in an airtight container in the refrigerator for 3 to 5 days.

Per Serving:
calorie: 496 | fat: 22g | protein: 13g | carbs: 69g | sugars: 9g | fiber: 13g | sodium: 33mg

Herbed Tomato Salad

Prep time: 7 minutes | Cook time: 0 minutes | Serves 2 to 4

1 pint cherry tomatoes, halved
1 bunch fresh parsley, leaves only (stems discarded)
1 cup cilantro, leaves only (stems discarded)
¼ cup fresh dill

1 teaspoon sumac (optional)
2 tablespoons extra-virgin olive oil
Kosher salt
Freshly ground black pepper

1. In a medium bowl, carefully toss together the tomatoes, parsley, cilantro, dill, sumac (if using), extra-virgin olive oil, and salt and pepper to taste. 2. Store any leftovers in an airtight container in the refrigerator for up to 3 days, but the salad is best consumed on the day it is dressed.

Per Serving:

calorie: 113 | fat: 10g | protein: 2g | carbs: 7g | sugars: 3g | fiber: 3g | sodium: 30mg

Raw Corn Salad with Black-Eyed Peas

Prep time: 15 minutes | Cook time: 0 minutes | Serves 8

2 ears fresh corn, kernels cut off
2 cups cooked black-eyed peas
1 green bell pepper, chopped
½ red onion, chopped
2 celery stalks, finely chopped
½ pint cherry tomatoes, halved
3 tablespoons white balsamic

vinegar
2 tablespoons extra-virgin olive oil
1 garlic clove, minced
¼ teaspoon smoked paprika
¼ teaspoon ground cumin
¼ teaspoon red pepper flakes

1. In a large salad bowl, combine the corn, black-eyed peas, bell pepper, onion, celery, and tomatoes. 2. In a small bowl, to make the dressing, whisk the vinegar, olive oil, garlic, paprika, cumin, and red pepper flakes together. 3. Pour the dressing over the salad, and toss gently to coat. Serve and enjoy.

Per Serving:

calorie: 127 | fat: 4g | protein: 5g | carbs: 19g | sugars: 5g | fiber: 5g | sodium: 16mg

Chicken, Spinach, and Berry Salad

Prep time: 5 minutes | Cook time: 0 minutes | Serves 4

For The Salad
8 cups baby spinach
2 cups shredded rotisserie chicken
½ cup sliced strawberries or other berries
½ cup sliced almonds

1 avocado, sliced
¼ cup crumbled feta (optional)
For The Dressing
2 tablespoons extra-virgin olive oil
2 teaspoons honey
2 teaspoons balsamic vinegar

To Make The Salad 1. In a large bowl, combine the spinach, chicken, strawberries, and almonds. 2. Pour the dressing over the salad and lightly toss. 3. Divide into four equal portions and top each with sliced avocado and 1 tablespoon of crumbled feta (if using). To Make The Dressing 4. In a small bowl, whisk together the olive oil, honey, and balsamic vinegar.

Per Serving:

calorie: 341 | fat: 22g | protein: 26g | carbs: 14g | sugars: 5g | fiber: 7g | sodium: 99mg

Celery and Apple Salad with Cider Vinaigrette

Prep time: 20 minutes | Cook time: 0 minutes | Serves 4

Dressing
2 tablespoons apple cider or apple juice
1 tablespoon cider vinegar
2 teaspoons canola oil
2 teaspoons finely chopped shallots
½ teaspoon Dijon mustard
½ teaspoon honey
½ teaspoon salt

Salad
2 cups chopped romaine lettuce
2 cups diagonally sliced celery
½ medium apple, unpeeled, sliced very thin (about 1 cup)
⅓ cup sweetened dried cranberries
2 tablespoons chopped walnuts
2 tablespoons crumbled blue cheese

1 In small bowl, beat all dressing ingredients with whisk until blended; set aside. 2 In medium bowl, place lettuce, celery, apple and cranberries; toss with dressing. To serve, arrange salad on 4 plates. Sprinkle with walnuts and blue cheese. Serve immediately.

Per Serving:

calorie: 130 | fat: 6g | protein: 2g | carbs: 17g | sugars: 13g | fiber: 3g | sodium: 410mg

Mediterranean Chicken Salad

Prep time: 5 minutes | Cook time: 0 minutes | Serves 3

8 ounces boneless, skinless, cooked chicken breast
2 tablespoons extra-virgin olive oil
2 tablespoons balsamic vinegar
¼ teaspoon dried basil
2 small garlic cloves, minced
¼ teaspoon freshly ground black

pepper
1 cup cooked green beans, cut into 2-inch pieces
1 cup cooked artichokes
¼ cup pine nuts, toasted
¼ cup sliced black olives
3 cherry tomatoes, halved
Tomato wedges (optional)

1. Cut the cooked chicken into bite-sized chunks, and set aside. 2. In a medium bowl, whisk together the oil, vinegar, basil, garlic, and pepper. Add the chicken, and toss with the dressing. 3. Add the green beans, artichokes, pine nuts, olives, and cherry tomatoes; toss well. Chill in the refrigerator for several hours. Garnish the salad with tomato wedges, and serve.

Per Serving:

calorie: 307 | fat: 19g | protein: 21g | carbs: 14g | sugars: 4g | fiber: 7g | sodium: 73mg

Power Salad

Prep time: 15 minutes | Cook time: 0 minutes | Serves 2

For the dressing
1 tablespoon extra-virgin olive oil
1 tablespoon freshly squeezed lemon juice
1 tablespoon balsamic vinegar
1 tablespoon chia seeds
1 teaspoon liquid stevia
Pinch salt
Freshly ground black pepper

For the salad
6 cups mixed baby greens
1 cup shelled edamame
1 cup chopped red cabbage
1 cup chopped red bell pepper
1 cup sliced fresh button mushrooms
½ cup sliced avocado
¼ cup sliced almonds
1 cup pea shoots, divided

To make the dressing 1. In a small bowl, whisk together the olive oil, lemon juice, balsamic vinegar, chia seeds, and stevia until well combined. Season with salt and pepper. To make the salad 2. In a large bowl, toss together the mixed greens, edamame, red cabbage, red bell pepper, mushrooms, avocado, and almonds. Drizzle the dressing over the salad. Toss again to coat well. 3. Divide the salad between 2 plates. Top each with ½ cup of pea shoots and serve.

Per Serving:

calorie: 449 | fat: 24g | protein: 22g | carbs: 47g | sugars: 11g | fiber: 16g | sodium: 86mg

Moroccan Carrot Salad

Prep time: 15 minutes | Cook time: 0 minutes | Serves 5

Dressing
¼ cup orange juice
2 tablespoons olive oil
1 teaspoon orange peel
1 teaspoon ground cumin
1 teaspoon paprika
¼ teaspoon salt
1/8 to ¼ teaspoon ground red pepper (cayenne)
1/8 teaspoon ground cinnamon
Salad

1 bag (10 ounces) julienne (matchstick-cut) carrots (5 cups)
1 can (15 ounces) chickpeas (garbanzo beans), drained, rinsed
¼ cup golden raisins
3 tablespoons salted roasted whole almonds, coarsely chopped
¼ cup coarsely chopped fresh cilantro or parsley

1 In small bowl, combine all dressing ingredients with whisk until blended; set aside. 2 In large bowl, combine carrots, chickpeas and raisins; toss to combine. Add dressing; mix thoroughly. Cover and refrigerate at least 2 hours or overnight, stirring occasionally. Just before serving, sprinkle with almonds and cilantro.

Per Serving:

calorie: 310 | fat: 11g | protein: 10g | carbs: 44g | sugars: 12g | fiber: 10g | sodium: 230mg

Blueberry and Chicken Salad on a Bed of Greens

Prep time: 10 minutes | Cook time: 0 minutes | Serves 4

2 cups chopped cooked chicken
1 cup fresh blueberries
¼ cup finely chopped almonds
1 celery stalk, finely chopped
¼ cup finely chopped red onion
1 tablespoon chopped fresh basil
1 tablespoon chopped fresh

cilantro
½ cup plain, nonfat Greek yogurt or vegan mayonnaise
¼ teaspoon salt
¼ teaspoon freshly ground black pepper
8 cups salad greens (baby spinach, spicy greens, romaine)

1. In a large mixing bowl, combine the chicken, blueberries, almonds, celery, onion, basil, and cilantro. Toss gently to mix. 2. In a small bowl, combine the yogurt, salt, and pepper. Add to the chicken salad and stir to combine. 3. Arrange 2 cups of salad greens on each of 4 plates and divide the chicken salad among the plates to serve.

Per Serving:

calories: 207 | fat: 6g | protein: 28g | carbs: 11g | sugars: 6g | fiber: 3g | sodium: 235mg

Three-Bean Salad with Black Bean Grilled Romaine with White Beans

Prep time: 5 minutes | Cook time: 8 minutes | Serves 4 to 6

3 tablespoons extra-virgin olive oil, divided
2 large heads romaine lettuce, halved lengthwise
2 tablespoons white miso

1 tablespoon water, plus more as needed
1 (15-ounce) can white beans, rinsed and drained
½ cup chopped fresh parsley

1. Preheat the grill or a grill pan. 2. Drizzle 2 tablespoons of extra-virgin olive oil over the cut sides of the romaine lettuce. 3. In a medium bowl, whisk the remaining 1 tablespoon of extra-virgin olive oil with the white miso and about 1 tablespoon of water. Add more water, if necessary, to reach a thin consistency. Add the white beans and parsley to the bowl, stir, adjust the seasonings as desired, and set aside. 4. When the grill is hot, put the romaine on the grill and cook for 1 to 2 minutes on each side or until lightly charred with grill marks. Remove the lettuce from the grill and repeat with remaining lettuce halves. Set the lettuce aside on a platter or individual plates and top with the beans.

Per Serving:

calorie: 242 | fat: 10g | protein: 11g | carbs: 31g | sugars: 4g | fiber: 11g | sodium: 282mg

Chapter 8 Snacks and Appetizers

Caramelized Onion-Shrimp Spread

Prep time: 30 minutes | Cook time: 20 minutes | Serves 18

1 tablespoon butter (do not use margarine)
½ medium onion, thinly sliced (about ½ cup)
1 clove garlic, finely chopped
¼ cup apple jelly
1 container (8 ounces) reduced-

fat cream cheese, softened
1 bag (4 ounces) frozen cooked salad shrimp, thawed, well drained (about 1 cup)
1 teaspoon chopped fresh chives
36 whole-grain crackers

1 In 1-quart saucepan, melt butter over medium-low heat. Add onion; cook 15 minutes, stirring frequently. Add garlic; cook 1 minute, stirring occasionally, until onion and garlic are tender and browned. Stir in apple jelly. Cook, stirring constantly, until melted. Remove from heat. Let stand 5 minutes to cool. 2 Meanwhile, in small bowl, stir together cream cheese and shrimp. On 8-inch plate, spread shrimp mixture into a 5-inch round. 3 Spoon onion mixture over shrimp mixture. Sprinkle with chives. Serve with crackers.

Per Serving:
calories: 90| fat: 4g | protein: 3g | carbs: 10g | sugars: 3g | fiber: 1g | sodium: 140mg

Green Goddess White Bean Dip

Prep time: 1 minutes | Cook time: 45 minutes | Makes 3 cups

1 cup dried navy, great Northern, or cannellini beans
4 cups water
2 teaspoons fine sea salt
3 tablespoons fresh lemon juice
¼ cup extra-virgin olive oil,

plus 1 tablespoon
¼ cup firmly packed fresh flat-leaf parsley leaves
1 bunch chives, chopped
Leaves from 2 tarragon sprigs
Freshly ground black pepper

1. Combine the beans, water, and 1 teaspoon of the salt in the Instant Pot and stir to dissolve the salt. 2. Secure the lid and set the Pressure Release to Sealing. Select the Bean/Chili, Pressure Cook, or Manual setting and set the cooking time for 30 minutes at high pressure if using navy or Great Northern beans or 40 minutes at high pressure if using cannellini beans. (The pot will take about 15 minutes to come up to pressure before the cooking program begins.) 3. When the cooking program ends, let the pressure release naturally for 15 minutes, then move the Pressure Release to Venting to release any remaining steam. Open the pot and scoop out and reserve ½ cup of the cooking liquid. Wearing heat-resistant mitts, lift out the inner pot and drain the beans in a colander. 4. In a food processor or blender, combine the beans, ½ cup cooking liquid, lemon juice, ¼ cup olive oil, ½ teaspoon parsley, chives, tarragon, remaining 1 teaspoon salt, and ½ teaspoon pepper. Process or blend on medium speed, stopping to scrape down the sides of the container as needed, for about 1 minute, until the mixture is

smooth. 5. Transfer the dip to a serving bowl. Drizzle with the remaining 1 tablespoon olive oil and sprinkle with a few grinds of pepper. The dip will keep in an airtight container in the refrigerator for up to 1 week. Serve at room temperature or chilled.

Per Serving:
calorie: 70 | fat: 5g | protein: 3g | carbs: 8g | sugars: 1g | fiber: 4g | sodium: 782mg

Lemony White Bean Puree

Prep time: 10 minutes | Cook time: 0 minutes | Makes 4 cups

1 (15-ounce) can white beans, drained and rinsed
1 small onion, coarsely chopped
1 garlic clove, minced
Zest and juice of 1 lemon

½ teaspoon herbs de Provence
3 tablespoons extra-virgin olive oil, divided
1 tablespoon chopped fresh parsley

1. Place the beans, onion, garlic, lemon zest and juice, and herbs in a food processor and pulse until smooth. While the machine is running, slowly stream in 2 tablespoons of extra-virgin olive oil. If the mixture is too thick, add water very slowly until you've reached the desired consistency. 2. Transfer the puree to a medium serving bowl. Top with the remaining 1 tablespoon of extra-virgin olive oil and the parsley. 3. Serve with your favorite vegetable or flatbread of choice. Store any leftovers in an airtight container in the refrigerator for up to 4 days.

Per Serving:
calorie: 121 | fat: 5g | protein: 5g | carbs: 15g | sugars: 1g | fiber: 3g | sodium: 4mg

Zucchini Hummus Dip with Red Bell Peppers

Prep time: 10 minutes | Cook time: 0 minutes | Serves 4

2 zucchini, chopped
3 garlic cloves
2 tablespoons extra-virgin olive oil
2 tablespoons tahini

Juice of 1 lemon
½ teaspoon sea salt
1 red bell pepper, seeded and cut into sticks

1. In a blender or food processor, combine the zucchini, garlic, olive oil, tahini, lemon juice, and salt. Blend until smooth. 2. Serve with the red bell pepper for dipping.

Per Serving:
calorie: 136 | fat: 11g | protein: 3g | carbs: 8g | sugars: 4g | fiber: 2g | sodium: 309mg

Cinnamon Toasted Pumpkin Seeds

Prep time: 5 minutes | Cook time: 45 minutes | Serves 4

1 cup pumpkin seeds
2 tablespoons canola oil
1 teaspoon cinnamon

2 (1-gram) packets stevia
¼ teaspoon sea salt

1. Preheat the oven to 300°F. 2. In a bowl, toss the pumpkin seeds with the oil, cinnamon, stevia, and salt. 3. Spread the seeds in a single layer on a rimmed baking sheet. Bake until browned and fragrant, stirring once or twice, about 45 minutes.

Per Serving:

calorie: 233 | fat: 21g | protein: 9g | carbs: 5g | sugars: 0g | fiber: 2g | sodium: 151mg

Ground Turkey Lettuce Cups

Prep time: 5 minutes | Cook time: 30 minutes | Serves 8

3 tablespoons water
2 tablespoons soy sauce, tamari, or coconut aminos
3 tablespoons fresh lime juice
2 teaspoons Sriracha, plus more for serving
2 tablespoons cold-pressed avocado oil
2 teaspoons toasted sesame oil
4 garlic cloves, minced
1-inch piece fresh ginger, peeled and minced
2 carrots, diced
2 celery stalks, diced

1 yellow onion, diced
2 pounds 93 percent lean ground turkey
½ teaspoon fine sea salt
Two 8-ounce cans sliced water chestnuts, drained and chopped
1 tablespoon cornstarch
2 hearts romaine lettuce or 2 heads butter lettuce, leaves separated
½ cup roasted cashews (whole or halves and pieces), chopped
1 cup loosely packed fresh cilantro leaves

1. In a small bowl, combine the water, soy sauce, 2 tablespoons of the lime juice, and the Sriracha and mix well. Set aside. 2. Select the Sauté setting on the Instant Pot and heat the avocado oil, sesame oil, garlic, and ginger for 2 minutes, until the garlic is bubbling but not browned. Add the carrots, celery, and onion and sauté for about 3 minutes, until the onion begins to soften. 3. Add the turkey and salt and sauté, using a wooden spoon or spatula to break up the meat as it cooks, for about 5 minutes, until cooked through and no streaks of pink remain. Add the water chestnuts and soy sauce mixture and stir to combine, working quickly so not too much steam escapes. 4. Secure the lid and set the Pressure Release to Sealing. Press the Cancel button to reset the cooking program, then select the Pressure Cook or Manual setting and set the cooking time for 5 minutes at high pressure. (The pot will take about 10 minutes to come up to pressure before the cooking program begins.) 5. When the cooking program ends, perform a quick pressure release by moving the Pressure Release to Venting, or let the pressure release naturally. Open the pot. 6. In a small bowl, stir together the remaining 1 tablespoon lime juice and the cornstarch, add the mixture to the pot, and stir to combine. Press the Cancel button to reset the cooking program, then select the Sauté setting. Let the mixture come to a boil and thicken, stirring often, for about 2 minutes, then press the Cancel button to turn off the pot. 7. Spoon the turkey mixture onto the lettuce leaves and sprinkle the cashews and cilantro on top. Serve right away, with additional Sriracha at the table.

Per Serving:

calories: 127 | fat: 7g | protein: 6g | carbs: 10g | sugars: 2g | fiber: 3g | sodium: 392mg

Vegetable Kabobs with Mustard Dip

Prep time: 35 minutes | Cook time: 10 minutes | Serves 9

Dip
⅔ cup plain fat-free yogurt
⅓ cup fat-free sour cream
1 tablespoon finely chopped fresh parsley
1 teaspoon onion powder
1 teaspoon garlic salt
1 tablespoon Dijon mustard
Kabobs

1 medium bell pepper, cut into 6 strips, then cut into thirds
1 medium zucchini, cut diagonally into ½-inch slices
1 package (8 ounces) fresh whole mushrooms
9 large cherry tomatoes
2 tablespoons olive or vegetable oil

1 In small bowl, mix dip ingredients. Cover; refrigerate at least 1 hour. 2 Heat gas or charcoal grill. On 5 (12-inch) metal skewers, thread vegetables so that one kind of vegetable is on the same skewer (use 2 skewers for mushrooms); leave space between each piece. Brush vegetables with oil. 3 Place skewers of bell pepper and zucchini on grill over medium heat. Cover grill; cook 2 minutes. Add skewers of mushrooms and tomatoes. Cover grill; cook 4 to 5 minutes, carefully turning every 2 minutes, until vegetables are tender. Transfer vegetables from skewers to serving plate. Serve with dip.

Per Serving:

calories: 60 | fat: 3.5g | protein: 2g | carbs: 6g | sugars: 3g | fiber: 1g | sodium: 180mg

Homemade Sun-Dried Tomato Salsa

Prep time: 5 minutes | Cook time: 0 minutes | Serves 4

½ (15-ounce/425-g) can no-salt-added diced tomatoes, drained
6 tablespoons (20 g) julienned sun-dried tomatoes (see Tip)
1½ cups (330 g) canned artichoke hearts, drained

1 clove garlic
⅛ cup (3 g) fresh basil leaves
1 teaspoon balsamic vinegar
2 tablespoons (30 ml) olive oil
Sea salt, as needed
Black pepper, as needed

1. In a food processor or blender, combine the diced tomatoes, sun-dried tomatoes, artichoke hearts, garlic, basil, vinegar, oil, sea salt, and black pepper. Process or blend the ingredients to the desired consistency.

Per Serving:

calorie: 131 | fat: 7g | protein: 2g | carbs: 13g | sugars: 3g | fiber: 4g | sodium: 279mg

Creamy Cheese Dip

Prep time: 5 minutes | Cook time: 5 minutes | Serves 40

1 cup plain fat-free yogurt, strained overnight in cheesecloth over a bowl set in the refrigerator
1 cup fat-free ricotta cheese
1 cup low-fat cottage cheese

1. Combine all the ingredients in a food processor; process until smooth. Place in a covered container, and refrigerate until ready to use (this cream cheese can be refrigerated for up to 1 week).

Per Serving:

calorie: 21 | fat: 1g | protein: 2g | carbs: 1g | sugars: 1g | fiber: 0g | sodium: 81mg

Baked Scallops

Prep time: 5 minutes | Cook time: 10 minutes | Serves 4

12 ounces fresh bay or dry sea scallops
1½ teaspoons salt-free pickling spices
½ cup cider vinegar
¼ cup water
1 tablespoon finely chopped

onion
1 red bell pepper, cut into thin strips
1 head butter lettuce, rinsed and dried
⅓ cup sesame seeds, toasted

1. Preheat the oven to 350 degrees. Wash the scallops in cool water, and cut any scallops that are too big in half. 2. Spread the scallops out in a large baking dish (be careful not to overlap them). In a small bowl, combine the spices, cider vinegar, water, onion, and pepper; pour the mixture over the scallops. Season with salt, if desired. 3. Cover the baking dish and bake for 7 minutes. Remove from the oven, and allow the scallops to chill in the refrigerator (leave them in the cooking liquid/vegetable mixture). 4. Just before serving, place the lettuce leaves on individual plates or a platter, and place the scallops and vegetables over the top. Sprinkle with sesame seeds before serving.

Per Serving:

calorie: 159 | fat: 8g | protein: 14g | carbs: 7g | sugars: 2g | fiber: 3g | sodium: 344mg

Turkey Rollups with Veggie Cream Cheese

Prep time: 10 minutes | Cook time: 0 minutes | Serves 2

¼ cup cream cheese, at room temperature
2 tablespoons finely chopped red onion
2 tablespoons finely chopped red bell pepper

1 tablespoon chopped fresh chives
1 teaspoon Dijon mustard
1 garlic clove, minced
¼ teaspoon sea salt
6 slices deli turkey

1. In a small bowl, mix the cream cheese, red onion, bell pepper,

chives, mustard, garlic, and salt. 2. Spread the mixture on the turkey slices and roll up.

Per Serving:

calorie: 146 | fat: 1g | protein: 24g | carbs: 8g | sugars: 6g | fiber: 1g | sodium: 572mg

Monterey Jack Cheese Quiche Squares

Prep time: 10 minutes | Cook time: 15 minutes | Serves 12

4 egg whites
1 cup plus 2 tablespoons low-fat cottage cheese
¼ cup plus 2 tablespoons flour
¾ teaspoon baking powder
1 cup shredded reduced-fat Monterey Jack cheese

½ cup diced green chilies
1 red bell pepper, diced
1 cup lentils, cooked
1 tablespoon extra-virgin olive oil
Parsley sprigs

1. Preheat the oven to 350 degrees. 2. In a medium bowl, beat the egg whites and cottage cheese for 2 minutes, until smooth. 3. Add the flour and baking powder, and beat until smooth. Stir in the cheese, green chilies, red pepper, and lentils. 4. Coat a 9-inch-square pan with the olive oil, and pour in the egg mixture. Bake for 30-35 minutes, until firm. 5. Remove the quiche from the oven, and allow to cool for 10 minutes (it will be easier to cut). Cut into 12 squares and transfer to a platter, garnish with parsley sprigs, and serve.

Per Serving:

calorie: 104 | fat: 6g | protein: 8g | carbs: 4g | sugars: 0g | fiber: 0g | sodium: 215mg

Smoky Spinach Hummus with Popcorn Chips

Prep time: 10 minutes | Cook time: 0 minutes | Serves 12

1 can (15 ounces) chickpeas (garbanzo beans), drained, liquid reserved
1 cup chopped fresh spinach leaves
2 tablespoons lemon juice
2 tablespoons sesame tahini paste (from 16-ounce jar)

2 teaspoons smoked Spanish paprika
1 teaspoon ground cumin
½ teaspoon salt
2 tablespoons chopped red bell pepper, if desired
6 ounces popcorn snack chips

1 In food processor, place chickpeas, ¼ cup of the reserved liquid, spinach, lemon juice, tahini paste, paprika, cumin and salt. Cover; process 30 seconds, using quick on-and-off motions; scrape side. 2 Add additional reserved bean liquid, 1 tablespoon at a time, covering and processing, using quick on-and-off motions, until smooth and desired dipping consistency. Garnish with bell pepper. Serve with popcorn snack chips.

Per Serving:

calories: 140 | fat: 3.5g | protein: 4g | carbs: 22g | sugars: 0g | fiber: 3g | sodium: 270mg

Lemon Artichokes

Prep time: 5 minutes | Cook time: 5 to 15 minutes | Serves 4

4 artichokes
1 cup water

2 tablespoons lemon juice
1 teaspoon salt

1. Wash and trim artichokes by cutting off the stems flush with the bottoms of the artichokes and by cutting ¾-1 inch off the tops. Stand upright in the bottom of the inner pot of the Instant Pot. 2. Pour water, lemon juice, and salt over artichokes. 3. Secure the lid and make sure the vent is set to sealing. On Manual, set the Instant Pot for 15 minutes for large artichokes, 10 minutes for medium artichokes, or 5 minutes for small artichokes. 4. When cook time is up, perform a quick release by releasing the pressure manually.

Per Serving:

calories: 60 | fat: 0g | protein: 4g | carbs: 13g | sugars: 1g | fiber: 6g | sodium: 397mg

Veggies with Cottage Cheese Ranch Dip

Prep time: 10 minutes | Cook time: 0 minutes | Serves 4

1 cup cottage cheese
2 tablespoons mayonnaise
Juice of ½ lemon
2 tablespoons chopped fresh chives
2 tablespoons chopped fresh dill

2 scallions, white and green parts, finely chopped
1 garlic clove, minced
½ teaspoon sea salt
2 zucchinis, cut into sticks
8 cherry tomatoes

1. In a small bowl, mix the cottage cheese, mayonnaise, lemon juice, chives, dill, scallions, garlic, and salt. 2. Serve with the zucchini sticks and cherry tomatoes for dipping.

Per Serving:

calorie: 88 | fat: 3g | protein: 6g | carbs: 10g | sugars: 4g | fiber: 2g | sodium: 495mg

Instant Popcorn

Prep time: 1 minutes | Cook time: 5 minutes | Serves 5

2 tablespoons coconut oil
½ cup popcorn kernels
¼ cup margarine spread, melted,

optional
Sea salt to taste

1. Set the Instant Pot to Sauté. 2. Melt the coconut oil in the inner pot, then add the popcorn kernels and stir. 3. Press Adjust to bring the temperature up to high. 4. When the corn starts popping, secure the lid on the Instant Pot. 5. When you no longer hear popping, turn off the Instant Pot, remove the lid, and pour the popcorn into a bowl. 6. Top with the optional melted margarine and season the popcorn with sea salt to your liking.

Per Serving:

calories: 161 | fat: 12g | protein: 1g | carbs: 13g | sugars: 0g | fiber: 3g | sodium: 89mg

Gruyere Apple Spread

Prep time: 5 minutes | Cook time: 5 minutes | Serves 20

4 ounces fat-free cream cheese, softened
½ cup low-fat cottage cheese
4 ounces Gruyere cheese
¼ teaspoon dry mustard
⅛ teaspoon freshly ground black

pepper
½ cup shredded apple (unpeeled)
2 tablespoons finely chopped pecans
2 teaspoons minced fresh chives

1. Place the cheeses in a food processor, and blend until smooth. Add the mustard and pepper, and blend for 30 seconds. 2. Transfer the mixture to a serving bowl, and fold in the apple and pecans. Sprinkle the dip with chives. 3. Cover, and refrigerate the mixture for 1-2 hours. Serve chilled with crackers, or stuff into celery stalks.

Per Serving:

calorie: 46 | fat: 3g | protein: 4g | carbs: 1g | sugars: 1g | fiber: 0g | sodium: 107mg

Cucumber Roll-Ups

Prep time: 5 minutes | Cook time: 0 minutes | Serves 2 to 4

2 (6-inch) gluten-free wraps
2 tablespoons cream cheese
1 medium cucumber, cut into

long strips
2 tablespoons fresh mint

1. Place the wraps on your work surface and spread them evenly with the cream cheese. Top with the cucumber and mint. 2. Roll the wraps up from one side to the other, kind of like a burrito. Slice into 1-inch bites or keep whole. 3. Serve. 4. Store any leftovers in an airtight container in the refrigerator for 1 to 2 days.

Per Serving:

calorie: 70 | fat: 1g | protein: 4g | carbs: 12g | sugars: 3g | fiber: 2g | sodium: 183mg

Peanut Butter Protein Bites

Prep time: 10 minutes | Cook time: 0 minutes | Makes 16 Balls

½ cup sugar-free peanut butter
¼ cup (1 scoop) sugar-free peanut butter powder or sugar-free protein powder
2 tablespoons unsweetened

cocoa powder
2 tablespoons canned coconut milk (or more to adjust consistency)

1. In a bowl, mix all ingredients until well combined. 2. Roll into 16 balls. Refrigerate before serving.

Per Serving:

calorie: 59 | fat: 5g | protein: 3g | carbs: 2g | sugars: 1g | fiber: 1g | sodium: 4mg

Chicken Kabobs

Prep time: 5 minutes | Cook time: 20 minutes | Serves 6

1 pound boneless, skinless chicken breast
3 tablespoons light soy sauce
One 1-inch cube of fresh ginger root, finely chopped
3 tablespoons extra-virgin olive

oil
3 tablespoons dry vermouth
1 large clove garlic, finely chopped
12 watercress sprigs
2 large lemons, cut into wedges

1. Cut the chicken into 1-inch cubes and place in a shallow bowl. 2. In a small bowl, combine the soy sauce, ginger root, oil, vermouth, and garlic and pour over the chicken. Cover the chicken, and let marinate for at least 1 hour (or overnight). 3. Thread the chicken onto 12 metal or wooden skewers (remember to soak wooden skewers in water before using). Grill or broil 6 inches from the heat source for 8 minutes, turning frequently. 4. Arrange the skewers on a platter and garnish with the watercress and lemon wedges. Serve hot with additional soy sauce, if desired.

Per Serving:
calorie: 187 | fat: 10g | protein: 18g | carbs: 4g | sugars: 2g | fiber: 1g | sodium: 158mg

Spicy Cajun Onion Dip

Prep time: 15 minutes | Cook time: 0 minutes | Serves 5

Dip
¾ cup plain low-fat yogurt
½ cup reduced-fat sour cream
3 medium green onions, chopped (3 tablespoons)
1½ teaspoons Cajun seasoning
2 cloves garlic, finely chopped
Vegetables and Shrimp

1 medium red bell pepper, cut into 20 strips
½ pound fresh sugar snap pea pods, strings removed
20 cooked deveined peeled large (21 to 30 count) shrimp, thawed if frozen

1 In small bowl, mix dip ingredients with whisk until smooth. Cover; refrigerate at least 15 minutes to blend flavors. 2 Serve dip with bell pepper, pea pods and shrimp.

Per Serving:
calories: 110 | fat: 4g | protein: 9g | carbs: 9g | sugars: 6g | fiber: 2g | sodium: 430mg

Creamy Spinach Dip

Prep time: 13 minutes | Cook time: 5 minutes | Serves 11

8 ounces low-fat cream cheese
1 cup low-fat sour cream
½ cup finely chopped onion
½ cup no-sodium vegetable broth
5 cloves garlic, minced
½ teaspoon salt

¼ teaspoon black pepper
10 ounces frozen spinach
12 ounces reduced-fat shredded Monterey Jack cheese
12 ounces reduced-fat shredded Parmesan cheese

1. Add cream cheese, sour cream, onion, vegetable broth, garlic, salt, pepper, and spinach to the inner pot of the Instant Pot. 2. Secure lid, make sure vent is set to sealing, and set to the Bean/Chili setting on high pressure for 5 minutes. 3. When done, do a manual release. 4. Add the cheeses and mix well until creamy and well combined.

Per Serving:
calorie: 274 | fat: 18g | protein: 19g | carbs: 10g | sugars: 3g | fiber: 1g | sodium: 948mg

Spinach and Artichoke Dip

Prep time: 5 minutes | Cook time: 4 minutes | Serves 11

8 ounces low-fat cream cheese
10-ounce box frozen spinach
½ cup no-sodium chicken broth
14-ounce can artichoke hearts, drained
½ cup low-fat sour cream
½ cup low-fat mayo

3 cloves of garlic, minced
1 teaspoon onion powder
16 ounces reduced-fat shredded Parmesan cheese
8 ounces reduced-fat shredded mozzarella

1. Put all ingredients in the inner pot of the Instant Pot, except the Parmesan cheese and the mozzarella cheese. 2. Secure the lid and set vent to sealing. Place on Manual high pressure for 4 minutes. 3. Do a quick release of steam. 4. Immediately stir in the cheeses.

Per Serving:
calories: 288 | fat: 18g | protein: 19g | carbs: 15g | sugars: 3g | fiber: 3g | sodium: 1007mg

Tuna, Hummus, and Veggie Wraps

Prep time: 10 minutes | Cook time: 0 minutes | Serves 2

FOR THE HUMMUS
1 cup from 1 (15-ounce) can low-sodium chickpeas, drained and rinsed
2 tablespoons tahini
1 tablespoon extra-virgin olive oil
1 garlic clove
Juice of ½ lemon

¼ teaspoon salt
2 tablespoons water
FOR THE WRAPS
4 large lettuce leaves
1 (5-ounce) can chunk light tuna packed in water, drained
1 red bell pepper, seeded and cut into strips
1 cucumber, sliced

TO MAKE THE HUMMUS In a blender jar, combine the chickpeas, tahini, olive oil, garlic, lemon juice, salt, and water. Process until smooth. Taste and adjust with additional lemon juice or salt, as needed. TO MAKE THE WRAPS 1. On each lettuce leaf, spread 1 tablespoon of hummus, and divide the tuna among the leaves. Top each with several strips of red pepper and cucumber slices. 2. Roll up the lettuce leaves, folding in the two shorter sides and rolling away from you, like a burrito. Serve.

Per Serving:
calories: 191 | fat: 5g | protein: 26g | carbs: 15g | sugars: 6g | fiber: 4g | sodium: 357mg

Grilled Nut Butter Sandwich

Prep time: 5 minutes | Cook time: 8 minutes | Serves 1

2-3 teaspoons almond or other nut butter (can substitute sunflower butter, Wowbutter, or tigernut butter)
2 slices sprouted grain bread

½ cup sliced ripe banana or apple
¼ teaspoon cinnamon
⅓ cup unsweetened applesauce

1. Place a nonstick skillet over medium-high heat. Spread about half of the nut butter on one slice of bread, then top with the banana or apple and cinnamon. Spread the remaining nut butter on the other slice of bread. Close up the sandwich, and place it in the skillet. Cook for 3 to 4 minutes, or until lightly browned. Flip and cook for another 3 to 4 minutes, or until lightly browned. Transfer to a cooling rack (so the underside doesn't soften) to cool slightly, then transfer to a plate and cut in half. Serve with the applesauce for dipping.

Per Serving:

calorie: 332 | fat: 8g | protein: 9g | carbs: 60g | sugars: 20g | fiber: 7g | sodium: 412mg

7-Layer Dip

Prep time: 10 minutes | Cook time: 35 minutes | Serves 6

Cashew Sour Cream
1 cup raw whole cashews, soaked in water to cover for 1 to 2 hours and then drained
½ cup avocado oil
½ cup water
¼ cup fresh lemon juice
2 tablespoons nutritional yeast
1 teaspoon fine sea salt
Beans
½ cup dried black beans
2 cups water
½ teaspoon fine sea salt

½ teaspoon chili powder
¼ teaspoon garlic powder
½ cup grape or cherry tomatoes, halved
1 avocado, diced
¼ cup chopped yellow onion
1 jalapeño chile, sliced
2 tablespoons chopped cilantro
6 ounces baked corn tortilla chips
1 English cucumber, sliced
2 carrots, sliced
6 celery stalks, cut into sticks

1. To make the cashew sour cream: In a blender, combine the cashews, oil, water, lemon juice, nutritional yeast, and salt. Blend on high speed, stopping to scrape down the sides of the container as needed, for about 2 minutes, until very smooth. (The sour cream can be made in advance and stored in an airtight container in the refrigerator for up to 5 days.) 2. To make the beans: Pour 1 cup water into the Instant Pot. In a 1½-quart stainless-steel bowl, combine the beans, the 2 cups water, and salt and stir to dissolve the salt. Place the bowl on a long-handled silicone steam rack, then, holding the handles of the steam rack, lower it into the Instant Pot. (If you don't have the long-handled rack, use the wire metal steam rack and a homemade sling) 3. Secure the lid and set the Pressure Release to Sealing. Select the Bean/Chili, Pressure Cook, or Manual setting and set the cooking time for 25 minutes at high pressure. (The pot will take about 10 minutes to come up to pressure before the cooking program begins.) 4. When the cooking program ends, let the pressure release naturally for at least 20 minutes, then move the Pressure Release to Venting to release any remaining steam. 5. Place a colander over a bowl. Open the pot and, wearing heat-resistant mitts, lift out the inner pot and drain the beans in the colander. Transfer the liquid captured in the bowl to a measuring cup, and pour the beans into the bowl. Add ¼ cup of the cooking liquid to the beans and, using a potato masher or fork, mash the beans to your desired consistency, adding more cooking liquid as needed. Stir in the chili powder and garlic powder. 6. Using a rubber spatula, spread the black beans in an even layer in a clear-glass serving dish. Spread the cashew sour cream in an even layer on top of the beans. Add layers of the tomatoes, avocado, onion, jalapeño, and cilantro. (At this point, you can cover and refrigerate the assembled dip for up to 1 day.) Serve accompanied with the tortilla chips, cucumber, carrots, and celery on the side.

Per Serving:

calories: 259 | fat: 8g | protein: 8g | carbs: 41g | sugars: 3g | fiber: 8g | sodium: 811mg

Porcupine Meatballs

Prep time: 20 minutes | Cook time: 15 minutes | Serves 8

1 pound ground sirloin or turkey
½ cup raw brown rice, parboiled
1 egg
¼ cup finely minced onion
1 or 2 cloves garlic, minced

¼ teaspoon dried basil and/or oregano, optional
10¾-ounce can reduced-fat condensed tomato soup
½ soup can of water

1. Mix all ingredients, except tomato soup and water, in a bowl to combine well. 2. Form into balls about 1½-inch in diameter. 3. Mix tomato soup and water in the inner pot of the Instant Pot, then add the meatballs. 4. Secure the lid and make sure the vent is turned to sealing. 5. Press the Meat button and set for 15 minutes on high pressure. 6. Allow the pressure to release naturally after cook time is up.

Per Serving:

calories: 141 | fat: 2g | protein: 16g | carbs: 14g | sugars: 3g | fiber: 1g | sodium: 176mg

No-Added-Sugar Berries and Cream Yogurt Bowl

Prep time: 5 minutes | Cook time: 0 minutes | Serves 1

1 cup (200 g) plain nonfat Greek yogurt
1 tablespoon (15 g) almond butter

½ cup (50 g) frozen mixed berries, thawed
Zest of ½ medium lemon

1. In a small bowl, combine the yogurt, almond butter, berries, and lemon zest.

Per Serving:

calorie: 270 | fat: 10g | protein: 27g | carbs: 21g | sugars: 15g | fiber: 3g | sodium: 89mg

Thai-Style Chicken Roll-Ups

Prep time: 15 minutes | Cook time: 0 minutes | Serves 4

1½ cups shredded cooked chicken breast
1 cup bean sprouts
1 cup shredded green cabbage
½ cup shredded carrots
¼ cup chopped scallions, both white and green parts
¼ cup chopped fresh cilantro

2 tablespoons natural peanut butter
2 tablespoons water
1 tablespoon rice wine vinegar
1 garlic clove, minced
¼ teaspoon salt
4 (8-inch) low-carb whole-wheat tortillas

1. In a large mixing bowl, toss the chicken breast, bean sprouts, cabbage, carrots, scallions, and cilantro. 2. In a medium bowl, whisk together the peanut butter, water, rice vinegar, garlic, and salt. 3. Fill each tortilla with about 1 cup of the chicken and vegetable mixture, and spoon a tablespoon of sauce over the filling. 4. Fold in two opposite sides of the tortilla and roll up. Serve.

Per Serving:

calories: 210 | fat: 8g | protein: 21g | carbs: 17g | sugars: 3g | fiber: 10g | sodium: 360mg

Hummus with Chickpeas and Tahini Sauce

Prep time: 10 minutes | Cook time: 55 minutes | Makes 4 cups

4 cups water
1 cup dried chickpeas
2½ teaspoons fine sea salt
½ cup tahini

3 tablespoons fresh lemon juice
1 garlic clove
¼ teaspoon ground cumin

1. Combine the water, chickpeas, and 1 teaspoon of the salt in the Instant Pot and stir to dissolve the salt. 2. Secure the lid and set the Pressure Release to Sealing. Select the Bean/Chili, Pressure Cook, or Manual setting and set the cooking time for 40 minutes at high pressure. (The pot will take about 15 minutes to come up to pressure before the cooking program begins.) 3. When the cooking program ends, let the pressure release naturally for 15 minutes, then move the Pressure Release to Venting to release any remaining steam. 4. Place a colander over a bowl. Open the pot and, wearing heat-resistant mitts, lift out the inner pot and drain the beans in the colander. Return the chickpeas to the inner pot and place it back in the Instant Pot housing on the Keep Warm setting. Reserve the cooking liquid. 5. In a blender or food processor, combine 1 cup of the cooking liquid, the tahini, lemon juice, garlic, cumin, and 1 teaspoon salt. Blend or process on high speed, stopping to scrape down the sides of the container as needed, for about 30 seconds, until smooth and a little fluffy. Scoop out and set aside ½ cup of this sauce for the topping. 6. Set aside ½ cup of the chickpeas for the topping. Add the remaining chickpeas to the tahini sauce in the blender or food processor along with ½ cup of the cooking liquid and the remaining ½ teaspoon salt. Blend or process on high speed, stopping to scrape down the sides of the container as needed, for about 1 minute, until very smooth. 7. Transfer the hummus to a shallow serving bowl. Spoon the reserved tahini mixture over the top, then sprinkle on the reserved chickpeas. The hummus will keep in an airtight container in the refrigerator for up to 3 days. Serve at

room temperature or chilled.

Per Serving:

calories: 107 | fat: 5g | protein: 4g | carbs: 10g | sugars: 3g | fiber: 4g | sodium: 753mg

Red Pepper, Goat Cheese, and Arugula Open-Faced Grilled Sandwich

Prep time: 5 minutes | Cook time: 15 minutes | Serves 1

½ red bell pepper, seeded
Nonstick cooking spray
1 slice whole-wheat thin-sliced bread (I love Ezekiel sprouted bread and Dave's Killer Bread)

2 tablespoons crumbled goat cheese
Pinch dried thyme
½ cup arugula

1. Preheat the broiler to high. Line a baking sheet with parchment paper. 2. Cut the ½ bell pepper lengthwise into two pieces and arrange on the prepared baking sheet with the skin facing up. 3. Broil for 5 to 10 minutes until the skin is blackened. Transfer to a covered container to steam for 5 minutes, then remove the skin from the pepper using your fingers. Cut the pepper into strips. 4. Heat a small skillet over medium-high heat. Spray it with nonstick cooking spray and place the bread in the skillet. Top with the goat cheese and sprinkle with the thyme. Pile the arugula on top, followed by the roasted red pepper strips. Press down with a spatula to hold in place. 5. Cook for 2 to 3 minutes until the bread is crisp and browned and the cheese is warmed through. (If you prefer, you can make a half-closed sandwich instead: Cut the bread in half and place one half in the skillet. Top with the cheese, thyme, arugula, red pepper, and the other half slice of bread. Cook for 4 to 6 minutes, flipping once, until both sides are browned.)

Per Serving:

calories: 109 | fat: 2g | protein: 4g | carbs: 21g | sugars: 5g | fiber: 6g | sodium: 123mg

Guacamole

Prep time: 5 minutes | Cook time: 5 minutes | Serves 8

2 large (8½-ounce) ripe avocados, peeled, pits removed, and mashed
½ cup chopped onion
2 medium jalapeño peppers, seeded and chopped
2 tablespoons minced fresh parsley
2 tablespoons fresh lime juice

⅛ teaspoon freshly ground black pepper
2 medium tomatoes, finely chopped
1 medium garlic clove, minced
1 tablespoon extra-virgin olive oil
½ teaspoon salt

1. In a large mixing bowl, combine all ingredients, blending well.

Per Serving:

calorie: 107 | fat: 9g | protein: 1g | carbs: 7g | sugars: 2g | fiber: 4g | sodium: 152mg

Low-Sugar Blueberry Muffins

Prep time: 5 minutes | Cook time: 20 to 25 minutes | Makes 12 muffins

2 large eggs
1½ cups (144 g) almond flour
1 cup (80 g) gluten-free rolled oats
½ cup (120 ml) pure maple syrup
½ cup (120 ml) avocado oil

1 teaspoon baking powder
1 teaspoon ground cinnamon
½ teaspoon pure vanilla extract
½ teaspoon pure almond extract
1 cup (150 g) fresh or frozen blueberries

1. Preheat the oven to 350°F (177°C). Line a 12-well muffin pan with paper liners or spray the wells with cooking oil spray. 2. In a blender, combine the eggs, almond flour, oats, maple syrup, oil, baking powder, cinnamon, vanilla, and almond extract. Blend the ingredients on high for 20 to 30 seconds, until the mixture is homogeneous. 3. Transfer the batter to a large bowl and gently stir in the blueberries. 4. Divide the batter evenly among the muffin wells. Bake the muffins for 20 to 25 minutes, until a toothpick inserted in the middle comes out clean. 5. Let the muffins rest for 5 minutes, then transfer them to a cooling rack.

Per Serving:

calorie: 240 | fat: 18g | protein: 5g | carbs: 19g | sugars: 10g | fiber: 3g | sodium: 19mg

Blackberry Baked Brie

Prep time: 5 minutes | Cook time: 15 minutes | Serves 5

8-ounce round Brie
1 cup water

¼ cup sugar-free blackberry preserves
2 teaspoons chopped fresh mint

1. Slice a grid pattern into the top of the rind of the Brie with a knife. 2. In a 7-inch round baking dish, place the Brie, then cover the baking dish securely with foil. 3. Insert the trivet into the inner pot of the Instant Pot; pour in the water. 4. Make a foil sling and arrange it on top of the trivet. Place the baking dish on top of the trivet and foil sling. 5. Secure the lid to the locked position and turn the vent to sealing. 6. Press Manual and set the Instant Pot for 15 minutes on high pressure. 7. When cooking time is up, turn off the Instant Pot and do a quick release of the pressure. 8. When the valve has dropped, remove the lid, then remove the baking dish. 9. Remove the top rind of the Brie and top with the preserves. Sprinkle with the fresh mint.

Per Serving:

calorie: 133 | fat: 10g | protein: 8g | carbs: 4g | sugars: 0g | fiber: 0g | sodium: 238mg

Chapter 9 Vegetables and Sides

Smashed Cucumber Salad

Prep time: 10 minutes | Cook time: 0 minutes | Serves 4 to 6

2 pounds mini cucumbers (English or Persian), unpeeled
½ teaspoon kosher salt
1 tablespoon extra-virgin olive oil
¾ teaspoon ground cumin
¼ teaspoon turmeric
Juice of 1 lime
½ cup cilantro leaves

1. Cut the cucumbers crosswise into 4-inch pieces and again in half lengthwise. 2. On a work surface, place one cucumber, flesh-side down. Place the side of the knife blade on the cucumber and carefully smash down lightly with your hand. Alternatively, put in a plastic bag, seal, and smash with a rolling pin or similar tool. Be careful not to break the bag. The skin of the cucumber should crack and flesh will break away. Repeat with all the cucumbers and cut the smashed pieces on a bias into bite-size pieces. 3. Transfer the cucumber pieces to a strainer and toss them with the salt. Allow the cucumbers to rest for at least 15 minutes. 4. Meanwhile, prepare the dressing by whisking together the extra-virgin olive oil, cumin, turmeric, and lime juice in a small bowl. 5. When the cucumbers are ready, shake them to remove any excess liquid. Transfer the cucumbers to a large bowl with the dressing and cilantro and toss to combine. Serve. 6. Store any leftovers in an airtight container in the refrigerator for up to 2 days.

Per Serving:

calories: 55 | fat: 2.99g | protein: 1.32g | carbs: 7.62g | sugars: 3.21g | fiber: 1.1g | sodium: 238mg

Green Beans with Garlic and Onion

Prep time: 5 minutes | Cook time: 12 minutes | Serves 8

1 pound fresh green beans, trimmed and cut into 2-inch pieces
1 tablespoon extra-virgin olive oil
1 small onion, chopped
1 large garlic clove, minced
1 tablespoon white vinegar
¼ cup Parmigiano-Reggiano cheese
⅛ teaspoon freshly ground black pepper

1. Steam the beans for 7 minutes or until just tender. Set aside. 2. In a skillet, heat the oil over low heat. Add the onion and garlic, and sauté for 4-5 minutes or until the onion is translucent. 3. Transfer the beans to a serving bowl, and add the onion mixture and vinegar, tossing well. Sprinkle with cheese and pepper, and serve.

Per Serving:

calories: 43 | fat: 2.87g | protein: 1.45g | carbs: 3.55g | sugars: 0.91g | fiber: 1.2g | sodium: 30mg

Italian Wild Mushrooms

Prep time: 30 minutes | Cook time: 3 minutes | Serves 10

2 tablespoons canola oil
2 large onions, chopped
4 garlic cloves, minced
3 large red bell peppers, chopped
3 large green bell peppers, chopped
12-ounce package oyster
mushrooms, cleaned and chopped
3 fresh bay leaves
10 fresh basil leaves, chopped
1 teaspoon salt
1½ teaspoons pepper
28-ounce can Italian plum tomatoes, crushed or chopped

1. Press Sauté on the Instant Pot and add in the oil. Once the oil is heated, add the onions, garlic, peppers, and mushroom to the oil. Sauté just until mushrooms begin to turn brown. 2. Add remaining ingredients. Stir well. 3. Secure the lid and make sure vent is set to sealing. Press Manual and set time for 3 minutes. 4. When cook time is up, release the pressure manually. Discard bay leaves.

Per Serving:

calories: 82 | fat: 3g | protein: 3g | carbs: 13g | sugars: 8g | fiber: 4g | sodium: 356mg

Vegetable-Stuffed Yellow Squash

Prep time: 10 minutes | Cook time: 30 minutes | Serves 6

6 small yellow squash
1 tomato, finely chopped
½ cup minced onion
½ cup finely chopped green bell pepper
½ cup shredded 50 percent reduced-fat sharp cheddar
¼ teaspoon salt
⅛ teaspoon freshly ground black pepper

1. Preheat the oven to 400 degrees. 2. Place the squash in a large pot of boiling water. Cover, reduce heat, and simmer for 5-7 minutes or until the squash is just tender. Drain, and allow to cool slightly. 3. Trim the stems from the squash, and cut in half lengthwise. Gently scoop out the pulp, leaving a firm shell. Drain, and chop the pulp. 4. In a large mixing bowl, combine the pulp and the remaining ingredients, blending well. 5. Place the squash shells in a 13-x-9-x-2-inch baking dish, gently spoon the vegetable mixture into the shells, and bake at 400 degrees for 15-20 minutes. Remove from the oven, and let cool slightly before serving.

Per Serving:

calories: 72 | fat: 3.94g | protein: 4.45g | carbs: 6.07g | sugars: 3.22g | fiber: 1.8g | sodium: 177mg

Roasted Delicata Squash

Prep time: 10 minutes | Cook time: 20 minutes | Serves 4

1 (1- to 1½-pound) delicata squash, halved, seeded, cut into ½-inch-thick strips
1 tablespoon extra-virgin olive oil
½ teaspoon dried thyme
¼ teaspoon salt
¼ teaspoon freshly ground black pepper

1. Preheat the oven to 400°F. Line a baking sheet with parchment paper. 2. In a large mixing bowl, toss the squash strips with the olive oil, thyme, salt, and pepper. Arrange on the prepared baking sheet in a single layer. 3. Roast for 10 minutes, flip, and continue to roast for 10 more minutes until tender and lightly browned.

Per Serving:
calories: 79 | fat: 4g | protein: 1g | carbs: 12g | sugars: 3g | fiber: 2g | sodium: 123mg

Coconut Curry Rice

Prep time: 5 minutes | Cook time: 45 minutes | Serves 3

1 cup uncooked brown rice or brown basmati rice
1⅓ cups water
1 small can (5.5 ounces) light coconut milk
2 tablespoons freshly squeezed lime juice
1 teaspoon mild curry powder
Rounded ¼ teaspoon sea salt
¼ teaspoon turmeric powder
3-4 tablespoons chopped cilantro for serving (optional)
Lime wedges for serving

1. In a saucepan, combine the rice, water, coconut milk, lime juice, curry powder, salt, and turmeric. Bring to a boil over high heat, stir, then reduce the heat to low. Cover and cook for 35 to 45 minutes, until the liquid is absorbed and the rice is tender. Turn off the heat and let the rice sit, covered, for 5 minutes. Stir in the cilantro (if using), and serve with the lime wedges.

Per Serving:
calorie: 298 | fat: 6g | protein: 6g | carbs: 56g | sugars: 2g | fiber: 4g | sodium: 303mg

Chipotle Twice-Baked Sweet Potatoes

Prep time: 20 minutes | Cook time: 1 hour | Serves 4

4 small sweet potatoes (about 1¾ pounds)
¼ cup fat-free half-and-half
1 chipotle chile in adobo sauce (from 7-ounce can), finely chopped
1 teaspoon adobo sauce (from
can of chipotle chiles)
½ teaspoon salt
8 teaspoons reduced-fat sour cream
4 teaspoons chopped fresh cilantro

1 Heat oven to 375°F. Gently scrub potatoes but do not peel. Pierce potatoes several times with fork to allow steam to escape while potatoes bake. Bake about 45 minutes or until potatoes are tender when pierced in center with a fork. 2 When potatoes are cool enough to handle, cut lengthwise down through center of potato to within ½ inch of ends and bottom. Carefully scoop out inside, leaving thin shell. In medium bowl, mash potatoes, half-and-half, chile, adobo sauce and salt with potato masher or electric mixer on low speed until light and fluffy. 3 Increase oven temperature to 400°F. In 13x9-inch pan, place potato shells. Divide potato mixture evenly among shells. Bake uncovered 20 minutes or until potato mixture is golden brown and heated through. 4 Just before serving, top each potato with 2 teaspoons sour cream and 1 teaspoon cilantro.

Per Serving:
calorie: 140 | fat: 1g | protein: 3g | carbs: 27g | sugars: 9g | fiber: 4g | sodium: 400mg

Sweet Potato Crisps

Prep time: 10 minutes | Cook time: 30 minutes | Serves 3

1 pound sweet potatoes
½ tablespoon balsamic vinegar
½ tablespoon pure maple syrup
Rounded ¼ teaspoon sea salt

1. Preheat the oven to 400°F. Line a large baking sheet with parchment paper. 2. Peel the sweet potatoes, then use the peeler to continue to make sweet potato peelings. (Alternatively, you can push peeled sweet potatoes through a food processor slicing blade.) Transfer the peelings to a large mixing bowl and use your hands to toss with the vinegar and syrup, coating them as evenly as possible. Spread the peelings on the prepared baking sheet, spacing well. Sprinkle with the salt. Bake for 30 minutes, tossing once or twice. The pieces around the edges of the pan can get brown quickly, so move the chips around during baking. Turn off the oven and let the chips sit in the residual heat for 20 minutes, stir again, and let sit for another 15 to 20 minutes, until they crisp up. Remove, and snack!

Per Serving:
calorie: 94 | fat: 0g | protein: 2g | carbs: 22g | sugars: 8g | fiber: 3g | sodium: 326mg

Perfect Sweet Potatoes

Prep time: 5 minutes | Cook time: 15 minutes | Serves 4 to 6

4-6 medium sweet potatoes
1 cup of water

1. Scrub skin of sweet potatoes with a brush until clean. Pour water into inner pot of the Instant Pot. Place steamer basket in the bottom of the inner pot. Place sweet potatoes on top of steamer basket. 2. Secure the lid and turn valve to seal. 3. Select the Manual mode and set to pressure cook on high for 15 minutes. 4. Allow pressure to release naturally (about 10 minutes). 5. Once the pressure valve lowers, remove lid and serve immediately.

Per Serving:
calories: 112 | fat: 0g | protein: 2g | carbs: 26g | sugars: 5g | fiber: 4g | sodium: 72mg

Mediterranean Zucchini Boats

Prep time: 5 minutes | Cook time: 10 minutes | Serves 4

1 large zucchini, ends removed, halved lengthwise
6 grape tomatoes, quartered
¼ teaspoon salt
¼ cup feta cheese
1 tablespoon balsamic vinegar
1 tablespoon olive oil

1. Use a spoon to scoop out 2 tablespoons from center of each zucchini half, making just enough space to fill with tomatoes and feta. 2. Place tomatoes evenly in centers of zucchini halves and sprinkle with salt. Place into ungreased air fryer basket. Adjust the temperature to 350°F (177°C) and roast for 10 minutes. When done, zucchini will be tender. 3. Transfer boats to a serving tray and sprinkle with feta, then drizzle with vinegar and olive oil. Serve warm.

Per Serving:

calories: 92 | fat: 6g | protein: 3g | carbs: 8g | fiber: 2g | sodium: 242mg

Spicy Roasted Cauliflower with Lime

Prep time: 5 minutes | Cook time: 10 minutes | Serves 4

1 cauliflower head, broken into small florets
2 tablespoons extra-virgin olive oil
½ teaspoon ground chipotle chili powder
½ teaspoon salt
Juice of 1 lime

1. Preheat the oven to 450°F. Line a rimmed baking sheet with parchment paper. 2. In a large mixing bowl, toss the cauliflower with the olive oil, chipotle chili powder, and salt. Arrange in a single layer on the prepared baking sheet. 3. Roast for 15 minutes, flip, and continue to roast for 15 more minutes until well-browned and tender. 4. Sprinkle with the lime juice, adjust the salt as needed, and serve.

Per Serving:

calories: 99 | fat: 7 | protein: 3g | carbs: 8g | sugars: 3g | fiber: 3g | sodium: 284mg

Lemon-Thyme Asparagus

Prep time: 5 minutes | Cook time: 4 to 8 minutes | Serves 4

1 pound (454 g) asparagus, woody ends trimmed off
1 tablespoon avocado oil
½ teaspoon dried thyme or ½ tablespoon chopped fresh thyme
Sea salt and freshly ground
black pepper, to taste
2 ounces (57 g) goat cheese, crumbled
Zest and juice of 1 lemon
Flaky sea salt, for serving (optional)

1. In a medium bowl, toss together the asparagus, avocado oil, and thyme, and season with sea salt and pepper. 2. Place the asparagus in the air fryer basket in a single layer. Set the air fryer to 400°F (204°C) and air fry for 4 to 8 minutes, to your desired doneness. 3. Transfer to a serving platter. Top with the goat cheese, lemon zest, and lemon juice. If desired, season with a pinch of flaky salt.

Per Serving:

calories: 121 | fat: 9g | protein: 7g | carbs: 6g | fiber: 3g | sodium: 208mg

Garlicky Cabbage and Collard Greens

Prep time: 10 minutes | Cook time: 10 minutes | Serves 8

2 tablespoons extra-virgin olive oil
1 collard greens bunch, stemmed and thinly sliced
½ small green cabbage, thinly
sliced
6 garlic cloves, minced
1 tablespoon low-sodium gluten-free soy sauce or tamari

1. In a large skillet, heat the oil over medium-high heat. 2. Add the collards to the pan, stirring to coat with oil. Sauté for 1 to 2 minutes until the greens begin to wilt. 3. Add the cabbage and stir to coat. Cover and reduce the heat to medium low. Continue to cook for 5 to 7 minutes, stirring once or twice, until the greens are tender. 4. Add the garlic and soy sauce and stir to incorporate. Cook until just fragrant, about 30 seconds longer. Serve warm and enjoy!

Per Serving:

calories: 72| fat: 4g | protein: 3g | carbs: 6g | sugars: 0g | fiber: 3g | sodium: 129mg

Zucchini Noodles with Lime-Basil Pesto

Prep time: 20 minutes | Cook time: 0 minutes | Serves 4

2 cups packed fresh basil leaves
½ cup pine nuts
2 teaspoons minced garlic
Zest and juice of 1 lime
Pinch sea salt
Pinch freshly ground black
pepper
¼ cup extra-virgin olive oil
4 green or yellow zucchini, rinsed, dried, and julienned or spiralized
1 tomato, diced

1. Place the basil, pine nuts, garlic, lime zest, lime juice, salt, and pepper in a food processor or a blender and pulse until very finely chopped. 2. While the machine is running, add the olive oil in a thin stream until a thick paste forms. 3. In a large bowl, combine the zucchini noodles and tomato. Add the pesto by the tablespoonful until you have the desired flavor. Serve the zucchini pasta immediately. 4. Store any leftover pesto in a sealed container in the refrigerator for up to 2 weeks.

Per Serving:

calories: 247 | fat: 25.18g | protein: 3.17g | carbs: 5.39g | sugars: 1.62g | fiber: 1.3g | sodium: 148mg

Dandelion Greens with Sweet Onion

Prep time: 15 minutes | Cook time: 15 minutes | Serves 4

1 tablespoon extra-virgin olive oil
1 Vidalia onion, thinly sliced
2 garlic cloves, minced
½ cup store-bought low-sodium
vegetable broth
2 bunches dandelion greens, roughly chopped
Freshly ground black pepper

1. In a large skillet, heat the olive oil over low heat. 2. Add the onion and garlic and cook, stirring to prevent the garlic from scorching, for 2 to 3 minutes, or until the onion is translucent. 3. Add the broth and greens and cook, stirring often, for 5 to 7 minutes, or until the greens are wilted. 4. Season with pepper, and serve warm.

Per Serving:
calories: 53 | fat: 3.7g | protein: 1.21g | carbs: 4.82g | sugars: 1.2g | fiber: 1.3g | sodium: 39mg

Lemony Roasted Cauliflower

Prep time: 5 minutes | Cook time: 25 to 30 minutes | Serves 3

3-4 tablespoons lemon juice
½ tablespoon tahini
¼ teaspoon smoked paprika
4½-5 cups cauliflower florets
(about 1 medium to large head)
¼ teaspoon sea salt
Freshly ground black pepper to taste (optional)

1. Preheat the oven to 450°F. Line a baking sheet with parchment paper. 2. In a large bowl, whisk together the lemon juice, tahini, and smoked paprika. Add the cauliflower and toss to coat. Transfer the cauliflower to the prepared baking sheet, scraping all of the lemon sauce over the cauliflower. Sprinkle with the salt. Bake for 25 to 30 minutes, stirring a couple of times, until golden. (Larger pieces will take longer to cook.) Remove, season with salt and pepper (if using) to taste, and serve.

Per Serving:
calorie: 51 | fat: 2g | protein: 3g | carbs: 7g | sugars: 3g | fiber: 4g | sodium: 368mg

Green Beans with Red Peppers

Prep time: 5 minutes | Cook time: 15 minutes | Serves 2

8 ounces fresh green beans, broken into 2-inch pieces
6 sun-dried tomatoes (not packed in oil), halved
1 medium red bell pepper, cut
into ¼-inch strips
1 teaspoon extra-virgin olive oil
Salt, to season
Freshly ground black pepper, to season

1. In a 1-quart saucepan set over high heat, add the green beans to 1 inch of water. Bring to a boil. Boil for 5 minutes, uncovered. 2. Add the sun-dried tomatoes. Cover and boil 5 to 7 minutes more, or until the beans are crisp-tender, and the tomatoes have softened. Drain.

Transfer to a serving bowl. 3. Add the red bell pepper and olive oil. Season with salt and pepper. Toss to coat. 4. Serve warm.

Per Serving:
calories: 82 | fat: 3.17g | protein: 2.83g | carbs: 12.57g | sugars: 5.65g | fiber: 4.4g | sodium: 601mg

Classic Oven-Roasted Carrots

Prep time: 10 minutes | Cook time: 15 minutes | Serves 4

1½ poundss (680 g) large carrots, trimmed and washed
Avocado oil spray, as needed
¼ teaspoon sea salt
1 tablespoon (3 g) dried rosemary

1. Preheat the oven to 400°F (204°C). Line a large baking sheet with parchment paper. 2. Arrange the carrots on the prepared baking sheet, making sure there is at least ½ inch (13 mm) between each of them. 3. Generously spray the carrots with the avocado oil spray, and then sprinkle them with the sea salt and rosemary. Roast the carrots for 15 minutes, or until they are fork-tender.

Per Serving:
calorie: 72 | fat: 1g | protein: 2g | carbs: 17g | sugars: 8g | fiber: 5g | sodium: 263mg

Cheesy Cauli Bake

Prep time: 10 minutes | Cook time: 25 to 30 minutes | Serves 6

3 tablespoons tahini
2 tablespoons nutritional yeast
1 tablespoon lemon juice
½ teaspoon pure maple syrup or agave nectar
½ teaspoon sea salt
½ cup + 1 tablespoon plain nondairy milk
3-3½ cups cauliflower florets, cut or broken in small pieces
Topping
1 tablespoon almond meal or breadcrumbs
½ tablespoon nutritional yeast
Pinch sea salt

1. Preheat the oven to 425°F. Use cooking spray to lightly coat the bottom and sides of an 8" x 8" (or similar size) baking dish. 2. In a small bowl, whisk together the tahini, nutritional yeast, lemon juice, maple syrup or agave nectar, and salt. Gradually whisk in the milk until it all comes together smoothly. In the baking dish, add the cauliflower and pour in the sauce, stir thoroughly to coat the cauliflower. Cover with foil and bake for 25 to 30 minutes, stirring only once, until the cauliflower is tender. 3. In a small bowl, toss together the topping ingredients. Remove the foil from the cauliflower, and sprinkle on the topping. Return to the oven and set oven to broil. Allow to cook for a minute or so until the topping is golden brown. Remove, let sit for a few minutes, then serve.

Per Serving:
calorie: 87 | fat: 5g | protein: 5g | carbs: 7g | sugars: 5g | fiber: 3g | sodium: 270mg

Marinated Green Beans

Prep time: 10 minutes | Cook time: 10 minutes | Serves 3

½-¾ pound green beans, ends trimmed	2 teaspoons coconut nectar or pure maple syrup
1 tablespoon nutritional yeast	Rounded ¼ teaspoon sea salt
1 teaspoon Dijon mustard	Freshly ground black pepper to taste (optional)
1 tablespoon apple cider vinegar	

1. Place a large pot of water over high heat, and bring to a boil. Add the green beans and cook for 2 to 3 minutes. Run the beans under cold water to stop the cooking process. Drain the beans and pat dry, if needed. In a large bowl, combine the yeast, mustard, vinegar, nectar or syrup, salt, and pepper (if using). Whisk until thoroughly combined. Add the green beans, and toss to coat thoroughly. Let sit for 30 minutes, then serve.

Per Serving:
calorie: 47 | fat: 0.4g | protein: 3g | carbs: 9g | sugars: 4g | fiber: 3g | sodium: 335mg

Roasted Beets, Carrots, and Parsnips

Prep time: 10 minutes | Cook time: 30 minutes | Serves 4

1 pound beets, peeled and quartered	1 tablespoon extra-virgin olive oil
½ pound carrots, peeled and cut into chunks	1 teaspoon apple cider vinegar
½ pound parsnips, peeled and cut into chunks	Sea salt
	Freshly ground black pepper

1. Preheat the oven to 375°F. Line a baking tray with aluminum foil. 2. In a large bowl, toss the beets, carrots, and parsnips with the oil and vinegar until everything is well coated. Spread them out on the baking sheet. 3. Roast until the vegetables are tender and lightly caramelized, about 30 minutes. 4. Transfer the vegetables to a serving bowl, season with salt and pepper, and serve warm.

Per Serving:
calories: 122 | fat: 3.84g | protein: 3.73g | carbs: 20.75g | sugars: 5.98g | fiber: 8.6g | sodium: 592mg

Chinese Asparagus

Prep time: 5 minutes | Cook time: 5 minutes | Serves 4

1 pound asparagus	2 teaspoons cornstarch
½ cup plus 1 tablespoon water, divided	1 tablespoon canola oil
1 tablespoon light soy sauce	2 teaspoons grated fresh ginger
1 tablespoon rice vinegar	1 scallion, minced

1. Trim the tough ends off the asparagus. Cut the stalks diagonally into 2-inch pieces. 2. In a small bowl, combine the ½ cup water, soy sauce, and rice vinegar. 3. In a measuring cup, combine the cornstarch and 1 tablespoon water. Set aside. 4. Heat the oil in a wok or skillet. Add the ginger and scallions, and stir-fry for 30 seconds. Add the asparagus and stir-fry for a few seconds more. Add the broth mixture, and bring to a boil. Cover, and simmer for 3-5 minutes, until the asparagus is just tender. 5. Add the cornstarch mixture, and cook until thickened. Serve.

Per Serving:
calories: 73 | fat: 4.37g | protein: 2.87g | carbs: 7.09g | sugars: 3.02g | fiber: 2.6g | sodium: 64mg

Broiled Asparagus

Prep time: 5 minutes | Cook time: 5 to 6 minutes | Serves 3

1 pound asparagus	¼ teaspoon sea salt
1 teaspoon lemon juice	Lemon pepper (optional)

1. Set the oven or toaster oven to broil. Line a baking sheet with parchment paper. 2. Wash and trim the asparagus. (Use a knife or break off ends where they naturally snap.) Pat the asparagus dry, and transfer to the prepared baking sheet. Sprinkle with the lemon juice, toss to coat, and then sprinkle with the salt. Broil for 5 to 6 minutes, or until the asparagus turns bright green. Remove, sprinkle with the lemon pepper (if using), and serve.

Per Serving:
calorie: 17 | fat: 0.2g | protein: 2g | carbs: 3g | sugars: 1g | fiber: 2g | sodium: 206mg

Mushroom "Bacon" Topper

Prep time: 10 minutes | Cook time: 16 to 17 minutes | Serves 4

½ pound shiitake mushrooms, stems removed	½ teaspoon smoked paprika
2½ teaspoons balsamic vinegar	½ teaspoon Dijon mustard
2½ teaspoons tamari	¼ teaspoon liquid smoke
1 tablespoon pure maple syrup	Freshly ground pepper or lemon pepper to taste

1. Preheat the oven to 400°F. Line a baking sheet with parchment paper. 2. Use a damp paper towel to clean the mushrooms. Slice the mushrooms thinly. In a large bowl, combine the vinegar, tamari, syrup, paprika, mustard, liquid smoke, and pepper. Whisk thoroughly. Add the mushrooms and stir to coat with the marinade. Transfer the mushrooms to the prepared baking sheet. Bake for 16 to 17 minutes, tossing once. Turn off the heat and let the mushrooms sit in the warm oven for 10 minutes, tossing once during this time. Remove and let cool. Serve on salads, soups, pizzas, and more.

Per Serving:
calorie: 45 | fat: 0.4g | protein: 2g | carbs: 9g | sugars: 6g | fiber: 2g | sodium: 233mg

Garlic Roasted Broccoli

Prep time: 8 minutes | Cook time: 10 to 14 minutes | Serves 6

1 head broccoli, cut into bite-size florets
1 tablespoon avocado oil
2 teaspoons minced garlic
⅛ teaspoon red pepper flakes
Sea salt and freshly ground black pepper, to taste
1 tablespoon freshly squeezed lemon juice
½ teaspoon lemon zest

1. In a large bowl, toss together the broccoli, avocado oil, garlic, red pepper flakes, salt, and pepper. 2. Set the air fryer to 375ºF (191ºC). Arrange the broccoli in a single layer in the air fryer basket, working in batches if necessary. Roast for 10 to 14 minutes, until the broccoli is lightly charred. 3. Place the florets in a medium bowl and toss with the lemon juice and lemon zest. Serve.

Per Serving:

calories: 58 | fat: 3g | protein: 3g | carbs: 7g | fiber: 3g | sodium: 34mg

"Honey" Mustard Sauce

Prep time: 5 minutes | Cook time: 0 minutes | Makes ½ cup

½ cup plain nonfat Greek yogurt
1 tablespoon apple cider vinegar
1 teaspoon dry mustard
¾ teaspoon garlic powder
⅛ teaspoon paprika
1 tablespoon granulated stevia

1. In a small bowl, whisk together the yogurt, apple cider vinegar, dry mustard, garlic powder, paprika, and stevia until smooth. 2. Refrigerate until needed.

Per Serving:

calories: 101 | fat: 0.48g | protein: 7.23g | carbs: 17.1g | sugars: 14.77g | fiber: 0.5g | sodium: 81mg

Orange-Scented Asparagus with Sweet Red Peppers

Prep time: 5 minutes | Cook time: 15 minutes | Serves 2

⅓ pound fresh asparagus, trimmed
1 teaspoon extra-virgin olive oil mixed with 1 teaspoon warm water
1 red bell pepper, seeded and julienned
1 tablespoon grated orange zest
Salt, to season
Freshly ground black pepper, to season
1 teaspoon granulated stevia, divided

1. Preheat the broiler to high. 2. In a steamer or large pot of boiling water, cook the asparagus for about 7 minutes, or until barely tender. Drain. Set aside. 3. In a small skillet set over medium-high heat, heat the olive oil and water. 4. Add the bell pepper. Cook for about 5 minutes, stirring frequently, until slightly softened. Remove from the heat. 5. Stir in the orange zest. Season with salt and pepper. 6. Evenly divided the asparagus between 2 gratin dishes. Spoon half of the red bell pepper and sauce over each. Sprinkle each with ½ teaspoon of stevia. Place the dished under the preheated broiler. Broil for 2 to 3 minutes, or until lightly browned. 7. Serve immediately.

Per Serving:

calories: 59 | fat: 2.49g | protein: 2.24g | carbs: 8.62g | sugars: 5.35g | fiber: 2.2g | sodium: 585mg

Spinach and Sweet Pepper Poppers

Prep time: 10 minutes | Cook time: 8 minutes | Makes 16 poppers

4 ounces (113 g) cream cheese, softened
1 cup chopped fresh spinach leaves
½ teaspoon garlic powder
8 mini sweet bell peppers, tops removed, seeded, and halved lengthwise

1. In a medium bowl, mix cream cheese, spinach, and garlic powder. Place 1 tablespoon mixture into each sweet pepper half and press down to smooth. 2. Place poppers into ungreased air fryer basket. Adjust the temperature to 400ºF (204ºC) and air fry for 8 minutes. Poppers will be done when cheese is browned on top and peppers are tender-crisp. Serve warm.

Per Serving:

calories: 31 | fat: 2g | protein: 1g | carbs: 3g | fiber: 0g | sodium: 34mg

Roasted Peppers and Eggplant

Prep time: 5 minutes | Cook time: 20 minutes | Serves 2

Extra-virgin olive oil cooking spray
1 small eggplant, halved and sliced
1 red bell pepper, cut into thick strips
1 yellow bell pepper, cut into thick strips
1 red onion, sliced
2 garlic cloves, quartered
1 tablespoon extra-virgin olive oil
Salt, to season
Freshly ground black pepper, to season
½ cup chopped fresh basil

1. Preheat the oven to 350°F. 2. Coat a nonstick baking dish with cooking spray. 3. To the prepared dish, add the eggplant, red bell pepper, yellow bell pepper, onion, and garlic. Drizzle with the olive oil. Toss to coat well. Spray any uncoated surfaces with cooking spray. 4. Place the dish in the preheated oven. Bake for 20 minutes, turning once halfway through cooking. 5. Transfer the vegetables to a serving dish. Season with salt and pepper. 6. Garnish with the basil and serve.

Per Serving:

calories: 185 | fat: 10.52g | protein: 3.88g | carbs: 22.17g | sugars: 12.42g | fiber: 10g | sodium: 651mg

Italian Roasted Vegetables

Prep time: 15 minutes | Cook time: 20 minutes | Serves 4

2 tablespoons extra-virgin olive oil
2 teaspoons chopped fresh oregano
1 teaspoon chopped fresh basil
1 teaspoon minced garlic
½ pound whole cremini

mushrooms
2 cups cauliflower florets
1 zucchini, cut into 1-inch chunks
2 cups cherry tomatoes
Sea salt
Freshly ground black pepper

1. Preheat the oven to 400°F. Line a baking sheet with aluminum foil. 2. In a large bowl, stir together the oil, oregano, basil, and garlic. 3. Add the mushrooms, cauliflower, zucchini, and cherry tomatoes and toss to coat. 4. Transfer the vegetables to the baking sheet and roast until they are tender and lightly browned, about 20 minutes. 5. Season with salt and pepper and serve.

Per Serving:

calories: 297 | fat: 7.79g | protein: 8.18g | carbs: 58.58g | sugars: 12.81g | fiber: 9.9g | sodium: 182mg

Soft-Baked Tamari Tofu

Prep time: 5 minutes | Cook time: 20 to 25 minutes | Serves 4

3 tablespoons tamari
1 package (16 ounces) medium-

firm tofu

1. Preheat the oven to 425°F. In an ovenproof dish just large enough to hold the tofu, add about half of the tamari. Use several paper towels to pat or squeeze some of the excess moisture from the tofu. Add the tofu to the dish, breaking it up slightly. Sprinkle the remaining tamari over the tofu. Bake for 20 to 25 minutes, or until the tofu is browned and drying in spots. Serve, spooning out tofu with some of the remaining tamari.

Per Serving:

calorie: 87 | fat: 5g | protein: 10g | carbs: 3g | sugars: 1g | fiber: 1g | sodium: 768mg

Focaccia

Prep time: 5 minutes | Cook time: 12 to 15 minutes | Serves 2

¾ cup warm water
1 packet quick-rise yeast (can use standard yeast)
½ tablespoon coconut sugar or pure maple syrup
2 cups white wheat flour
Rounded ¼ teaspoon sea salt

1½-2 teaspoons chopped fresh rosemary leaves (can substitute thyme)
Scant ½ teaspoon coarse salt
Freshly ground black pepper (to taste) or lemon pepper

1. In a small bowl, combine the warm water, yeast, and sugar or syrup. (The water should be warm but not hot, as hot will kill the yeast but water that is too cold will not activate it.) Whisk well, and let stand for about 5 minutes, or until foamy. 2. Meanwhile, in a large bowl, combine the flour and sea salt, and mix. Once the yeast mixture is foamy, add it to the flour. Use a large spoon to work the mixture together. Once the dough comes together, either knead the dough inside the bowl or lightly flour the countertop and transfer the dough there for kneading. Knead for just a couple of minutes. Lightly coat the inside of a large bowl with cooking spray and transfer the dough to that bowl. Cover with plastic wrap. Place the bowl on a countertop in a warm but not hot area to rest and rise for 30 minutes or more. 3. Preheat the oven to 450°F for at least a half-hour. Lightly coat a large piece of parchment with cooking spray. 4. Transfer the dough to the prepared parchment, and begin to press it into shape with your fingers. Focaccia can be round, or squarish, or whatever shape you like. Use your fingers to poke into the surface of the dough, leaving small indentations all over. Sprinkle on the rosemary, coarse salt, and pepper. Bake for 12 to 15 minutes, or until golden on the edges. Remove, let cool slightly, and cut to serve.

Per Serving:

calorie: 434 | fat: 3g | protein: 17g | carbs: 91g | sugars: 4g | fiber: 14g | sodium: 973mg

Sesame Bok Choy with Almonds

Prep time: 15 minutes | Cook time: 7 minutes | Serves 4

2 teaspoons sesame oil
2 pounds bok choy, cleaned and quartered
2 teaspoons low-sodium soy

sauce
Pinch red pepper flakes
½ cup toasted sliced almonds

1. Place a large skillet over medium heat and add the oil. 2. When the oil is hot, sauté the bok choy until tender-crisp, about 5 minutes. 3. Stir in the soy sauce and red pepper flakes and sauté 2 minutes more. 4. Remove the bok choy to a serving bowl and top with the sliced almonds.

Per Serving:

calories: 56 | fat: 3g | protein: 4g | carbs: 6g | sugars: 3g | fiber: 3g | sodium: 229mg

Best Brown Rice

Prep time: 5 minutes | Cook time: 22 minutes | Serves 6 to 12

2 cups brown rice

2½ cups water

1. Rinse brown rice in a fine-mesh strainer. 2. Add rice and water to the inner pot of the Instant Pot. 3. Secure the lid and make sure vent is on sealing. 4. Use Manual setting and select 22 minutes cooking time on high pressure. 5. When cooking time is done, let the pressure release naturally for 10 minutes, then press Cancel and manually release any remaining pressure.

Per Serving:

calorie: 114 | fat: 1g | protein: 2g | carbs: 23g | sugars: 0g | fiber: 1g | sodium: 3mg

Carrots Marsala

Prep time: 5 minutes | Cook time: 10 minutes | Serves 6

10 carrots (about 1 pound), peeled and diagonally sliced
¼ cup Marsala wine
¼ cup water
1 tablespoon extra-virgin olive

oil
⅛ teaspoon freshly ground black pepper
1 tablespoon finely chopped fresh parsley

1. In a large saucepan, combine the carrots, wine, water, oil, and pepper. Bring to a boil, cover, reduce the heat, and simmer for 8-10 minutes, until the carrots are just tender, basting occasionally. Taste, and add salt, if desired. 2. Transfer to a serving dish, spoon any juices on top, and sprinkle with parsley.

Per Serving:

calories: 48 | fat: 2.4g | protein: 0.66g | carbs: 6.49g | sugars: 2.76g | fiber: 2.3g | sodium: 46mg

Mushroom Cassoulets

Prep time: 5 minutes | Cook time: 30 minutes | Serves 6

1 pound mushrooms, sliced
½ cup lentils, cooked
1 medium onion, chopped
1 cup low-sodium chicken broth
1 sprig thyme
1 bay leaf
Leaves from 1 celery stalk

2 tablespoons lemon juice
⅛ teaspoon freshly ground black pepper
½ cup wheat germ
2 tablespoons extra-virgin olive oil

1. Preheat the oven to 350 degrees. 2. In a saucepan, combine the mushrooms, lentils, onion, and chicken broth. Tie together the thyme, bay leaf, and celery leaves and add to the mushrooms. 3. Add the lemon juice and pepper, and bring to a boil. Boil until the liquid is reduced, about 10 minutes. Remove the bundle of herbs. 4. Divide the mushroom mixture equally into small ramekins. Mix the wheat germ and oil together, and sprinkle on top of each casserole. 5. Bake at 350 degrees for 20 minutes or until the tops are golden brown. Remove from the oven, and let cool slightly before serving. Add salt if desired.

Per Serving:

calories: 114 | fat: 6.01g | protein: 6.19g | carbs: 11.63g | sugars: 2.49g | fiber: 2.5g | sodium: 21mg

Herb-Roasted Root Vegetables

Prep time: 15 minutes | Cook time: 45 to 55 minutes | Serves 6

2 medium turnips, peeled, cut into 1-inch pieces (3 cups)
2 medium parsnips, peeled, cut into ½-inch pieces (1½ cups)
1 medium red onion, cut into 1-inch wedges (1 cup)

1 cup ready-to-eat baby-cut carrots
Cooking spray
2 teaspoons Italian seasoning
½ teaspoon coarse salt

1 Heat oven to 425°F. Spray 15x10x1-inch pan with cooking spray. Arrange vegetables in single layer in pan. Spray with cooking spray (2 or 3 seconds). Sprinkle with Italian seasoning and salt. 2 Bake uncovered 45 to 55 minutes, stirring once, until vegetables are tender.

Per Serving:

calorie: 70 | fat: 0g | protein: 1g | carbs: 15g | sugars: 7g | fiber: 4g | sodium: 260mg

Not Slow-Cooked Collards

Prep time: 10 minutes | Cook time: 20 minutes | Serves 4

1 cup store-bought low-sodium vegetable broth, divided
½ onion, thinly sliced
2 garlic cloves, thinly sliced
1 large bunch collard greens including stems, roughly

chopped
1 medium tomato, chopped
1 teaspoon ground cumin
½ teaspoon freshly ground black pepper

1. In a Dutch oven, bring ½ cup of broth to a simmer over medium heat. 2. Add the onion and garlic and cook for 3 to 5 minutes, or until translucent. 3. Add the collard greens, tomato, cumin, pepper, and the remaining ½ cup of broth, and gently stir. 4. Reduce the heat to low and cook, uncovered, for 15 minutes.

Per Serving:

calories: 27 | fat: 0.45g | protein: 1.33g | carbs: 5.32g | sugars: 2.83g | fiber: 1.2g | sodium: 53mg

Sautéed Spinach with Parmesan and Almonds

Prep time: 5 minutes | Cook time: 5 minutes | Serves 2

2 teaspoons extra-virgin olive oil
2 tablespoons sliced almonds
2 garlic cloves, minced
2 (5-ounce) bags prewashed spinach

2 teaspoons balsamic vinegar
⅛ teaspoon salt
2 tablespoons soy Parmesan cheese
Freshly ground black pepper, to season

1. In a large nonstick skillet or Dutch oven set over medium-high heat, heat the olive oil. 2. Add the almonds and garlic. Cook for 30 seconds, stirring, or until fragrant. 3. Add the spinach. Cook for about 2 minutes, stirring, until just wilted. Remove the pan from the heat. 4. Stir in the balsamic vinegar and salt. 5. Sprinkle with the soy Parmesan cheese. Season with pepper and serve immediately.

Per Serving:

calories: 84 | fat: 6.62g | protein: 2.55g | carbs: 4.26g | sugars: 0.96g | fiber: 0.9g | sodium: 262mg

Summer Squash Casserole

Prep time: 15 minutes | Cook time: 30 minutes | Serves 8

1 tablespoon extra-virgin olive oil
6 yellow summer squash, thinly sliced
1 large portobello mushroom, thinly sliced
1 Vidalia onion, thinly sliced
1 cup shredded Parmesan cheese, divided

1 cup shredded reduced-fat extra-sharp Cheddar cheese
½ cup whole-wheat bread crumbs
½ cup tri-color quinoa
1 tablespoon Creole seasoning

1. Preheat the oven to 350°F. 2. In a large cast iron pan, heat the oil over medium heat. 3. Add the squash, mushroom, and onion, and sauté for 7 to 10 minutes, or until softened. 4. Remove from the heat. Add ½ cup of Parmesan cheese and the Cheddar cheese and mix well. 5. In a small bowl, whisk the bread crumbs, quinoa, the remaining ½ cup of Parmesan, and the Creole seasoning together. Evenly distribute over the casserole. 6. Transfer the pan to the oven, and bake for 20 minutes, or until browned. Serve warm and enjoy.

Per Serving:

calories: 163 | fat: 7.2g | protein: 10.08g | carbs: 14.45g | sugars: 0.53g | fiber: 1.7g | sodium: 484mg

Stuffed Portobellos

Prep time: 10 minutes | Cook time: 8 minutes | Serves 4

3 ounces (85 g) cream cheese, softened
½ medium zucchini, trimmed and chopped
¼ cup seeded and chopped red bell pepper
1½ cups chopped fresh spinach

leaves
4 large portobello mushrooms, stems removed
2 tablespoons coconut oil, melted
½ teaspoon salt

1. In a medium bowl, mix cream cheese, zucchini, pepper, and spinach. 2. Drizzle mushrooms with coconut oil and sprinkle with salt. Scoop ¼ zucchini mixture into each mushroom. 3. Place mushrooms into ungreased air fryer basket. Adjust the temperature to 400°F (204°C) and air fry for 8 minutes. Portobellos will be tender and tops will be browned when done. Serve warm.

Per Serving:

calories: 151 | fat: 13g | protein: 4g | carbs: 6g | fiber: 2g | sodium: 427mg

Instant Pot Hoppin' John with Skillet Cauli "Rice"

Prep time: 0 minutes | Cook time: 30 minutes | Serves 6

Hoppin' John
1 pound dried black-eyed peas (about 2¼ cups)
8⅔ cups water
1½ teaspoons fine sea salt
2 tablespoons extra-virgin olive oil
2 garlic cloves, minced
8 ounces shiitake mushrooms, stemmed and chopped, or cremini mushrooms, chopped
1 small yellow onion, diced
1 green bell pepper, seeded and diced
2 celery stalks, diced
2 jalapeño chiles, seeded and

diced
½ teaspoon smoked paprika
½ teaspoon dried thyme
½ teaspoon dried sage
¼ teaspoon cayenne pepper
2 cups low-sodium vegetable broth
Cauli "Rice"
1 tablespoon vegan buttery spread or unsalted butter
1 pound riced cauliflower
½ teaspoon fine sea salt
2 green onions, white and green parts, sliced
Hot sauce (such as Tabasco or Crystal) for serving

1. To make the Hoppin' John: In a large bowl, combine the black-eyed peas, 8 cups of the water, and 1 teaspoon of the salt and stir to dissolve the salt. Let soak for at least 8 hours or up to overnight. 2. Select the Sauté setting on the Instant Pot and heat the oil and garlic for 3 minutes, until the garlic is bubbling but not browned. Add the mushrooms and the remaining ½ teaspoon salt and sauté for 5 minutes, until the mushrooms have wilted and begun to give up their liquid. Add the onion, bell pepper, celery, and jalapeños and sauté for 4 minutes, until the onion is softened. Add the paprika, thyme, sage, and cayenne and sauté for 1 minute. 3. Drain the black-eyed peas and add them to the pot along with the broth and remaining ⅔ cup water. The liquid should just barely cover the beans. (Add an additional splash of water if needed.) 4. Secure the lid and set the Pressure Release to Sealing. Press the Cancel button to reset the cooking program, then select the Bean/Chili, Pressure Cook, or Manual setting and set the cooking time for 5 minutes at high pressure. (The pot will take about 10 minutes to come up to pressure before the cooking program begins.) 5. When the cooking program ends, let the pressure release naturally for 10 minutes, then move the Pressure Release to Venting to release any remaining steam. 6. To make the cauli "rice": While the pressure is releasing, in a large skillet over medium heat, melt the buttery spread. Add the cauliflower and salt and sauté for 3 to 5 minutes, until cooked through and piping hot. (If using frozen riced cauliflower, this may take another 2 minutes or so.) 7. Spoon the cauli "rice" onto individual plates. Open the pot and spoon the black-eyed peas on top of the cauli "rice". Sprinkle with the green onions and serve right away, with the hot sauce on the side.

Per Serving:

calories: 287 | fat: 7g | protein: 23g | carbs: 56g | sugars: 8g | fiber: 24g | sodium: 894mg

Orange Tofu

Prep time: 10 minutes | Cook time: 20 minutes | Serves 4

⅓ cup freshly squeezed orange juice (zest orange first; see orange zest ingredient below)
1 tablespoon tamari
1 tablespoon tahini
½ tablespoon coconut nectar or pure maple syrup
2 tablespoons apple cider vinegar
½ tablespoon freshly grated

ginger
1 large clove garlic, grated
½-1 teaspoon orange zest
¼ teaspoon sea salt
Few pinches of crushed red-pepper flakes (optional)
1 package (12 ounces) extra-firm tofu, sliced into ¼"-½" thick squares and patted to remove excess moisture

1. Preheat the oven to 400°F. 2. In a small bowl, combine the orange juice, tamari, tahini, nectar or syrup, vinegar, ginger, garlic, orange zest, salt, and red-pepper flakes (if using). Whisk until well combined. Pour the sauce into an 8" x 12" baking dish. Add the tofu and turn to coat both sides. Bake for 20 minutes. Add salt to taste.

Per Serving:

calorie: 122 | fat: 7g | protein: 10g | carbs: 7g | sugars: 4g | fiber: 1g | sodium: 410mg

Grilled Vegetables on White Bean Mash

Prep time: 15 minutes | Cook time: 30 minutes | Serves 2

2 medium zucchini, sliced
1 red bell pepper, seeded and quartered
2 portobello mushroom caps, quartered
3 teaspoons extra-virgin olive oil, divided
1 (8-ounce) can cannellini beans, drained and rinsed
1 garlic clove, minced
½ cup low-sodium vegetable broth
4 cups baby spinach, divided
Salt, to season
Freshly ground black pepper, to season
1 tablespoon chopped fresh parsley
2 lemon wedges, divided, for garnish

1. Preheat the grill. Use a stove-top grill pan or broiler if a grill is not available. 2. Lightly brush the zucchini, red bell pepper, and mushrooms with 1½ teaspoons of olive oil. Arrange them in a barbecue grill pan. Place the pan on the preheated grill. Cook the vegetables for 5 to 8 minutes, or until lightly browned. Turn the vegetables. Brush with the remaining 1½ teaspoons of olive oil. Cook for 5 to 8 minutes more, or until tender. 3. To a small pan set over high heat, add the cannellini beans, garlic, and vegetable broth. Bring to a boil. Reduce the heat to low. Simmer for 10 minutes, uncovered. Using a potato masher, roughly mash the beans, adding a little more broth if they seem too dry. 4. Place 2 cups of spinach on each serving plate. 5. Top each with half of the bean mash and half of the grilled vegetables. Season with salt and pepper. Garnish with parsley. 6. Place 1 lemon wedge on each plate and serve.

Per Serving:
calories: 289.5 | fat: 8.55g | protein: 11.3g | carbs:28.91 g | sugars: 7.88g | fiber: 4.4g | sodium: 398mg

Palak Tofu

Prep time: 5 minutes | Cook time: 40 minutes | Serves 4

One 14-ounce package extra-firm tofu, drained
5 tablespoons cold-pressed avocado oil
1 yellow onion, diced
1-inch piece fresh ginger, peeled and minced
3 garlic cloves, minced
1 teaspoon fine sea salt
½ teaspoon freshly ground black pepper
¼ teaspoon cayenne pepper
One 16-ounce bag frozen chopped spinach
⅓ cup water
One 14½-ounce can fire-roasted diced tomatoes and their liquid
¼ cup coconut milk
2 teaspoons garam masala
Cooked brown rice or cauliflower "rice" or whole-grain flatbread for serving

1. Cut the tofu crosswise into eight ½-inch-thick slices. Sandwich the slices between double layers of paper towels or a folded kitchen towel and press firmly to wick away as much moisture as possible. Cut the slices into ½-inch cubes. 2. Select the Sauté setting on the Instant Pot and and heat 4 tablespoons of the oil for 2 minutes. Add the onion and sauté for about 10 minutes, until it begins to brown. 3. While the onion is cooking in the Instant Pot, in a large nonstick skillet over medium-high heat, warm the remaining 1 tablespoon oil. Add the tofu in a single layer and cook without stirring for about 3 minutes, until lightly browned. 4. Using a spatula, turn the cubes over and cook for about 3 minutes more, until browned on the other side. Remove from the heat and set aside. 5. Add the ginger and garlic to the onion in the Instant Pot and sauté for about 2 minutes, until the garlic is bubbling but not browned. Add the sautéed tofu, salt, black pepper, and cayenne and stir gently to combine, taking care not to break up the tofu. Add the spinach and stir gently. Pour in the water and then pour the tomatoes and their liquid over the top in an even layer. Do not stir them in. 6. Secure the lid and set the Pressure Release to Sealing. Press the Cancel button to reset the cooking program, then select the Manual or Pressure Cook setting and set the cooking time for 10 minutes at low pressure. (The pot will take about 15 minutes to come up to pressure before the cooking program begins.) 7. When the cooking program ends, let the pressure release naturally for 10 minutes, then move the Pressure Release to Venting to release any remaining steam. Open the pot, add the coconut milk and garam masala, and stir to combine. 8. Ladle the tofu onto plates or into bowls. Serve piping hot, with the "rice" alongside.

Per Serving:
calories: 345 | fat: 24g | protein: 14g | carbs: 18g | sugars: 5g | fiber: 6g | sodium: 777mg

Asparagus, Sun-Dried Tomato, and Green Pea Sauté

Prep time: 10 minutes | Cook time: 10 minutes | Serves 2

6 packaged sun-dried tomatoes (not packed in oil)
½ cup boiling water
1 tablespoon extra-virgin olive oil
2 garlic cloves, minced
¾ pound fresh asparagus, trimmed and cut into 2-inch pieces
¼ cup chopped red bell pepper
½ cup sliced fresh button
mushrooms
¼ cup reduced-sodium vegetable broth
2 tablespoons sliced almonds
1 large tomato, diced (about 1 cup)
1½ teaspoons dried tarragon
½ cup frozen peas
Freshly ground black pepper, to season

1. In a small heatproof bowl, place the sun-dried tomatoes. Cover with the boiling water. Set aside. 2. In a large skillet or wok set over high heat, heat the olive oil. 3. Add the garlic. Swirl in the oil for a few seconds. 4. Toss in the asparagus, red bell pepper, and mushrooms. Stir-fry for 30 seconds. 5. Add the vegetable broth and almonds. Cover and steam for about 2 minutes. Uncover the skillet. 6. Add the tomato and tarragon. Cook for 2 to 3 minutes to reduce the liquid. 7. Drain and chop the sun-dried tomatoes. Add them and the peas to the skillet. Stir-fry for 3 to 4 minutes, or until the vegetables are crisp-tender and the liquid is reduced to a sauce. 8. Season with pepper and serve immediately.

Per Serving:
calories: 165 | fat: 8.22g | protein: 7.51g | carbs: 20g | sugars: 9.15g | fiber: 7.3g | sodium: 46mg

Soybeans with Plums and Peppers

Prep time: 15 minutes | Cook time: 40 minutes | Serves 2

2 medium purple plums	2 whole cloves
1 tablespoon extra-virgin olive oil	2 teaspoons ground cumin
1 medium onion, chopped	½ cup minced fresh cilantro leaves
1 small yellow bell pepper, chopped	2 teaspoons freshly squeezed lemon juice
1 small red bell pepper, chopped	½ teaspoon liquid stevia
1 garlic clove, chopped	1 cup cooked black soybeans

1. Fill a deep pot with water and bring to a boil over high heat. 2. Add the plums. Boil for 30 seconds to loosen their skins. With a slotted spoon, remove the plums. Set aside to cool. 3. In a large skillet set over low heat, heat the olive oil. 4. Add the onion, yellow bell pepper, red bell pepper, garlic, whole cloves, cumin, and cilantro. Cook for 5 to 10 minutes, stirring frequently, until the onion softens. 5. Peel the plums. Remove the pits and chop the fruit. 6. Add the plum, lemon juice, and stevia to the onions and peppers. 7. Stir in the black soybeans. Cover and cook for about 30 minutes, or until the peppers are soft, stirring frequently to prevent sticking. 8. Remove the 2 whole cloves. Serve hot or chilled and enjoy!

Per Serving:
calories: 255 | fat: 4.78g | protein: 10.27g | carbs: 46.3g | sugars: 14.41g | fiber: 10.8g | sodium: 22mg

Vegan Dal Makhani

Prep time: 0 minutes | Cook time: 55 minutes | Serves 6

1 cup dried kidney beans	diced
⅓ cup urad dal or beluga or Puy lentils	1 tablespoon garam masala
4 cups water	1 teaspoon ground turmeric
1 teaspoon fine sea salt	¼ teaspoon cayenne pepper (optional)
1 tablespoon cold-pressed avocado oil	One 15-ounce can fire-roasted diced tomatoes and liquid
1 tablespoon cumin seeds	2 tablespoons vegan buttery spread
1-inch piece fresh ginger, peeled and minced	Cooked cauliflower "rice" for serving
4 garlic cloves, minced	2 tablespoons chopped fresh cilantro
1 large yellow onion, diced	
2 jalapeño chiles, seeded and diced	6 tablespoons plain coconut yogurt
1 green bell pepper, seeded and	

1. In a medium bowl, combine the kidney beans, urad dal, water, and salt and stir to dissolve the salt. Let soak for 12 hours. 2. Select the Sauté setting on the Instant Pot and heat the oil and cumin seeds for 3 minutes, until the seeds are bubbling, lightly toasted, and aromatic. Add the ginger and garlic and sauté for 1 minute, until bubbling and fragrant. Add the onion, jalapeños, and bell pepper and sauté for 5 minutes, until the onion begins to soften. 3. Add the garam masala, turmeric, cayenne (if using), and the soaked beans and their liquid and stir to mix. Pour the tomatoes and their liquid on top. Do not stir them in. 4. Secure the lid and set the Pressure

Release to Sealing. Press the Cancel button to reset the cooking program, then select the Pressure Cook or Manual setting and set the cooking time for 30 minutes at high pressure. (The pot will take about 15 minutes to come up to pressure before the cooking program begins.) 5. When the cooking program ends, let the pressure release naturally for 30 minutes, then move the Pressure Release to Venting to release any remaining steam. Open the pot and stir to combine, then stir in the buttery spread. If you prefer a smoother texture, ladle 1½ cups of the dal into a blender and blend until smooth, about 30 seconds, then stir the blended mixture into the rest of the dal in the pot. 6. Spoon the cauliflower "rice" into bowls and ladle the dal on top. Sprinkle with the cilantro, top with a dollop of coconut yogurt, and serve.

Per Serving:
calorie: 245 | fat: 7g | protein: 11g | carbs: 37g | sugars: 4g | fiber: 10g | sodium: 518mg

Roasted Veggie Bowl

Prep time: 10 minutes | Cook time: 15 minutes | Serves 2

1 cup broccoli florets	seeded and sliced ¼ inch thick
1 cup quartered Brussels sprouts	1 tablespoon coconut oil
½ cup cauliflower florets	2 teaspoons chili powder
¼ medium white onion, peeled and sliced ¼ inch thick	½ teaspoon garlic powder
½ medium green bell pepper,	½ teaspoon cumin

1. Toss all ingredients together in a large bowl until vegetables are fully coated with oil and seasoning. 2. Pour vegetables into the air fryer basket. 3. Adjust the temperature to 360ºF (182ºC) and roast for 15 minutes. 4. Shake two or three times during cooking. Serve warm.

Per Serving:
calories: 112 | fat: 7.68g | protein: 3.64g | carbs: 10.67g | sugars: 3.08g | fiber: 4.6g | sodium: 106mg

Southwest Tofu

Prep time: 10 minutes | Cook time: 20 minutes | Serves 4

3½ tablespoons freshly squeezed lime juice	½ teaspoon sea salt
2 teaspoons pure maple syrup	⅛ teaspoon allspice
1½ teaspoons ground cumin	1 package (12 ounces) extra-firm tofu, sliced into ¼"-½" thick squares and patted to remove excess moisture
1 teaspoon dried oregano leaves	
1 teaspoon chili powder	
½ teaspoon paprika	

1. In a 9" x 12" baking dish, combine the lime juice, syrup, cumin, oregano, chili powder, paprika, salt, and allspice. Add the tofu and turn to coat both sides. Bake uncovered for 20 minutes, or until the marinade is absorbed, turning once.

Per Serving:
calorie: 78 | fat: 4g | protein: 7g | carbs: 6g | sugars: 3g | fiber: 1g | sodium: 324mg

Caprese Eggplant Stacks

Prep time: 5 minutes | Cook time: 12 minutes | Serves 4

1 medium eggplant, cut into ¼-inch slices
2 large tomatoes, cut into ¼-inch slices
4 ounces (113 g) fresh

Mozzarella, cut into ½-ounce / 14-g slices
2 tablespoons olive oil
¼ cup fresh basil, sliced

1. In a baking dish, place four slices of eggplant on the bottom. Place a slice of tomato on top of each eggplant round, then Mozzarella, then eggplant. Repeat as necessary. 2. Drizzle with olive oil. Cover dish with foil and place dish into the air fryer basket. 3. Adjust the temperature to 350ºF (177ºC) and bake for 12 minutes. 4. When done, eggplant will be tender. Garnish with fresh basil to serve.

Per Serving:
calories: 97 | fat: 7g | protein: 2g | carbs: 8g | fiber: 4g | sodium: 11mg

Vegetable Burgers

Prep time: 10 minutes | Cook time: 12 minutes | Serves 4

8 ounces (227 g) cremini mushrooms
2 large egg yolks
½ medium zucchini, trimmed and chopped
¼ cup peeled and chopped

yellow onion
1 clove garlic, peeled and finely minced
½ teaspoon salt
¼ teaspoon ground black pepper

1. Place all ingredients into a food processor and pulse twenty times until finely chopped and combined. 2. Separate mixture into four equal sections and press each into a burger shape. Place burgers into ungreased air fryer basket. Adjust the temperature to 375ºF (191ºC) and air fry for 12 minutes, turning burgers halfway through cooking. Burgers will be browned and firm when done. 3. Place burgers on a large plate and let cool 5 minutes before serving.

Per Serving:
calories: 50 | fat: 3g | protein: 3g | carbs: 4g | fiber: 1g | sodium: 299mg

Stuffed Portobello Mushrooms

Prep time: 5 minutes | Cook time: 20 minutes | Serves 4

8 large portobello mushrooms
3 teaspoons extra-virgin olive oil, divided

4 cups fresh spinach
1 medium red bell pepper, diced
¼ cup crumbled feta

1. Preheat the oven to 450ºF. 2. Remove the stems from the mushrooms, and gently scoop out the gills and discard. Coat the mushrooms with 2 teaspoons of olive oil. 3. On a baking sheet, place the mushrooms cap-side down, and roast for 20 minutes. 4.

Meanwhile, heat the remaining 1 teaspoon of olive oil in a medium skillet over medium heat. When hot, sauté the spinach and red bell pepper for 8 to 10 minutes, stirring occasionally. 5. Remove the mushrooms from the oven. Drain, if necessary. Spoon the spinach and pepper mix into the mushrooms, and top with feta.

Per Serving:
calories: 91 | fat: 4.24g | protein: 6.04g | carbs: 9.77g | sugars: 5.96g | fiber: 3.5g | sodium: 155mg

Italian Tofu with Mushrooms and Peppers

Prep time: 5 minutes | Cook time: 10 minutes | Serves 2

1 teaspoon extra-virgin olive oil
¼ cup chopped bell pepper, any color
¼ cup chopped onions
1 garlic clove, minced
8 ounces firm tofu, drained and rinsed
½ cup sliced fresh button

mushrooms
1 portobello mushroom cap, chopped
1 tablespoon balsamic vinegar
1 teaspoon dried basil
Salt, to season
Freshly ground black pepper, to season

1. In a medium skillet set over medium heat, heat the olive oil. 2. Add the bell pepper, onions, and garlic. Sauté for 5 minutes, or until soft. 3. Add the tofu, button mushrooms, and portobello mushrooms, tossing and stirring. Reduce the heat to low. 4. Stir in the balsamic vinegar and basil. Season with salt and pepper. Simmer for 2 minutes. 5. Enjoy!

Per Serving:
calories: 142 | fat: 7.81g | protein: 12.76g | carbs: 8.58g | sugars: 3.77g | fiber: 1.8g | sodium: 326mg

Chickpea-Spinach Curry

Prep time: 5 minutes | Cook time: 10 minutes | Serves 2

1 cup frozen chopped spinach, thawed
1 cup canned chickpeas, drained and rinsed
½ cup frozen green beans
½ cup frozen broccoli florets
½ cup no-salt-added canned

chopped tomatoes, undrained
1 tablespoon curry powder
1 tablespoon granulated garlic
Salt, to season
Freshly ground black pepper, to season
½ cup chopped fresh parsley

1. In a medium saucepan set over high heat, stir together the spinach, chickpeas, green beans, broccoli, tomatoes and their juice, curry powder, and garlic. Season with salt and pepper. Bring to a fast boil. Reduce the heat to low. Cover and simmer for 10 minutes, or until heated through. 2. Top with the parsley, serve, and enjoy!

Per Serving:
calories: 203 | fat: 3.42g | protein: 12.63g | carbs: 34.72g | sugars: 6.94g | fiber: 13g | sodium: 375mg

Quinoa-White Bean Loaf

Prep time: 15 minutes | Cook time: 1 hour | Serves 2

Extra-virgin olive oil cooking spray
2 teaspoons extra-virgin olive oil
2 garlic cloves, minced
½ cup sliced fresh button mushrooms
6 ounces extra-firm tofu, crumbled
Salt, to season

Freshly ground black pepper, to season
1 (8-ounce) can cannellini beans, drained and rinsed
2 tablespoons coconut flour
1 tablespoon chia seeds
⅓ cup water
½ cup cooked quinoa
¼ cup chopped red onion
¼ cup chopped fresh parsley

1. Preheat the oven to 350°F. 2. Lightly coat 2 mini loaf pans with cooking spray. Set aside. 3. In a large skillet set over medium-high heat, heat the olive oil. 4. Add the garlic, mushrooms, and tofu. Season with salt and pepper. 5. Cook for 6 to 8 minutes, stirring occasionally, until the mushrooms and tofu are golden brown. 6. In a food processor, combine the cannellini beans, coconut flour, chia seeds, and water. Pulse until almost smooth. 7. In a large bowl, mix together the mushroom and tofu mixture, cannellini bean mixture, quinoa, red onion, and parsley. Season with salt and pepper. 8. Evenly divide the mixture between the 2 prepared loaf pans, gently pressing down and mounding the mixture in the middle. 9. Place the pans in the preheated oven. Bake for about 1 hour, or until firm and golden brown. Remove from the oven. Let rest for 10 minutes. 10. Slice and serve.

Per Serving:

calories: 193 | fat: 8.42g | protein: 12.26g | carbs: 20.3g | sugars: 4.02g | fiber: 4g | sodium: 366mg

Chile Relleno Casserole with Salsa Salad

Prep time: 10 minutes | Cook time: 55 minutes | Serves 4

Casserole
½ cup gluten-free flour (such as King Arthur or Cup4Cup brand)
1 teaspoon baking powder
6 large eggs
½ cup nondairy milk or whole milk
Three 4-ounce cans fire-roasted diced green chiles, drained
1 cup nondairy cheese shreds or shredded mozzarella cheese
Salad
1 head green leaf lettuce, shredded

2 Roma tomatoes, seeded and diced
1 green bell pepper, seeded and diced
½ small yellow onion, diced
1 jalapeño chile, seeded and diced (optional)
2 tablespoons chopped fresh cilantro
4 teaspoons extra-virgin olive oil
4 teaspoons fresh lime juice
⅛ teaspoon fine sea salt

1. To make the casserole: Pour 1 cup water into the Instant Pot. Butter a 7-cup round heatproof glass dish or coat with nonstick cooking spray and place the dish on a long-handled silicone steam rack. (If you don't have the long-handled rack, use the wire metal steam rack and a homemade sling) 2. In a medium bowl, whisk together the flour and baking powder. Add the eggs and milk and whisk until well blended, forming a batter. Stir in the chiles and ¾ cup of the cheese. 3. Pour the batter into the prepared dish and cover tightly with aluminum foil. Holding the handles of the steam rack, lower the dish into the Instant Pot. 4. Secure the lid and set the Pressure Release to Sealing. Select the Pressure Cook or Manual setting and set the cooking time for 40 minutes at high pressure. (The pot will take about 10 minutes to come up to pressure before the cooking program begins.) 5. When the cooking program ends, let the pressure release naturally for at least 10 minutes, then move the Pressure Release to Venting to release any remaining steam. Open the pot and, wearing heat-resistant mitts, grasp the handles of the steam rack and lift it out of the pot. Uncover the dish, taking care not to get burned by the steam or to drip condensation onto the casserole. While the casserole is still piping hot, sprinkle the remaining ¼ cup cheese evenly on top. Let the cheese melt for 5 minutes. 6. To make the salad: While the cheese is melting, in a large bowl, combine the lettuce, tomatoes, bell pepper, onion, jalapeño (if using), cilantro, oil, lime juice, and salt. Toss until evenly combined. 7. Cut the casserole into wedges. Serve warm, with the salad on the side.

Per Serving:

calorie: 361 | fat: 22g | protein: 21g | carbs: 23g | sugars: 8g | fiber: 3g | sodium: 421mg

Stuffed Peppers

Prep time: 20 minutes | Cook time: 50 minutes | Serves 2

½ cup water
¼ cup uncooked quinoa, thoroughly rinsed
1 tablespoon extra-virgin olive oil
1 garlic clove, minced
6 ounces extra-firm tofu, drained and sliced
½ cup marinara sauce, divided
¼ cup finely chopped walnuts
1 teaspoon dried basil

Salt, to season
Freshly ground black pepper, to season
1 red bell pepper, halved and seeded
1 orange bell pepper, halved and seeded
½ cup nonfat shredded mozzarella cheese, divided
4 tomato slices, divided

1. Preheat the oven to 350°F. 2. In a small pot set over high heat, bring the water to a boil. 3. Add the quinoa. Reduce the heat to low. Cover and simmer for about 15 minutes, or until tender and all the water is absorbed. Let cool. Fluff with a fork. Set aside. 4. In a skillet set over medium heat, stir together the olive oil, garlic, and tofu. Cook for about 5 minutes, or until the tofu is evenly brown. 5. Mix in ¼ cup of marinara, the walnuts, and basil. Season with salt and pepper. Cook for 5 minutes more, stirring. 6. Using a wooden spoon or spatula, press one-quarter of the cooked quinoa into each pepper half. 7. Top each with about 1 tablespoon of the remaining ¼ cup of marinara. 8. Sprinkle each with about 1 tablespoon of mozzarella cheese. 9. Place 1 tomato slice on each filled pepper. 10. Finish with about 1 tablespoon of the remaining ¼ cup of mozzarella cheese. 11. Transfer the stuffed peppers to a baking dish. Place the dish in the preheated oven. Bake for 25 minutes, or until the cheese melts. 12. Serve 1 stuffed red bell pepper half and 1 stuffed orange bell pepper half to each person and enjoy!

Per Serving:

calories: 399 | fat: 20.88g | protein: 24.71g | carbs: 33.3g | sugars: 6.65g | fiber: 6.2g | sodium: 535mg

Black-Eyed Pea Sauté with Garlic and Olives

Prep time: 5 minutes | Cook time: 5 minutes | Serves 2

2 teaspoons extra-virgin olive oil
1 garlic clove, minced
½ red onion, chopped
1 cup cooked black-eyed peas; if canned, drain and rinse
½ teaspoon dried thyme
¼ cup water
¼ teaspoon salt
¼ teaspoon freshly ground black pepper
6 Kalamata olives, pitted and halved

1. In a medium saucepan set over medium heat, stir together the olive oil, garlic, and red onion. Cook for 2 minutes, continuing to stir. 2. Add the black-eyed peas and thyme. Cook for 1 minute. 3. Stir in the water, salt, pepper, and olives. Cook for 2 minutes more, or until heated through.

Per Serving:
calories: 140 | fat: 6.13g | protein: 4.65g | carbs: 18.02g | sugars: 7.75g | fiber: 4.6g | sodium: 426mg

Edamame Falafel with Roasted Vegetables

Prep time: 10 minutes | Cook time: 55 minutes | Serves 2

For the roasted vegetables
1 cup broccoli florets
1 medium zucchini, sliced
½ cup cherry tomatoes, halved
1½ teaspoons extra-virgin olive oil
Salt, to season
Freshly ground black pepper, to season
Extra-virgin olive oil cooking spray
For the falafel
1 cup frozen shelled edamame, thawed
1 small onion, chopped
1 garlic clove, chopped
1 tablespoon freshly squeezed lemon juice
2 tablespoons hemp hearts
1 teaspoon ground cumin
2 tablespoons oat flour
¼ teaspoon salt
Pinch freshly ground black pepper
2 tablespoons extra-virgin olive oil, divided
Prepared hummus, for serving (optional)

To make the roasted vegetables 1. Preheat the oven to 425°F. 2. In a large bowl, toss together the broccoli, zucchini, tomatoes, and olive oil to coat. Season with salt and pepper. 3. Spray a baking sheet with cooking spray. 4. Spread the vegetables evenly atop the sheet. Place the sheet in the preheated oven. Roast for 35 to 40 minutes, stirring every 15 minutes, or until the vegetables are soft and cooked through. 5. Remove from the oven. Set aside. To make the falafel 1. In a food processor, pulse the edamame until coarsely ground. 2. Add the onion, garlic, lemon juice, and hemp hearts. Process until finely ground. Transfer the mixture to a medium bowl. 3. By hand, mix in the cumin, oat flour, salt, and pepper. 4. Roll the dough into 1-inch balls. Flatten slightly. You should have about 12 silver dollar-size patties. 5. In a large skillet set over medium heat, heat 1 tablespoon of olive oil. 6. Add 4 falafel patties to the pan at a time (or as many as will fit without crowding), and cook for about 3 minutes on each side, or until lightly browned. Remove from the pan. Repeat with the remaining 1 tablespoon of olive oil and falafel patties. 7. Serve immediately with the roasted vegetables and hummus (if using) and enjoy!

Per Serving:
calories: 316 | fat: 22.48g | protein: 11.78g | carbs: 20.68g | sugars: 3.73g | fiber: 5.8g | sodium: 649mg

Chickpea Coconut Curry

Prep time: 5 minutes | Cook time: 15 minutes | Serves 4

3 cups fresh or frozen cauliflower florets
2 cups unsweetened almond milk
1 (15-ounce) can coconut milk
1 (15-ounce) can low-sodium
chickpeas, drained and rinsed
1 tablespoon curry powder
¼ teaspoon ground ginger
¼ teaspoon garlic powder
⅛ teaspoon onion powder
¼ teaspoon salt

1. In a large stockpot, combine the cauliflower, almond milk, coconut milk, chickpeas, curry, ginger, garlic powder, and onion powder. Stir and cover. 2. Cook over medium-high heat for 10 minutes. 3. Reduce the heat to low, stir, and cook for 5 minutes more, uncovered. Season with up to ¼ teaspoon salt.

Per Serving:
calories: 225 | fat: 6.9g | protein: 12.46g | carbs: 30.99g | sugars: 14.27g | fiber: 9.3g | sodium: 489mg

Cheesy Zucchini Patties

Prep time: 10 minutes | Cook time: 20 minutes | Serves 2

1 cup grated zucchini
1 cup chopped fresh mushrooms
½ cup grated carrot
½ cup nonfat shredded mozzarella cheese
¼ cup finely ground flaxseed
1 large egg, beaten
1 garlic clove, minced
Salt, to season
Freshly ground black pepper, to season
1 tablespoon extra-virgin olive oil
4 cup mixed baby greens, divided

1. In a medium bowl, stir together the zucchini, mushrooms, carrot, mozzarella cheese, flaxseed, egg, and garlic. Season with salt and pepper. Stir again to combine. 2. In a large skillet set over medium-high heat, heat the olive oil. 3. Drop 1 tablespoon of the zucchini mixture into the skillet. Continue dropping tablespoon-size portions in the pan until it is full, but not crowded. Cook for 2 to 3 minutes on each side, or until golden. Transfer to a serving plate. Repeat with the remaining mixture. 4. Place 2 cups of greens on each serving plate. Top each with zucchini patties. 5. Enjoy!

Per Serving:
calories: 252 | fat: 14.61g | protein: 18.96g | carbs: 14.36g | sugars: 3.67g | fiber: 8.6g | sodium: 644mg

Greek Stuffed Eggplant

Prep time: 15 minutes | Cook time: 20 minutes | Serves 2

1 large eggplant
2 tablespoons unsalted butter
¼ medium yellow onion, diced
¼ cup chopped artichoke hearts
1 cup fresh spinach
2 tablespoons diced red bell pepper
½ cup crumbled feta

1. Slice eggplant in half lengthwise and scoop out flesh, leaving enough inside for shell to remain intact. Take eggplant that was scooped out, chop it, and set aside. 2. In a medium skillet over medium heat, add butter and onion. Sauté until onions begin to soften, about 3 to 5 minutes. Add chopped eggplant, artichokes, spinach, and bell pepper. Continue cooking 5 minutes until peppers soften and spinach wilts. Remove from the heat and gently fold in the feta. 3. Place filling into each eggplant shell and place into the air fryer basket. 4. Adjust the temperature to 320°F (160°C) and air fry for 20 minutes. 5. Eggplant will be tender when done. Serve warm.

Per Serving:

calories: 259 | fat: 16.32g | protein: 9.81g | carbs: 22.16g | sugars: 12.44g | fiber: 10.1g | sodium: 386mg

Easy Cheesy Vegetable Frittata

Prep time: 10 minutes | Cook time: 15 minutes | Serves 2

Extra-virgin olive oil cooking spray
½ cup sliced onion
½ cup sliced green bell pepper
½ cup sliced eggplant
½ cup frozen spinach
½ cup sliced fresh mushrooms
1 tablespoon chopped fresh
basil
Pinch freshly ground black pepper
½ cup liquid egg substitute
½ cup nonfat cottage cheese
¼ cup fat-free evaporated milk
¼ cup nonfat shredded Cheddar cheese

1. Coat an ovenproof 10-inch skillet with cooking spray. Place it over medium-low heat until hot. 2. Add the onion, green bell pepper, eggplant, spinach, and mushrooms. Sauté for 2 to 3 minutes, or until lightly browned. 3. Add the basil. Season with pepper. Stir to combine. Cook for 2 to 3 minutes more, or until the flavors blend. Remove from the heat. 4. Preheat the broiler. 5. In a blender, combine the egg substitute, cottage cheese, Cheddar cheese, and evaporated milk. Process until smooth. Pour the egg mixture over the vegetables in the skillet. 6. Return the skillet to medium-low heat. Cover and cook for about 5 minutes, or until the bottom sets and the top is still slightly wet. 7. Transfer the ovenproof skillet to the broiler. Broil for 2 to 3 minutes, or until the top is set. 8. Serve one-half of the frittata per person and enjoy!

Per Serving:

calories: 177 | fat: 7.23g | protein: 17.07g | carbs: 12.4g | sugars: 6.22g | fiber: 2.6g | sodium: 408mg

Chickpea and Tofu Bolognese

Prep time: 5 minutes | Cook time: 25 minutes | Serves 4

1 (3- to 4-pound) spaghetti squash
½ teaspoon ground cumin
1 cup no-sugar-added spaghetti
sauce
1 (15-ounce) can low-sodium chickpeas, drained and rinsed
6 ounces extra-firm tofu

1. Preheat the oven to 400°F. 2. Cut the squash in half lengthwise. Scoop out the seeds and discard. 3. Season both halves of the squash with the cumin, and place them on a baking sheet cut-side down. Roast for 25 minutes. 4. Meanwhile, heat a medium saucepan over low heat, and pour in the spaghetti sauce and chickpeas. 5. Press the tofu between two layers of paper towels, and gently squeeze out any excess water. 6. Crumble the tofu into the sauce and cook for 15 minutes. 7. Remove the squash from the oven, and comb through the flesh of each half with a fork to make thin strands. 8. Divide the "spaghetti" into four portions, and top each portion with one-quarter of the sauce.

Per Serving:

calories: 221 | fat: 6.39g | protein: 12.46g | carbs: 31.8g | sugars: 6.36g | fiber: 7.8g | sodium: 405mg

Veggie Fajitas

Prep time: 10 minutes | Cook time: 15 minutes | Serves 4

For The Guacamole
2 small avocados pitted and peeled
1 teaspoon freshly squeezed lime juice
¼ teaspoon salt
9 cherry tomatoes, halved
For The Fajitas
1 red bell pepper
1 green bell pepper
1 small white onion
Avocado oil cooking spray
1 cup canned low-sodium black beans, drained and rinsed
½ teaspoon ground cumin
¼ teaspoon chili powder
¼ teaspoon garlic powder
4 (6-inch) yellow corn tortillas

To Make The Guacamole 1. In a medium bowl, use a fork to mash the avocados with the lime juice and salt. 2. Gently stir in the cherry tomatoes. To Make The Fajitas 1. Cut the red bell pepper, green bell pepper, and onion into ½-inch slices. 2. Heat a large skillet over medium heat. When hot, coat the cooking surface with cooking spray. Put the peppers, onion, and beans into the skillet. 3. Add the cumin, chili powder, and garlic powder, and stir. 4. Cover and cook for 15 minutes, stirring halfway through. 5. Divide the fajita mixture equally between the tortillas, and top with guacamole and any preferred garnishes.

Per Serving:

calories: 269 | fat: 15g | protein: 8g | carbs: 30g | sugars: 5g | fiber: 11g | sodium: 175mg

Crispy Eggplant Rounds

Prep time: 15 minutes | Cook time: 10 minutes | Serves 4

1 large eggplant, ends trimmed, cut into ½-inch slices
½ teaspoon salt
2 ounces (57 g) Parmesan 100%
cheese crisps, finely ground
½ teaspoon paprika
¼ teaspoon garlic powder
1 large egg

1. Sprinkle eggplant rounds with salt. Place rounds on a kitchen towel for 30 minutes to draw out excess water. Pat rounds dry. 2. In a medium bowl, mix cheese crisps, paprika, and garlic powder. In a separate medium bowl, whisk egg. Dip each eggplant round in egg, then gently press into cheese crisps to coat both sides. 3. Place eggplant rounds into ungreased air fryer basket. Adjust the temperature to 400°F (204°C) and air fry for 10 minutes, turning rounds halfway through cooking. Eggplant will be golden and crispy when done. Serve warm.

Per Serving:

calories: 113 | fat: 5g | protein: 7g | carbs: 10g | fiber: 4g | sodium: 567mg

The Ultimate Veggie Burger

Prep time: 5 minutes | Cook time: 10 minutes | Serves 2

¾ cup shelled edamame
¾ cup frozen mixed vegetables, thawed
3 tablespoons hemp hearts
2 tablespoons quick-cook oatmeal
¼ teaspoon salt
¼ teaspoon onion powder
¼ teaspoon ground cumin
1 scallion, sliced
2 teaspoons chopped fresh cilantro
2 tablespoons coconut flour
2 large egg whites
Extra-virgin olive oil cooking spray

1. In a food processor, combine the edamame, mixed vegetables, hemp hearts, oatmeal, salt, onion powder, cumin, scallion, cilantro, coconut flour, and egg whites. Pulse until blended, but not completely puréed. You want some texture. 2. Spray a nonstick skillet with cooking spray. Place it over medium-high heat. 3. Spoon half of the mixture into the pan. Using the back of a spoon, spread it out to form a patty. Repeat with the remaining half of the mixture. 4. Cook for 3 to 5 minutes, or until golden, and flip. Cook for about 3 minutes more, or until golden. Turn off the heat. 5. Transfer to serving plates and enjoy!

Per Serving:

calories: 154 | fat: 3.64g | protein: 12.86g | carbs: 18.69g | sugars: 4.25g | fiber: 7g | sodium: 467mg

Tofu and Bean Chili

Prep time: 10 minutes | Cook time 30 minutes | Serves 4

1 (15-ounce) can low-sodium dark red kidney beans, drained and rinsed, divided
2 (15-ounce) cans no-salt-added diced tomatoes
1½ cups low-sodium vegetable broth
½ teaspoon chili powder
½ teaspoon ground cumin
½ teaspoon garlic powder
½ teaspoon dried oregano
¼ teaspoon onion powder
¼ teaspoon salt
8 ounces extra-firm tofu

1. In a small bowl, mash ⅓ of the beans with a fork. 2. Put the mashed beans, the remaining whole beans, and the diced tomatoes with their juices in a large stockpot. 3. Add the broth, chili powder, cumin, garlic powder, dried oregano, onion powder, and salt. Simmer over medium-high heat for 15 minutes. 4. Press the tofu between 3 or 4 layers of paper towels to squeeze out any excess moisture. 5. Crumble the tofu into the stockpot and stir. Simmer for another 10 to 15 minutes.

Per Serving:

calories: 207 | fat: 4.73g | protein: 14.71g | carbs: 31.18g | sugars: 10.97g | fiber: 11.6g | sodium: 376mg

Seitan Curry

Prep time: 10 minutes | Cook time: 15 minutes | Serves 2

1 tablespoon extra-virgin olive oil
½ cup chopped onion
2 garlic cloves, chopped
1 cup cauliflower florets
½ cup diced carrots
6 ounces seitan (wheat gluten), finely chopped
2 teaspoons garam masala
1 cup diced tomatoes
⅓ cup unsweetened light canned coconut milk
¼ cup water
Salt, to season
Freshly ground black pepper, to season
2 tablespoons chopped cashews, for garnish

1. In a large wok or skillet set over high heat, heat the olive oil. 2. Add the onion and garlic. Sauté for 3 minutes. 3. Add the cauliflower, carrots, seitan, and garam masala. Mix well. Reduce the heat to medium-high. 4. Stir in the tomatoes, coconut milk, and water. Cover and bring to a simmer. Cook for about 10 minutes, covered, or until the cauliflower and carrots are tender. 5. Season with salt and pepper. Garnish with the cashews. 6. Serve and enjoy!

Per Serving:

calories: 617 | fat: 28.29g | protein:5.32 g | carbs: 43g | sugars: 8.31g | fiber: 5.7g | sodium: 434.3mg

Green Ginger Soup

Prep time: 10 minutes | Cook time: 30 minutes | Serves 2

½ cup chopped onion
½ cup peeled, chopped fennel
1 small zucchini, chopped
½ cup frozen lima beans
¼ cup uncooked brown rice
1 bay leaf
1 teaspoon dried basil
⅛ teaspoon freshly ground black pepper
2 cups water

1 cup frozen green beans
¼ cup fresh parsley, chopped
1 (3-inch) piece fresh ginger, peeled, grated, and pressed through a strainer to extract the juice (about 2 to 3 tablespoons)
Salt, to season
2 tablespoons chopped fresh chives

1. In a large pot set over medium-high heat, stir together the onion, fennel, zucchini, lima beans, rice, bay leaf, basil, pepper, and water. Bring to a boil. Reduce the heat to low. Simmer for 15 minutes. 2. Add the green beans. Simmer for about 5 minutes, uncovered, until tender. 3. Stir in the parsley. 4. Remove and discard the bay leaf. 5. In a blender or food processor, purée the soup in batches until smooth, adding water if necessary to thin. 6. Blend in the ginger juice. 7. Season with salt. Garnish with the chives. 8. Serve hot and enjoy immediately!

Per Serving:

calories: 189 | fat: 1.52g | protein: 7.14g | carbs: 38.58g | sugars: 3.1g | fiber: 6.8g | sodium: 338mg

Turkey and Pinto Chili

Prep time: 0 minutes | Cook time: 60 minutes | Serves 8

2 tablespoons cold-pressed avocado oil
4 garlic cloves, diced
1 large yellow onion, diced
4 jalapeño chiles, seeded and diced
2 carrots, diced
4 celery stalks, diced
2 teaspoons fine sea salt
2 pounds 93 percent lean ground turkey
Two 4-ounce cans fire-roasted diced green chiles

4 tablespoons chili powder
2 teaspoons ground cumin
2 teaspoons ground coriander
1 teaspoon dried oregano
1 teaspoon dried sage
1 cup low-sodium chicken broth
3 cups drained cooked pinto beans, or two 15-ounce cans pinto beans, drained and rinsed
Two 14½-ounce cans no-salt petite diced tomatoes and their liquid
¼ cup tomato paste

1. Select the Sauté setting on the Instant Pot and heat the oil and garlic for 3 minutes, until the garlic is bubbling but not browned. Add the onion, jalapeños, carrots, celery, and salt and sauté for 5 minutes, until the onion begins to soften. Add the turkey and sauté, using a wooden spoon or spatula to break up the meat as it cooks, for 6 minutes, until cooked through and no streaks of pink remain. Stir in the green chiles, chili powder, cumin, coriander, oregano, sage, and broth, using a wooden spoon or spatula to nudge any browned bits from the bottom of the pot. 2. Pour in the beans in a layer on top of the turkey. Pour in the tomatoes and their liquid and add the tomato paste in a dollop on top. Do not stir in the beans, tomatoes, or tomato paste. 3. Secure the lid and set the Pressure Release to Sealing. Press the Cancel button to reset the cooking program, then select the Pressure Cook or Manual setting and set the cooking time for 15 minutes at high pressure. (The pot will take about 15 minutes to come up to pressure before the cooking program begins.) 4. When the cooking program ends, let the pressure release naturally for at least 20 minutes, then move the Pressure Release to Venting to release any remaining steam. Open the pot and stir the chili to mix all of the ingredients. 5. Press the Cancel button to reset the cooking program, then select the Sauté setting and set the cooking time for 10 minutes. Allow the chili to reduce and thicken. Do not stir the chili while it is cooking, as this will cause it to sputter more. 6. When the cooking program ends, the pot will turn off. Wearing heat-resistant mitts, remove the inner pot from the housing. Wait for about 2 minutes to allow the chili to stop simmering, then give it a final stir. 7. Ladle the chili into bowls and serve hot.

Per Serving:

calories: 354 | fat: 14g | protein: 30g | carbs: 28g | sugars: 6g | fiber: 9g | sodium: 819mg

Ham and Potato Chowder

Prep time: 25 minutes | Cook time: 8 hour s | Serves 5

5-ounce package scalloped potatoes
Sauce mix from potato package
1 cup extra-lean, reduced-sodium, cooked ham, cut into narrow strips
4 teaspoons sodium-free

bouillon powder
4 cups water
1 cup chopped celery
⅓ cup chopped onions
Pepper to taste
2 cups fat-free half-and-half
⅓ cup flour

1. Combine potatoes, sauce mix, ham, bouillon powder, water, celery, onions, and pepper in the inner pot of the Instant Pot. 2. Secure the lid and cook using the Slow Cook function on low for 7 hours. 3. Combine half-and-half and flour. Remove the lid and gradually add to the inner pot, blending well. 4. Secure the lid once more and cook on the low Slow Cook function for up to 1 hour more, stirring occasionally until thickened.

Per Serving:

calories: 241 | fat: 3g | protein: 11g | carbs: 41g | sugars: 8g | fiber: 3g | sodium: 836mg

Buttercup Squash Soup

Prep time: 15 minutes | Cook time: 10 minutes | Serves 6

2 tablespoons extra-virgin olive oil
1 medium onion, chopped
4 to 5 cups Vegetable Broth or Chicken Bone Broth
1½ pounds buttercup squash,
peeled, seeded, and cut into 1-inch chunks
½ teaspoon kosher salt
¼ teaspoon ground white pepper
Whole nutmeg, for grating

1. Set the electric pressure cooker to the Sauté setting. When the pot is hot, pour in the olive oil. 2. Add the onion and sauté for 3 to 5 minutes, until it begins to soften. Hit Cancel. 3. Add the broth, squash, salt, and pepper to the pot and stir. (If you want a thicker soup, use 4 cups of broth. If you want a thinner, drinkable soup, use 5 cups.) 4. Close and lock the lid of the pressure cooker. Set the valve to sealing. 5. Cook on high pressure for 10 minutes. 6. When the cooking is complete, hit Cancel and allow the pressure to release naturally. 7. Once the pin drops, unlock and remove the lid. 8. Use an immersion blender to purée the soup right in the pot. If you don't have an immersion blender, transfer the soup to a blender or food processor and purée. (Follow the instructions that came with your machine for blending hot foods.) 9. Pour the soup into serving bowls and grate nutmeg on top.

Per Serving:

calories: 320 | fat: 15.86g | protein: 36.2g | carbs: 7g | sugars: 3.37g | fiber: 1.6g | sodium: 856mg

Hearty Beef and Veggie Stew

Prep time: 15 minutes | Cook time: 45 minutes | Serves 4

2 tablespoons (30 ml) avocado oil
1 pound (454 g) extra lean beef stew meat
1 medium yellow onion, cut into large chunks
4 large carrots, cut into 2-inch (5-cm) chunks
5 to 6 small red potatoes,
quartered
3 cups (720 ml) low-sodium beef broth
½ teaspoon salt
½ teaspoon black pepper
¼ to ⅓ cup (16 to 21 g) finely chopped fresh herbs of choice (see Tip)

1. Heat the oil in a large Dutch oven or pot over medium-high heat. 2. Add the stew meat and cook it for 2 to 3 minutes on each side, until it is brown on all sides but still pink in the center. Remove the stew meat from the Dutch oven and set it aside. 3. Add the onion and carrots to the Dutch oven and cook them for 5 to 10 minutes, until they start to soften. 4. Add the potatoes, broth, salt, black pepper, and herbs. Bring the mixture to a boil. Reduce the heat to low and simmer the stew for 30 minutes, until the vegetables are fork-tender. 5. Add the stew meat to the stew and cook it for 5 to 10 minutes to warm the meat through. Serve the stew immediately.

Per Serving:

calorie: 400 | fat: 11g | protein: 32g | carbs: 45g | sugars: 8g | fiber: 6g | sodium: 742mg

Tasty Tomato Soup

Prep time: 10 minutes | Cook time: 1 hour 25 minutes | Serves 2

3 cups chopped tomatoes
1 red bell pepper, cut into chunks
2 tablespoons extra-virgin olive oil, divided
Salt, to season
Freshly ground black pepper, to season
1 medium onion, chopped
1 garlic clove, minced
2 cups low-sodium vegetable broth
1 cup sliced fresh button mushrooms
½ cup fresh chopped basil

1. Preheat the oven to 400°F. 2. On a baking sheet, spread out the tomatoes and red bell pepper. 3. Drizzle with 1 tablespoon of olive oil. Toss to coat. Season with salt and pepper. Place the sheet in the preheated oven. Roast for 45 minutes. 4. In a large stockpot set over medium heat, heat the remaining 1 tablespoon of olive oil. 5. Add the onion. Cook for 2 to 3 minutes, or until tender. 6. Stir in the garlic. Cook for 2 minutes more. 7. Add the vegetable broth, mushrooms, and basil. 8. Stir in the roasted tomatoes and peppers. Reduce the heat to medium-low. Cook for 30 minutes. 9. To a blender or food processor, carefully transfer the soup in batches, blending until smooth. Return the processed soup to the pot. Simmer for 5 minutes. 10. Serve warm and enjoy!

Per Serving:

calories: 255 | fat: 15.09g | protein: 5.97g | carbs: 28.64g | sugars: 17.95g | fiber: 6.6g | sodium: 738mg

Down South Corn Soup

Prep time: 10 minutes | Cook time: 35 minutes | Serves 8 to 10

1 tablespoon extra-virgin olive oil
½ Vidalia onion, minced
2 garlic cloves, minced
3 cups chopped cabbage
1 small cauliflower, broken into florets or 1 (10-ounce) bag frozen cauliflower
1 (10-ounce) bag frozen corn
1 cup store-bought low-sodium vegetable broth
1 teaspoon smoked paprika
1 teaspoon ground cumin
1 teaspoon dried dill
½ teaspoon freshly ground black pepper
1 cup plain unsweetened cashew milk

1. In a large stockpot, heat the oil over medium heat. 2. Add the onion and garlic, and sauté, stirring to prevent the garlic from scorching, for 3 to 5 minutes, or until translucent. 3. Add the cabbage and a splash of water, cover, and cook for 5 minutes, or until tender. 4. Add the cauliflower, corn, broth, paprika, cumin, dill, and pepper. Cover and cook for 20 minutes, or until tender. 5. Add the cashew milk and stir well. Cover and cook for 5 minutes, letting the flavors come together. 6. Serve with a heaping plate of greens and seafood of your choice.

Per Serving:

calories: 98 | fat: 3.41g | protein: 3.52g | carbs: 14.83g | sugars: 6.17g | fiber: 2.5g | sodium: 53mg

Pasta e Fagioli with Ground Beef

Prep time: 0 minutes | Cook time: 30 minutes | Serves 8

2 tablespoons extra-virgin olive oil
4 garlic cloves, minced
1 yellow onion, diced
2 large carrots, diced
4 celery stalks, diced
1½ pounds 95 percent extra-lean ground beef
4 cups low-sodium vegetable broth
2 teaspoons Italian seasoning
½ teaspoon freshly ground black pepper

1¼ cups chickpea-based elbow pasta or whole-wheat elbow pasta
1½ cups drained cooked kidney beans, or one 15-ounce can kidney beans, rinsed and drained
One 28-ounce can whole San Marzano tomatoes and their liquid
2 tablespoons chopped fresh flat-leaf parsley

1. Select the Sauté setting on the Instant Pot and heat the oil and garlic for 2 minutes, until the garlic is bubbling but not browned. Add the onion, carrots, and celery and sauté for 5 minutes, until the onion begins to soften. Add the beef and sauté, using a wooden spoon or spatula to break up the meat as it cooks, for 5 minutes; it's fine if some streaks of pink remain, the beef does not need to be cooked through. 2. Stir in the broth, Italian seasoning, pepper, and pasta, making sure all of the pasta is submerged in the liquid. Add the beans and stir to mix. Add the tomatoes and their liquid, crushing the tomatoes with your hands as you add them to the pot. Do not stir them in. 3. Secure the lid and set the Pressure Release to Sealing. Press the Cancel button to reset the cooking program, then select the Pressure Cook or Manual setting and set the cooking time for 2 minutes at low pressure. (The pot will take about 15 minutes to come up to pressure before the cooking program begins.) 4. When the cooking program ends, let the pressure release naturally for 10 minutes, then move the Pressure Release to Venting to release any remaining steam. Open the pot and stir the soup to mix all of the ingredients. 5. Ladle the soup into bowls, sprinkle with the parsley, and serve right away.

Per Serving:

calories: 278 | fat: 9g | protein: 26g | carbs: 25g | sugars: 4g | fiber: 6g | sodium: 624mg

Turkey Barley Vegetable Soup

Prep time: 5 minutes | Cook time: 20 minutes | Serves 8

2 tablespoons avocado oil
1 pound ground turkey
4 cups Chicken Bone Broth, low-sodium store-bought chicken broth, or water
1 (28-ounce) carton or can diced tomatoes
2 tablespoons tomato paste
1 (15-ounce) package frozen

chopped carrots (about 2½ cups)
1 (15-ounce) package frozen peppers and onions (about 2½ cups)
⅓ cup dry barley
1 teaspoon kosher salt
¼ teaspoon freshly ground black pepper
2 bay leaves

1. Set the electric pressure cooker to the Sauté/More setting. When

the pot is hot, pour in the avocado oil. 2. Add the turkey to the pot and sauté, stirring frequently to break up the meat, for about 7 minutes or until the turkey is no longer pink. Hit Cancel. 3. Add the broth, tomatoes and their juices, and tomato paste. Stir in the carrots, peppers and onions, barley, salt, pepper, and bay leaves. 4. Close and lock the lid of the pressure cooker. Set the valve to sealing. 5. Cook on high pressure for 20 minutes. 6. When the cooking is complete, hit Cancel and allow the pressure to release naturally for 10 minutes, then quick release any remaining pressure. 7. Once the pin drops, unlock and remove the lid. Discard the bay leaves. 8. Spoon into bowls and serve.

Per Serving:

calories: 203 | fat: 8.73g | protein: 14.62g | carbs: 18.17g | sugars: 7.62g | fiber: 5.6g | sodium: 793mg

Minestrone with Parmigiano-Reggiano

Prep time: 25 minutes | Cook time: 3 to 8 hours | Serves 8

2 tablespoons extra-virgin olive oil
3 cloves garlic, minced
1 cup coarsely chopped sweet onion
1 cup coarsely chopped carrots
1 cup coarsely chopped celery
1 tablespoon finely chopped fresh rosemary
1 (14- to 15-ounce / 397- to 425-g) can plum tomatoes, with their juice
¼ cup dry white wine
2 medium zucchini, cut into ½-inch rounds
1 (14- to 15-ounce / 397- to 425-g) can small white beans, drained and rinsed
1 head escarole or Savoy

cabbage, cut into small pieces
8 ounces (227 g) green beans, ends snipped, cut into 1-inch pieces
1 medium head cauliflower, cut into florets
Rind from Parmigiano-Reggiano cheese, cut into ½-inch pieces, plus ½ to 1 cup finely grated Parmigiano-Reggiano cheese, for garnish
2 cups vegetable broth
1 teaspoon salt
½ teaspoon freshly ground black pepper
8 ounces (227 g) cooked small pasta (shells, ditalini, or other short tubular pasta)

1. Heat the oil in a large skillet over medium-high heat. Add the garlic, onion, carrots, celery, and rosemary and sauté until the vegetables begin to soften, 4 to 5 minutes. 2. Add the tomatoes and wine and allow some of the liquid to evaporate in the pan. 3. Transfer the contents of the skillet to the insert of a 5- to 7-quart slow cooker. Add the zucchini, white beans, cabbage, green beans, cauliflower, Parmigiano-Reggiano rind, broth, salt, and pepper. 4. Cover the slow cooker and cook on high for 3 to 4 hours or on low for 6 to 8 hours. 5. Stir in the cooked pasta at the end of the cooking time, cover, and set on warm until ready to serve. Serve the soup garnished with the grated Parmigiano-Reggiano.

Per Serving:

calories: 224 | fat: 5g | protein: 9g | carbs: 40g | net carbs: 29g | sugars: 11g | fiber: g | sodium: 552mg | cholesterol: 0mg

Quick Moroccan-Inspired Chicken Stew

Prep time: 5 minutes | Cook time: 15 minutes | Serves 4 to 6

2 teaspoons ground cumin
1 teaspoon ground cinnamon
½ teaspoon turmeric
½ teaspoon paprika
1½ pounds boneless, skinless chicken, cut into strips
2 tablespoons extra-virgin olive oil

5 garlic cloves, smashed and coarsely chopped
2 onions, thinly sliced
1 tablespoon fresh lemon zest
½ cup coarsely chopped olives
2 cups low-sodium chicken broth
Cilantro, for garnish (optional)

1. In a medium bowl, mix together the cumin, cinnamon, turmeric, and paprika until well blended. Add the chicken, tossing to coat, and set aside. 2. Heat the extra-virgin olive oil in a large skillet or medium Dutch oven over medium-high heat. Add the chicken and garlic in one layer and cook, browning on all sides, about 2 minutes. 3. Add the onions, lemon zest, olives, and broth and bring the soup to a boil. Reduce the heat to medium low, cover, and simmer for 8 minutes. 4. Uncover the soup and let it simmer for another 2 to 3 minutes for the sauce to thicken slightly. Adjust the seasonings as desired and serve garnished with cilantro (if using). 5. Store the cooled soup in an airtight container in the refrigerator for up to 5 days.

Per Serving:
calories: 252 | fat: 10.35g | protein: 12.62g | carbs: 27.57g | sugars: 6.45g | fiber: 2.6g | sodium: 451mg

Manhattan Clam Chowder

Prep time: 10 minutes | Cook time: 1 hour 30 minutes | Serves 8

3 medium carrots, peeled and coarsely chopped
3 large white or russet potatoes, peeled and coarsely chopped
4 celery stalks, coarsely chopped

2½ cups minced clams, drained
2 cups canned tomatoes, slightly crushed
½ teaspoon dried thyme or 1 teaspoon minced fresh thyme
Freshly ground black pepper

1. Add all the ingredients to a large stockpot. Cover and let simmer for 1½ hours. Taste and add a dash of salt if needed. Serve hot.

Per Serving:
calories: 164 | fat: 0.42g | protein: 4.05g | carbs: 37.36g | sugars: 5.54g | fiber: 3.4g | sodium: 305mg

Jamaican Stew

Prep time: 10 minutes | Cook time: 20 minutes | Serves 4

1½ cups chopped onions
3-4 cups cubed plantains (see Note; can substitute sweet potatoes)
1¼ teaspoons sea salt

1½ teaspoons ground coriander
½ teaspoon ground cumin
½ teaspoon ground turmeric
1 teaspoon dried thyme
½ teaspoon ground allspice

¼ teaspoon crushed red-pepper flakes (or to taste)
1 small can (5.5 ounces) light coconut milk
3½ cups water
2 cans (15 ounces each) black beans or adzuki beans, rinsed and drained
3 cups cauliflower florets

2 tablespoons freshly grated ginger
3 tablespoons freshly squeezed lime juice
3 cups baby spinach leaves
¼ cup freshly chopped cilantro (optional)
Lime wedges for serving

1. In a large pot over medium or medium-high heat, combine the onion, plantains, salt, coriander, cumin, turmeric, thyme, allspice, red-pepper flakes, and a few tablespoons of the coconut milk. Cook for 6 to 7 minutes, stirring occasionally. Add the water, beans, cauliflower, ginger, and remaining coconut milk. Increase the heat to high to bring to a boil, then reduce the heat to low, cover, and cook for 12 to 15 minutes, or until the plantains are cooked through. Add the lime juice, spinach, and cilantro (if using), and stir just until the spinach wilts. Serve immediately, with the lime wedges.

Per Serving:
calorie: 426 | fat: 5g | protein: 16g | carbs: 88g | sugars: 22g | fiber: 22g | sodium: 1053mg

Creamy Sweet Potato Soup

Prep time: 15 minutes | Cook time: 10 minutes | Serves 6

2 tablespoons avocado oil
1 small onion, chopped
2 celery stalks, chopped
2 teaspoons minced garlic
1 teaspoon kosher salt
½ teaspoon freshly ground black pepper
1 teaspoon ground turmeric
½ teaspoon ground cinnamon
2 pounds sweet potatoes, peeled

and cut into 1-inch cubes
3 cups Vegetable Broth or Chicken Bone Broth
Plain Greek yogurt, to garnish (optional)
Chopped fresh parsley, to garnish (optional)
Pumpkin seeds (pepitas), to garnish (optional)

1. Set the electric pressure cooker to the Sauté setting. When the pot is hot, pour in the avocado oil. 2. Sauté the onion and celery for 3 to 5 minutes or until the vegetables begin to soften. 3. Stir in the garlic, salt, pepper, turmeric, and cinnamon. Hit Cancel. 4. Stir in the sweet potatoes and broth. 5. Close and lock the lid of the pressure cooker. Set the valve to sealing. 6. Cook on high pressure for 10 minutes. 7. When the cooking is complete, hit Cancel and allow the pressure to release naturally. 8. Once the pin drops, unlock and remove the lid. 9. Use an immersion blender to purée the soup right in the pot. If you don't have an immersion blender, transfer the soup to a blender or food processor and purée. (Follow the instructions that came with your machine for blending hot foods.) 10. Spoon into bowls and serve topped with Greek yogurt, parsley, and/or pumpkin seeds (if using).

Per Serving:
calories: 175 | fat: 5.26g | protein: 4.69g | carbs: 28.87g | sugars: 3.99g | fiber: 3.5g | sodium: 706mg

Pasta e Fagioli

Prep time: 10 minutes | Cook time: 25 minutes | Serves 12

1 tablespoon extra-virgin olive oil
1 large onion, chopped
3 cloves garlic, crushed
2 medium carrots, sliced
2 medium zucchini, sliced
2 tablespoons finely chopped fresh basil
2 teaspoons finely chopped

fresh oregano
Two 14.5-ounce cans unsalted tomatoes with liquid
Two 15-ounce cans low-sodium white cannellini or navy beans, drained and rinsed
¾ pound whole-wheat uncooked rigatoni or shell pasta

1. In a large saucepan, heat the oil and sauté the onion and garlic for 5 minutes. 2. Add the carrots, zucchini, basil, oregano, tomatoes with their liquid, and beans. Cook until the vegetables are just tender, about 15-17 minutes. 3. In a separate saucepan, cook the pasta according to package directions (without adding salt). Add the pasta to the soup, and mix thoroughly. Serve warm with crusty bread.

Per Serving:

calories: 84 | fat: 1.2g | protein: 3.81g | carbs: 15.64g | sugars: 1.16g | fiber: 3.1g | sodium: 68mg

Hot and Sour Soup

Prep time: 0 minutes | Cook time: 30 minutes | Serves 6

4 cups boiling water
1 ounce dried shiitake mushrooms
2 tablespoons cold-pressed avocado oil
3 garlic cloves, chopped
4 ounces cremini or button mushrooms, sliced
1 pound boneless pork loin, sirloin, or tip, thinly sliced against the grain into ¼-inch-thick, ½-inch-wide, 2-inch-long strips
1 teaspoon ground ginger
½ teaspoon ground white pepper
2 cups low-sodium chicken

broth or vegetable broth
One 8-ounce can sliced bamboo shoots, drained and rinsed
2 tablespoons low-sodium soy sauce
1 tablespoon chile garlic sauce
1 teaspoon toasted sesame oil
2 teaspoons Lakanto Monkfruit Sweetener Classic
2 large eggs
¼ cup rice vinegar
2 tablespoons cornstarch
4 green onions, white and green parts, thinly sliced
¼ cup chopped fresh cilantro

1. In a large liquid measuring cup or heatproof bowl, pour the boiling water over the shiitake mushrooms. Cover and let soak for 30 minutes. Drain the mushrooms, reserving the soaking liquid. Remove and discard the stems and thinly slice the caps. 2. Select the Sauté setting on the Instant Pot and heat the avocado oil and garlic for 2 minutes, until the garlic is bubbling but not browned. Add the cremini and shiitake mushrooms and sauté for 3 minutes, until the mushrooms are beginning to wilt. Add the pork, ginger, and white pepper and sauté for about 5 minutes, until the pork is opaque and cooked through. 3. Pour the mushroom soaking liquid into the pot, being careful to leave behind any sediment at the bottom of the measuring cup or bowl. Using a wooden spoon,

nudge any browned bits from the bottom of the pot. Stir in the broth, bamboo shoots, soy sauce, chile garlic sauce, sesame oil, and sweetener. 4. Secure the lid and set the Pressure Release to Sealing. Press the Cancel button to reset the cooking program, then select the Pressure Cook or Manual setting and set the cooking time for 5 minutes at high pressure. (The pot will take about 10 minutes to come up to pressure before the cooking program begins.) 5. While the soup is cooking, in a small bowl, beat the eggs until no streaks of yolk remain. 6. When the cooking program ends, let the pressure release naturally for at least 15 minutes, then move the Pressure Release to Venting to release any remaining steam. 7. In a small bowl, stir together the vinegar and cornstarch until the cornstarch dissolves. Open the pot and stir the vinegar mixture into the soup. Press the Cancel button to reset the cooking program, then select the Sauté setting. Bring the soup to a simmer and cook, stirring occasionally, for about 3 minutes, until slightly thickened. While stirring the soup constantly, pour in the beaten eggs in a thin stream. Press the Cancel button to turn off the pot and then stir in the green onions and cilantro. 8. Ladle the soup into bowls and serve hot.

Per Serving:

calories: 231 | fat: 13g | protein: 21g | carbs: 14g | sugars: 2g | fiber: 3g | sodium: 250mg

Beef, Mushroom, and Wild Rice Soup

Prep time: 0 minutes | Cook time: 55 minutes | Serves 6

2 tablespoons extra-virgin olive oil or unsalted butter
2 garlic cloves, minced
8 ounces shiitake mushrooms, stems removed and sliced
1 teaspoon fine sea salt
2 carrots, diced
2 celery stalks, diced
1 yellow onion, diced
1 teaspoon dried thyme

1½ pounds beef stew meat, larger pieces halved, or beef chuck, trimmed of fat and cut into ¾-inch pieces
4 cups low-sodium roasted beef bone broth
1 cup wild rice, rinsed
1 tablespoon Worcestershire sauce
2 tablespoons tomato paste

1. Select the Sauté setting on the Instant Pot and heat the oil and garlic for about 1 minute, until the garlic is bubbling but not browned. Add the mushrooms and salt and sauté for 5 minutes, until the mushrooms have wilted and given up some of their liquid. Add the carrots, celery, and onion and sauté for 4 minutes, until the onion begins to soften. Add the thyme and beef and sauté for 3 minutes more, until the beef is mostly opaque on the outside. Stir in the broth, rice, Worcestershire sauce, and tomato paste, using a wooden spoon to nudge any browned bits from the bottom of the pot. 2. Secure the lid and set the Pressure Release to Sealing. Press the Cancel button to reset the cooking program, then select the Pressure Cook or Manual setting and set the cooking time for 25 minutes at high pressure. (The pot will take about 15 minutes to come up to pressure before the cooking program begins.) 3. When the cooking program ends, let the pressure release naturally for at least 15 minutes, then move the Pressure Release to Venting to release any remaining steam. Open the pot. Ladle the soup into bowls and serve hot.

Per Serving:

calories: 316 | fat: 8g | protein: 29g | carbs: 32g | sugars: 6g | fiber: 8g | sodium: 783mg

Chicken Noodle Soup

Prep time: 15 minutes | Cook time: 20 minutes | Serves 12

2 tablespoons avocado oil
1 medium onion, chopped
3 celery stalks, chopped
1 teaspoon kosher salt
¼ teaspoon freshly ground black pepper
2 teaspoons minced garlic
5 large carrots, peeled and cut into ¼-inch-thick rounds

3 pounds bone-in chicken breasts (about 3)
4 cups Chicken Bone Broth or low-sodium store-bought chicken broth
4 cups water
2 tablespoons soy sauce
6 ounces whole grain wide egg noodles

1. Set the electric pressure cooker to the Sauté setting. When the pot is hot, pour in the avocado oil. 2. Sauté the onion, celery, salt, and pepper for 3 to 5 minutes or until the vegetables begin to soften. 3. Add the garlic and carrots, and stir to mix well. Hit Cancel. 4. Add the chicken to the pot, meat-side down. Add the broth, water, and soy sauce. Close and lock the lid of the pressure cooker. Set the valve to sealing. 5. Cook on high pressure for 20 minutes. 6. When the cooking is complete, hit Cancel and quick release the pressure. Unlock and remove the lid. 7. Using tongs, remove the chicken breasts to a cutting board. Hit Sauté/More and bring the soup to a boil. 8. Add the noodles and cook for 4 to 5 minutes or until the noodles are al dente. 9. While the noodles are cooking, use two forks to shred the chicken. Add the meat back to the pot and save the bones to make more bone broth. 10. Season with additional pepper, if desired, and serve.

Per Serving:
calories: 294 | fat: 13.92g | protein: 26.68g | carbs: 15.28g | sugars: 2.8g | fiber: 2.7g | sodium: 640mg

Fresh Fish Chowder

Prep time: 10 minutes | Cook time: 50 minutes | Serves 6

2 tablespoons extra-virgin olive oil
1 large garlic clove, minced
1 small onion, chopped
1 large green bell pepper, chopped
One 14.5-ounce can no-salt-added crushed tomatoes
1 tablespoon tomato paste
½ teaspoon dried basil

½ teaspoon dried oregano
¼ cup dry red wine
 teaspoon salt
 teaspoon freshly ground black pepper
½ cup uncooked brown rice
½ pound fresh halibut, cubed
2 tablespoons freshly chopped parsley

1. In a 3-quart saucepan, heat the olive oil over medium-high heat. Add the garlic, onion, and green pepper; sauté for 10 minutes over low heat until the vegetables are just tender. 2. Add the tomatoes, tomato paste, basil, oregano, wine, salt, and pepper. Let simmer for 15 minutes. Add the rice and continue to cook for 15 minutes. 3. Add the halibut, and cook for about 5-7 minutes, until the fish is cooked through. Garnish the stew with chopped parsley and serve.

Per Serving:
calories: 166 | fat: 7.43g | protein: 7.74g | carbs: 17.26g | sugars: 3.1g | fiber: 2.5g | sodium: 430mg

Pumpkin Soup

Prep time: 15 minutes | Cook time: 30 minutes | Serves 6

2 cups store-bought low-sodium seafood broth, divided
1 bunch collard greens, stemmed and cut into ribbons
1 tomato, chopped
1 garlic clove, minced
1 butternut squash or other

winter squash, peeled and cut into 1-inch cubes
1 teaspoon paprika
1 teaspoon dried dill
2 (5-ounce) cans boneless, skinless salmon in water, rinsed

1. In a heavy-bottomed large stockpot, bring ½ cup of broth to a simmer over medium heat. 2. Add the collard greens, tomato, and garlic and cook for 5 minutes, or until the greens are wilted and the garlic is softened. 3. Add the squash, paprika, dill, and remaining 1½ cups of broth. Cover and cook for 20 minutes, or until the squash is tender. 4. Add the salmon and cook for 3 minutes, or just enough for the flavors to come together.

Per Serving:
calories: 161 | fat: 5.5g | protein: 23.92g | carbs: 4.51g | sugars: 1.18g | fiber: 1g | sodium: 579mg

Roasted Tomato and Sweet Potato Soup

Prep time: 10 minutes | Cook time: 40 to 50 minutes | Serves 4

1½ cups onions, finely chopped
2 cups cubed red or yellow potatoes (not russet)
2 cups cubed sweet potatoes (can use frozen)
3-4 large cloves garlic, minced
1¼ teaspoons sea salt
1½ cups peeled, quartered onion (roughly 1 large onion)
4 cups cubed sweet potato (roughly 1-1¼ pounds before peeling)
4 cups (about 1½ pounds)

quartered Roma or other tomatoes, juices squeezed out
1½ teaspoons dried basil
1½ teaspoons dried oregano
1 tablespoon balsamic vinegar
1 teaspoon blackstrap molasses
Freshly ground black pepper to taste
1⅛ teaspoons sea salt
2¼-2½ cups water
¼ cup chopped fresh basil (optional)

1. Preheat the oven to 450°F. 2. In a large baking dish, combine the onion, sweet potato, tomatoes, basil, oregano, vinegar, molasses, pepper, and 1 teaspoon of the salt. Cook for 40 to 50 minutes, stirring a couple of times, until the sweet potatoes are softened and the mixture is becoming caramelized. Transfer the vegetables and any juices they've released in the pan to a medium soup pot, add 2¼ cups of the water and the remaining ⅛ teaspoon salt, and use an immersion blender to puree. (Alternatively, you can transfer everything to a blender to puree.) Blend to the desired smoothness, using the additional ¼ cup water if needed. Stir in fresh basil, if using, and serve.

Per Serving:
calorie: 152 | fat: 0.4g | protein: 4g | carbs: 35g | sugars: 14g | fiber: 5g | sodium: 648mg

Kickin' Chili

Prep time: 10 minutes | Cook time: 45 minutes | Serves 2

1 tablespoon extra-virgin olive oil
½ cup chopped onions
1 garlic clove, minced
1 celery stalk, chopped
½ cup chopped bell peppers, any color
1 cup diced tomatoes, undrained
1 cup frozen broccoli florets
1 (15-ounce) can pinto beans, drained and rinsed
2 cups water
2 teaspoons ground cumin
2 teaspoons chili powder
½ teaspoon cayenne pepper
Salt, to season
Freshly ground black pepper, to season

1. In a large pot set over medium heat, heat the olive oil. 2. Add the onions. Cook for about 5 minutes, or until tender. 3. Add the garlic. Cook for 2 to 3 minutes, or until lightly browned. 4. Add the celery and bell peppers. Cook for 5 minutes, or until the vegetables are soft. 5. Stir in the tomatoes, broccoli, pinto beans, and water. 6. Add the cumin, chili powder, and cayenne pepper. Season with salt and pepper. Stir to combine. Simmer for 30 minutes, stirring frequently. 7. Serve hot and enjoy!

Per Serving:

calories: 249 | fat: 4.9g | protein: 14.08g | carbs: 42.04g | sugars: 5.97g | fiber: 13.1g | sodium: 739mg

Black Bean, Turmeric, and Cauliflower Tortilla Soup

Prep time: 10 minutes | Cook time: 45 minutes | Serves 4

1 medium head cauliflower, chopped into medium florets
2 teaspoons (10 ml) extra virgin olive oil, divided
½ teaspoon ground turmeric
½ teaspoon garlic powder
1 medium yellow onion, coarsely chopped
1 clove garlic, minced
1 medium red bell pepper, coarsely chopped
2 cups (480 ml) low-sodium salsa
1 teaspoon chipotle chili powder (see Tips)
4 cups (960 ml) water
Juice of ½ medium lime
1 (15-ounce/425-g) can black beans, drained and rinsed
½ cup (60 g) shredded Cheddar cheese
Finely chopped fresh cilantro, as needed
Avocado, sliced (optional)
4 lime wedges

1. Preheat the oven to 425°F (218°C). 2. Place the cauliflower florets in a large bowl. Add 1 teaspoon of the oil, turmeric, and garlic powder and toss the cauliflower florets to coat them in the seasonings. Transfer the cauliflower to a large baking sheet. Bake the cauliflower for 25 minutes, until it is golden brown. 3. Meanwhile, heat the remaining 1 teaspoon of oil in a large pot over medium heat. Add the onion, garlic, and bell pepper and sauté the vegetables for 5 to 10 minutes, or until the onion is translucent with charred edges. Add the salsa, chipotle chili powder, water, lime juice, and black beans and bring the soup to a simmer. 4. When the cauliflower is done, add it and the Cheddar cheese to the soup. Simmer the soup for at least 15 to 20 minutes to allow the flavors to meld. 5. Serve the soup with the cilantro sprinkled on top, avocado if desired, and a lime wedge on the side of each serving.

Per Serving:

calorie: 347 | fat: 7g | protein: 13g | carbs: 62g | sugars: 15g | fiber: 13g | sodium: 268mg

Vegetarian Chili

Prep time: 25 minutes | Cook time: 10 minutes | Serves 6

2 teaspoons olive oil
3 garlic cloves, minced
2 onions, chopped
1 green bell pepper, chopped
1 cup textured vegetable protein (T.V.P.)
1-pound can beans of your choice, drained
1 jalapeño pepper, seeds removed, chopped
28-ounce can diced Italian tomatoes
1 bay leaf
1 tablespoon dried oregano
½ teaspoons salt
¼ teaspoons pepper

1. Set the Instant Pot to the Sauté function. As it's heating, add the olive oil, garlic, onions, and bell pepper. Stir constantly for about 5 minutes as it all cooks. Press Cancel. 2. Place all of the remaining ingredients into the inner pot of the Instant pot and stir. 3. Secure the lid and make sure vent is set to sealing. Cook on Manual mode for 10 minutes. 4. When cook time is up, let the steam release naturally for 5 minutes and then manually release the rest.

Per Serving:

calories: 242 | fat: 2g | protein: 17g | carbs: 36g | sugars: 9g | fiber: 12g | sodium: 489mg

Unstuffed Cabbage Soup

Prep time: 15 minutes | Cook time: 20 minutes | Serves 5

2 tablespoons coconut oil
1 pound ground sirloin or turkey
1 medium onion, diced
2 cloves garlic, minced
1 small head cabbage, chopped, cored, cut into roughly 2-inch pieces.
6-ounce can low-sodium tomato paste
32-ounce can low-sodium diced tomatoes, with liquid
2 cups low-sodium beef broth
1½ cups water
¾ cup brown rice
1-2 teaspoons salt
½ teaspoon black pepper
1 teaspoon oregano
1 teaspoon parsley

1. Melt coconut oil in the inner pot of the Instant Pot using Sauté function. Add ground meat. Stir frequently until meat loses color, about 2 minutes. 2. Add onion and garlic and continue to sauté for 2 more minutes, stirring frequently. 3. Add chopped cabbage. 4. On top of cabbage layer tomato paste, tomatoes with liquid, beef broth, water, rice, and spices. 5. Secure the lid and set vent to sealing. Using Manual setting, select 20 minutes. 6. When time is up, let the pressure release naturally for 10 minutes, then do a quick release.

Per Serving:

calories: 282 | fat: 6g | protein: 23g | carbs: 34g | sugars: 6g | fiber: 3g | sodium: 898mg

Four-Bean Field Stew

Prep time: 10 minutes | Cook time: 40 minutes | Serves 8 to 10

6 cups store-bought low-sodium vegetable broth
1 cup dried lima beans
1 cup dried black beans
1 cup dried pinto beans
1 cup dried kidney beans
1 cup roughly chopped tomato
2 carrots, peeled and roughly chopped
1 zucchini, chopped
½ cup chopped white onion
1 celery stalk, roughly chopped
2 garlic cloves, minced
1 teaspoon dried oregano
1 teaspoon dried thyme
¼ teaspoon freshly ground black pepper

1. In an electric pressure cooker, combine the broth, lima beans, black beans, pinto beans, kidney beans, tomato, carrots, zucchini, onion, celery, garlic, oregano, thyme, and pepper. 2. Close and lock the lid, and set the pressure valve to sealing. 3. Select the Manual/Pressure Cook setting, and cook for 40 minutes. 4. Once cooking is complete, quick-release the pressure. Carefully remove the lid. 5. Serve.

Per Serving:

calories: 262 | fat: 2.98g | protein: 14.57g | carbs: 46.7g | sugars: 7.74g | fiber: 10.4g | sodium: 143mg

Ground Turkey Stew

Prep time: 5 minutes | Cook time: 25 minutes | Serves 5

1 tablespoon olive oil
1 onion, chopped
1 pound ground turkey
½ teaspoon garlic powder
1 teaspoon chili powder
¾ teaspoon cumin
2 teaspoons coriander
1 teaspoon dried oregano
½ teaspoon salt
1 green pepper, chopped
1 red pepper, chopped
1 tomato, chopped
1½ cups reduced-sodium tomato sauce
1 tablespoon low-sodium soy sauce
1 cup water
2 handfuls cilantro, chopped
15-ounce can reduced-salt black beans

1. Press the Sauté function on the control panel of the Instant Pot. 2. Add the olive oil to the inner pot and let it get hot. Add onion and sauté for a few minutes, or until light golden. 3. Add ground turkey. Break the ground meat using a wooden spoon to avoid formation of lumps. Sauté for a few minutes, until the pink color has faded. 4. Add garlic powder, chili powder, cumin, coriander, dried oregano, and salt. Combine well. Add green pepper, red pepper, and chopped tomato. Combine well. 5. Add tomato sauce, soy sauce, and water; combine well. 6. Close and secure the lid. Click on the Cancel key to cancel the Sauté mode. Make sure the pressure release valve on the lid is in the sealing position. 7. Click on Manual function first and then select high pressure. Click the + button and set the time to 15 minutes. 8. You can either have the steam release naturally (it will take around 20 minutes) or, after 10 minutes, turn the pressure release valve on the lid to venting and release steam. Be careful as the steam is very hot. After the pressure has released completely, open the lid. 9. If the stew is watery, turn on the Sauté function and let it cook for a few more minutes with the lid off. 10. Add cilantro

and can of black beans, combine well, and let cook for a few minutes.

Per Serving:

calories: 209 | fat: 3g | protein: 24g | carbs: 21g | sugars: 8g | fiber: 6g | sodium: 609mg

French Onion Soup

Prep time: 10 minutes | Cook time: 20 minutes | Serves 10

½ cup light, soft tub margarine
8-10 large onions, sliced
3 14-ounce cans 98% fat-free, lower-sodium beef broth
2½ cups water
3 teaspoons sodium-free
chicken bouillon powder
1½ teaspoons Worcestershire sauce
3 bay leaves
10 (1-ounce) slices French bread, toasted

1. Turn the Instant Pot to the Sauté function and add in the margarine and onions. Cook about 5 minutes, or until the onions are slightly soft. Press Cancel. 2. Add the beef broth, water, bouillon powder, Worcestershire sauce, and bay leaves and stir. 3. Secure the lid and make sure vent is set to sealing. Cook on Manual mode for 20 minutes. 4. Let the pressure release naturally for 15 minutes, then do a quick release. Open the lid and discard bay leaves. 5. Ladle into bowls. Top each with a slice of bread and some cheese if you desire.

Per Serving:

calories: 178 | fat: 4g | protein: 6g | carbs: 31g | sugars: 10g | fiber: 4g | sodium: 476mg

Egg Drop Soup

Prep time: 10 minutes | Cook time: 15 minutes | Serves 4

3½ cups low-sodium vegetable broth, divided
1 teaspoon grated fresh ginger (optional)
2 garlic cloves, minced
3 teaspoons low-sodium soy
sauce or tamari
1 tablespoon cornstarch
2 large eggs, lightly beaten
2 scallions, both white and green parts, thinly sliced

1. In a large saucepan, bring 3 cups plus 6 tablespoons of vegetable broth and the ginger (if using), garlic, and tamari to a boil over medium-high heat. 2. In a small bowl, make a slurry by combining the cornstarch and the remaining 2 tablespoons of broth. Stir until dissolved. Slowly add the cornstarch mixture to the rest of the heated soup, stirring until thickened, 2 to 3 minutes. 3. Reduce the heat to low and simmer. While stirring the soup, pour the eggs in slowly. Turn off the heat, add the scallions, and serve. 4. Store the cooled soup in an airtight container in the refrigerator for up to 3 days.

Per Serving:

calories: 82 | fat: 2.99g | protein: 3.79g | carbs: 11.42g | sugars: 6.33g | fiber: 1.2g | sodium: 248mg

Creamy Chicken Wild Rice Soup

Prep time: 15 minutes | Cook time: 15 minutes | Serves 5

2 tablespoons margarine
½ cup yellow onion, diced
¾ cup carrots, diced
¾ cup sliced mushrooms (about 3-4 mushrooms)
½ pound chicken breast, diced into 1-inch cubes
6.2-ounce box Uncle Ben's

Long Grain & Wild Rice Fast Cook
2 14-ounce cans low-sodium chicken broth
1 cup skim milk
1 cup evaporated skim milk
2 ounces fat-free cream cheese
2 tablespoons cornstarch

1. Select the Sauté feature and add the margarine, onion, carrots, and mushrooms to the inner pot. Sauté for about 5 minutes until onions are translucent and soft. 2. Add the cubed chicken and seasoning packet from the Uncle Ben's box and stir to combine. 3. Add the rice and chicken broth. Select Manual, high pressure, then lock the lid and make sure the vent is set to sealing. Set the time for 5 minutes. 4. After the cooking time ends, allow it to stay on Keep Warm for 5 minutes and then quick release the pressure. 5. Remove the lid; change the setting to the Sauté function again. 6. Add the skim milk, evaporated milk, and cream cheese. Stir to melt. 7. In a small bowl, mix the cornstarch with a little bit of water to dissolve, then add to the soup to thicken.

Per Serving:

calories: 316 | fat: 7g | protein: 27g | carbs: 35g | sugars: 10g | fiber: 1g | sodium: 638mg

Golden Lentil-Pea Soup

Prep time: 10 minutes | Cook time: 50 minutes | Serves 6

1 cup diced onion
1 cup chopped celery
1 tablespoon smoked paprika
1 teaspoon dried rosemary
1 teaspoon ground cumin
¼ teaspoon allspice
¼ teaspoon sea salt
2-3 tablespoons + 4 cups water
4 cups chopped yellow sweet

potato (or 2 cups chopped sweet potato and 2 cups chopped carrot)
1½ cups dried red lentils
1 cup dried yellow split peas
2 cups vegetable broth
1½ tablespoons apple cider vinegar

1. In a large soup pot over medium-high heat, combine the onion, celery, paprika, rosemary, cumin, allspice, salt, and 2 to 3 tablespoons of the water, and stir. Cook for 8 to 9 minutes, then add the potato, lentils, split peas, broth, and the remaining 4 cups of water. Stir to combine. Increase the heat to high to bring to a boil. Reduce the heat to low, cover, and simmer for 40 to 45 minutes, or until the peas are completely softened. Stir in the apple cider vinegar, season with additional salt and pepper if desired, and serve.

Per Serving:

calorie: 340 | fat: 1g | protein: 21g | carbs: 64g | sugars: 8g | fiber: 20g | sodium: 363mg

Freshened-Up French Onion Soup

Prep time: 15 minutes | Cook time: 30 minutes | Serves 2

1 tablespoon extra-virgin olive oil
2 medium onions, sliced
2 cups low-sodium beef broth
1 (8-ounce) can chickpeas, drained and rinsed

½ teaspoon dried thyme
Salt
Freshly ground black pepper
4 slices nonfat Swiss deli-style cheese

1. In a medium soup pot set over medium-low heat, heat the olive oil. 2. Add the onions. Stir to coat them in oil. Cook for about 10 minutes, or until golden brown. 3. Add the beef broth, chickpeas, and thyme. Bring to a simmer. 4. Taste the broth. Season with salt and pepper. Cook for 10 minutes more. 5. Preheat the broiler to high. 6. Ladle the soup into 2 ovenproof soup bowls. 7. Top each with 2 slices of Swiss cheese. Place the bowls on a baking sheet. Carefully transfer the sheet to the preheated oven. Melt the cheese under the broiler for 2 minutes. Alternately, you can melt the cheese in the microwave (in microwave-safe bowls) on high in 30-second intervals until melted. 8. Enjoy immediately.

Per Serving:

calories: 278 | fat: 13.52g | protein: 15.39g | carbs: 28.6g | sugars: 3.04g | fiber: 1.8g | sodium: 804mg

Spicy Turkey Chili

Prep time: 10 minutes | Cook time: 50 minutes | Serves 6

2 onions, chopped
2 garlic cloves, minced
½ cup chopped green bell pepper
1 tablespoon extra-virgin olive oil
1 pound lean ground turkey breast meat

2 cups cooked (not canned) kidney or pinto beans
2 cups canned tomatoes with liquid
1 cup low-sodium chicken broth
2 tablespoon chili powder
2 teaspoons cumin
Freshly ground black pepper

1. In a large saucepan, sauté the onion, garlic, and green pepper in the oil for 10 minutes. Add the turkey, and sauté until the turkey is cooked, about 5-10 minutes. Drain any fat away. 2. Add the remaining ingredients, bring to a boil, lower the heat, and simmer uncovered for 30 minutes. Add additional chili powder if you like your chili extra spicy.

Per Serving:

calories: 214 | fat: 9.94g | protein: 20.55g | carbs: 11.57g | sugars: 4.11g | fiber: 2.2g | sodium: 363mg

Green Chile Corn Chowder

Prep time: 20 minutes | Cook time: 7 to 8 hours | Serves 8

16-ounce can cream-style corn
3 potatoes, peeled and diced
2 tablespoons chopped fresh chives
4-ounce can diced green chilies, drained
2-ounce jar chopped pimentos, drained

½ cup chopped cooked ham
2 10½-ounce cans 100% fat-free lower-sodium chicken broth
Pepper to taste
Tabasco sauce to taste
1 cup fat-free milk

1. Combine all ingredients, except milk, in the inner pot of the Instant Pot. 2. Secure the lid and cook using the Slow Cook function on low 7-8 hours or until potatoes are tender. 3. When cook time is up, remove the lid and stir in the milk. Cover and let simmer another 20 minutes.

Per Serving:

calories: 124 | fat: 2g | protein: 6g | carbs: 21g | sugars: 7g | fiber: 2g | sodium: 563mg

Potlikker Soup

Prep time: 15 minutes | Cook time: 20 minutes | Serves 6

3 cups store-bought low-sodium chicken broth, divided
1 medium onion, chopped
3 garlic cloves, minced
1 bunch collard greens or mustard greens including stems, roughly chopped

1 fresh ham bone
5 carrots, peeled and cut into 1-inch rounds
2 fresh thyme sprigs
3 bay leaves
Freshly ground black pepper

1. Select the Sauté setting on an electric pressure cooker, and combine ½ cup of chicken broth, the onion, and garlic and cook for 3 to 5 minutes, or until the onion and garlic are translucent. 2. Add the collard greens, ham bone, carrots, remaining 2½ cups of broth, the thyme, and bay leaves. 3. Close and lock the lid and set the pressure valve to sealing. 4. Change to the Manual/Pressure Cook setting, and cook for 15 minutes. 5. Once cooking is complete, quick-release the pressure. Carefully remove the lid. Discard the bay leaves. 6. Serve.

Per Serving:

calories: 107 | fat: 2.61g | protein: 11.74g | carbs: 11.83g | sugars: 2.62g | fiber: 4.7g | sodium: 556mg

Chapter 12 Desserts

Cream Cheese Swirl Brownies

Prep time: 10 minutes | Cook time: 20 minutes | Serves 12

2 eggs
¼ cup unsweetened applesauce
¼ cup coconut oil, melted
3 tablespoons pure maple syrup, divided
¼ cup unsweetened cocoa
powder
¼ cup coconut flour
¼ teaspoon salt
1 teaspoon baking powder
2 tablespoons low-fat cream cheese

1. Preheat the oven to 350°F. Grease an 8-by-8-inch baking dish. 2. In a large mixing bowl, beat the eggs with the applesauce, coconut oil, and 2 tablespoons of maple syrup. 3. Stir in the cocoa powder and coconut flour, and mix well. Sprinkle the salt and baking powder evenly over the surface and mix well to incorporate. Transfer the mixture to the prepared baking dish. 4. In a small, microwave-safe bowl, microwave the cream cheese for 10 to 20 seconds until softened. Add the remaining 1 tablespoon of maple syrup and mix to combine. 5. Drop the cream cheese onto the batter, and use a toothpick or chopstick to swirl it on the surface. Bake for 20 minutes, until a toothpick inserted in the center comes out clean. Cool and cut into 12 squares. 6. Store refrigerated in a covered container for up to 5 days.

Per Serving:

calories: 84 | fat: 6g | protein: 2g | carbs: 6g | sugars: 4g | fiber: 2g | sodium: 93mg

Instant Pot Tapioca

Prep time: 10 minutes | Cook time: 7 minutes | Serves 6

2 cups water
1 cup small pearl tapioca
½ cup sugar
4 eggs
½ cup evaporated skim milk
Sugar substitute to equal ¼ cup sugar
1 teaspoon vanilla
Fruit of choice, optional

1. Combine water and tapioca in Instant Pot. 2. Secure lid and make sure vent is set to sealing. Press Manual and set for 5 minutes. 3. Perform a quick release. Press Cancel, remove lid, and press Sauté. 4. Whisk together eggs and evaporated milk. SLOWLY add to the Instant Pot, stirring constantly so the eggs don't scramble. 5. Stir in the sugar substitute until it's dissolved, press Cancel, then stir in the vanilla. 6. Allow to cool thoroughly, then refrigerate at least 4 hours.

Per Serving:

calorie: 262 | fat: 3g | protein: 6g | carbs: 50g | sugars: 28g | fiber: 0g | sodium: 75mg

Blueberry Chocolate Clusters

Prep time: 5 minutes | Cook time: 5 minutes | Serves 10

1½ cups dark chocolate chips
1 tablespoon coconut oil, melted
½ cups chopped, toasted pecans
2 cups blueberries

1. Line a baking sheet with parchment paper. 2. Melt the chocolate in a microwave-safe bowl in 20- to 30-second intervals. 3. In a medium bowl, combine the melted chocolate with the coconut oil and pecans. 4. Spoon a small amount of chocolate mixture (about 1 teaspoon) on the prepared baking sheet. 5. Place a cluster of about 5 blueberries on top of the chocolate. You should get about 20 clusters in total. 6. Drizzle a small amount of chocolate over the berries. 7. Freeze until set, about 15 minutes. 8. Store in an airtight container in the refrigerator for up to 5 days or in the freezer for up to 1 month.

Per Serving:

calories: 224 | fat: 17g | protein: 3g | carbs: 17g | sugars: 9g | fiber: 4g | sodium: 6mg

Simple Bread Pudding

Prep time: 25 minutes | Cook time: 40 minutes | Serves 8

6-8 slices bread, cubed
2 cups fat-free milk
2 eggs
¼ cup sugar
1 teaspoon ground cinnamon
1 teaspoon vanilla
1½ cups water
Sauce:
1 tablespoon cornstarch
6-ounce can concentrated grape juice

1. Place bread cubes in greased 1.6-quart baking dish. 2. Beat together milk and eggs. Stir in sugar, cinnamon and vanilla. Pour over bread and stir. 3. Cover with foil. 4. Place the trivet into your Instant Pot and pour in 1½ cup of water. Place a foil sling on top of the trivet, then place the baking dish on top. 5. Secure the lid and make sure lid is set to sealing. Press Manual and set time for 30 minutes. 6. When cook time is up, let the pressure release naturally for 15 minutes, then release any remaining pressure manually. Carefully remove the springform pan by using hot pads to lift the baking dish out by the foil sling. Let sit for a few minutes, uncovered, while you make the sauce. 7. Combine cornstarch and concentrated juice in saucepan. Heat until boiling, stirring constantly, until sauce is thickened. Serve drizzled over bread pudding.

Per Serving:

calories: 179 | fat: 2g | protein: 5g | carbs: 35g | sugars: 24g | fiber: 1g | sodium: 153mg

Pineapple Pear Medley

Prep time: 10 minutes | Cook time: 10 minutes | Serves 12

1 large orange
15 ounces canned unsweetened pineapple chunks, undrained
32 ounces canned unsweetened pear halves, drained
16 ounces canned unsweetened apricot halves, drained
6 whole cloves
2 cinnamon sticks

1. Peel the orange, and reserve the rind. Divide the orange into sections, and remove the membrane. 2. Drain the pineapple, reserve the juice, and set aside. 3. In a large bowl, combine the orange sections, pineapple, pears, and apricots. Toss, and set aside. 4. In a small saucepan over medium heat, combine the orange rind, pineapple juice, cloves, and cinnamon. Let simmer for 5-10 minutes; then strain the juices, and pour over the fruit. 5. Cover, and refrigerate for at least 2-3 hours. Toss before serving.

Per Serving:

calories: 67 | fat: 0g | protein: 1g | carbs: 67g | sugars: 11g | fiber: 4g | sodium: 2mg

Coffee and Cream Pops

Prep time: 10 minutes | Cook time: 5 minutes | Serves 4

2 teaspoons espresso powder (or to taste)
2 cups canned coconut milk
½ teaspoon vanilla extract
½ teaspoon cinnamon
3 (1 g) packets stevia

1. In a medium saucepan over medium-low heat, heat all of the ingredients, stirring constantly, until the espresso powder is completely dissolved, about 5 minutes. 2. Pour the mixture into 4 ice pop molds. Freeze for 6 hours before serving.

Per Serving:

calories: 230 | fat: 24g | protein: 2g | carbs: 1g | sugars: 0g | fiber: 1g | sodium: 16mg

Pineapple-Peanut Nice Cream

Prep time: 10 minutes | Cook time: 0 minutes | Serves 6

2 cups frozen pineapple
1 cup peanut butter (no added sugar, salt, or fat)
½ cup unsweetened almond milk

1. In a blender or food processor, combine the frozen pineapple and peanut butter and process. 2. Add the almond milk, and blend until smooth. The end result should be a smooth paste.

Per Serving:

calories: 143 | fat: 3g | protein: 10g | carbs: 15g | sugars: 7g | fiber: 3g | sodium: 22mg

Chewy Barley-Nut Cookies

Prep time: 45 minutes | Cook time: 10 to 14 minutes | Makes 2 dozen cookies

⅓ cup canola oil
½ cup granulated sugar
¼ cup packed brown sugar
¼ cup reduced-fat mayonnaise or salad dressing
1 teaspoon vanilla
1 egg
2 cups rolled barley flakes or 2 cups plus 2 tablespoons old-
fashioned oats
¾ cup whole wheat flour
½ teaspoon baking soda
½ teaspoon salt
¼ teaspoon ground cinnamon
⅓ cup "heart-healthy" mixed nuts (peanuts, almonds, pistachios, pecans, hazelnuts)

1 Heat oven to 350°F. Spray cookie sheet with cooking spray. 2 In medium bowl, mix oil, sugars, mayonnaise, vanilla and egg with spoon. Stir in barley, flour, baking soda, salt and cinnamon. Stir in nuts. 3 Drop dough by rounded tablespoonfuls 2 inches apart onto cookie sheet. 4 Bake 10 to 14 minutes or until edges are golden brown. Cool 2 minutes; transfer from cookie sheet to cooling rack.

Per Serving:

1 Cookie: calorie: 150 | fat: 5g | protein: 2g | carbs: 23g | sugars: 7g | fiber: 3g | sodium: 110mg

Banana Pudding

Prep time: 30 minutes | Cook time: 20 minutes | Serves 10

FOR THE PUDDING
¾ cup erythritol or other sugar replacement
5 teaspoons almond flour
¼ teaspoon salt
2½ cups fat-free milk
6 tablespoons prepared egg replacement
½ teaspoon vanilla extract
2 (8-ounce) containers sugar-free spelt hazelnut biscuits, crushed
5 medium bananas, sliced
FOR THE MERINGUE
5 medium egg whites (1 cup)
¼ cup erythritol or other sugar replacement
½ teaspoon vanilla extract

TO MAKE THE PUDDING 1. In a saucepan, whisk the erythritol, almond flour, salt, and milk together. Cook over medium heat until the sugar is dissolved. 2. Whisk in the egg replacement and cook for about 10 minutes, or until thickened. 3. Remove from the heat and stir in the vanilla. 4. Spread the thickened pudding onto the bottom of a 3 × 6-inch casserole dish. 5. Arrange a layer of crushed biscuits on top of the pudding. 6. Place a layer of sliced bananas on top of the biscuits. TO MAKE THE MERINGUE 1. Preheat the oven to 350°F. 2. In a medium bowl, beat the egg whites for about 5 minutes, or until stiff. 3. Add the erythritol and vanilla while continuing to beat for about 3 more minutes. 4. Spread the meringue on top of the banana pudding. 5. Transfer the casserole dish to the oven, and bake for 7 to 10 minutes, or until the top is lightly browned.

Per Serving:

calories: 323 | fat: 14g | protein: 12g | carbs: 42g | sugars: 11g | fiber: 3g | sodium: 148mg

Crustless Key Lime Cheesecake

Prep time: 15 minutes | Cook time: 35 minutes | Serves 8

Nonstick cooking spray
16 ounces light cream cheese (Neufchâtel), softened
⅔ cup granulated erythritol sweetener
¼ cup unsweetened Key lime juice (I like Nellie & Joe's

Famous Key West Lime Juice)
½ teaspoon vanilla extract
¼ cup plain Greek yogurt
1 teaspoon grated lime zest
2 large eggs
Whipped cream, for garnish (optional)

1. Spray a 7-inch springform pan with nonstick cooking spray. Line the bottom and partway up the sides of the pan with foil. 2. Put the cream cheese in a large bowl. Use an electric mixer to whip the cream cheese until smooth, about 2 minutes. Add the erythritol, lime juice, vanilla, yogurt, and zest, and blend until smooth. Stop the mixer and scrape down the sides of the bowl with a rubber spatula. With the mixer on low speed, add the eggs, one at a time, blending until just mixed. (Don't overbeat the eggs.) 3. Pour the mixture into the prepared pan. Drape a paper towel over the top of the pan, not touching the cream cheese mixture, and tightly wrap the top of the pan in foil. (Your goal here is to keep out as much moisture as possible.) 4. Pour 1 cup of water into the electric pressure cooker. 5. Place the foil-covered pan onto the wire rack and carefully lower it into the pot. 6. Close and lock the lid of the pressure cooker. Set the valve to sealing. 7. Cook on high pressure for 35 minutes. 8. When the cooking is complete, hit Cancel. Allow the pressure to release naturally for 20 minutes, then quick release any remaining pressure. 9. Once the pin drops, unlock and remove the lid. 10. Using the handles of the wire rack, carefully transfer the pan to a cooling rack. Cool to room temperature, then refrigerate for at least 3 hours. 11. When ready to serve, run a thin rubber spatula around the rim of the cheesecake to loosen it, then remove the ring. 12. Slice into wedges and serve with whipped cream (if using).

Per Serving:

calories: 127 | fat: 2g | protein: 11g | carbs: 17g | sugars: 14g | fiber: 0g | sodium: 423mg

No-Bake Chocolate Peanut Butter Cookies

Prep time: 10 minutes | Cook time: 0 minutes | Makes 12 Cookies

¾ cup unsweetened shredded coconut
½ cup peanut butter
2 tablespoons cream cheese, at room temperature
2 tablespoons unsalted butter,

melted
2 tablespoons unsweetened cocoa powder
2 tablespoons pure maple syrup
½ teaspoon vanilla extract

1. In a medium bowl, mix all of the ingredients until well combined. 2. Spoon into 12 cookies on a platter lined with parchment paper. Refrigerate to set, about 2 hours.

Per Serving:

1 cookie: calories: 113 | fat: 9g | protein: 3g | carbs: 6g | sugars: 4g | fiber: 1g | sodium: 25mg

Grilled Watermelon with Avocado Mousse

Prep time: 10 minutes | Cook time: 10 minutes | Serves 8

1 small, seedless watermelon, halved and cut into 1-inch rounds
2 ripe avocados, pitted and

peeled
½ cup fat-free plain yogurt
¼ teaspoon cayenne pepper

1. On a hot grill, grill the watermelon slices for 2 to 3 minutes on each side, or until you can see the grill marks. 2. To make the avocado mousse, in a blender, combine the avocados, yogurt, and cayenne and process until smooth. 3. To serve, cut each watermelon round in half. Top each with a generous dollop of avocado mousse.

Per Serving:

calories: 162 | fat: 8g | protein: 3g | carbs: 22g | sugars: 14g | fiber: 5g | sodium: 13mg

Pumpkin Cheesecake Smoothie

Prep time: 10 minutes | Cook time: 0 minutes | Serves 1

2 tablespoons cream cheese, at room temperature
½ cup canned pumpkin purée (not pumpkin pie mix)

1 cup almond milk
1 teaspoon pumpkin pie spice
½ cup crushed ice

1. In a blender, combine all of the ingredients. Blend until smooth.

Per Serving:

calories: 230 | fat: 11g | protein: 11g | carbs: 25g | sugars: 16g | fiber: 4g | sodium: 216mg

Crustless Peanut Butter Cheesecake

Prep time: 10 minutes | Cook time: 10 minutes | Serves 2

4 ounces (113 g) cream cheese, softened
2 tablespoons confectioners' erythritol

1 tablespoon all-natural, no-sugar-added peanut butter
½ teaspoon vanilla extract
1 large egg, whisked

1. In a medium bowl, mix cream cheese and erythritol until smooth. Add peanut butter and vanilla, mixing until smooth. Add egg and stir just until combined. 2. Spoon mixture into an ungreased springform pan and place into air fryer basket. Adjust the temperature to 300°F (149°C) and bake for 10 minutes. Edges will be firm, but center will be mostly set with only a small amount of jiggle when done. 3. Let pan cool at room temperature 30 minutes, cover with plastic wrap, then place into refrigerator at least 2 hours. Serve chilled.

Per Serving:

calories: 281 | fat: 26g | protein: 8g | carbs: 4g | net carbs: 4g | fiber: 0g

Oatmeal Cookies

Prep time: 5 minutes | Cook time: 15 minutes | Serves 16

¾ cup almond flour
¾ cup old-fashioned oats
¼ cup shredded unsweetened coconut
1 teaspoon baking powder
1 teaspoon ground cinnamon
¼ teaspoon salt
¼ cup unsweetened applesauce
1 large egg
1 tablespoon pure maple syrup
2 tablespoons coconut oil, melted

1. Preheat the oven to 350°F. 2. In a medium mixing bowl, combine the almond flour, oats, coconut, baking powder, cinnamon, and salt, and mix well. 3. In another medium bowl, combine the applesauce, egg, maple syrup, and coconut oil, and mix. Stir the wet mixture into the dry mixture. 4. Form the dough into balls a little bigger than a tablespoon and place on a baking sheet, leaving at least 1 inch between them. Bake for 12 minutes until the cookies are just browned. Remove from the oven and let cool for 5 minutes. 5. Using a spatula, remove the cookies and cool on a rack.

Per Serving:

calorie: 76 | fat: 6g | protein: 2g | carbs: 5g | sugars: 1g | fiber: 1g | sodium: 57mg

Almond Butter Blondies

Prep time: 10 minutes | Cook time: 20 minutes | Serves 8

½ cup creamy natural almond butter, at room temperature
4 large eggs
¾ cup Lakanto Monkfruit Sweetener Golden
1 teaspoon pure vanilla extract
½ teaspoon fine sea salt
1¼ cups almond flour
¾ cup stevia-sweetened chocolate chips

1. Pour 1 cup water into the Instant Pot. Line the base of a 7 by 3-inch round cake pan with a circle of parchment paper. Butter the sides of the pan and the parchment or coat with nonstick cooking spray. 2. Put the almond butter into a medium bowl. One at a time, whisk the eggs into the almond butter, then whisk in the sweetener, vanilla, and salt. Stir in the flour just until it is fully incorporated, followed by the chocolate chips. 3. Transfer the batter to the prepared pan and, using a rubber spatula, spread it in an even layer. Cover the pan tightly with aluminum foil. Place the pan on a long-handled silicone steam rack, then, holding the handles of the steam rack, lower it into the Instant Pot. 4. Secure the lid and set the Pressure Release to Sealing. Select the Cake, Pressure Cook, or Manual setting and set the cooking time for 40 minutes at high pressure. (The pot will take about 10 minutes to come up to pressure before the cooking program begins.) 5. When the cooking program ends, let the pressure release naturally for 10 minutes, then move the Pressure Release to Venting to release any remaining steam. Open the pot and, wearing heat-resistant mitts, grasp the handles of the steam rack and lift it out of the pot. Uncover the pan, taking care not to get burned by the steam or to drip condensation onto the blondies. Let the blondies cool in the pan on a cooling rack for about 5 minutes. 6. Run a butter knife around the edge of pan to make sure the blondies are not sticking to the pan sides. Invert the blondies onto the rack, lift off the pan, and peel off the parchment paper. Let cool for 15 minutes, then invert the blondies onto a serving plate and cut into eight wedges. The blondies will keep, stored in an airtight container in the refrigerator for up to 5 days, or in the freezer for up to 4 months.

Per Serving:

calories: 211 | fat: 17g | protein: 8g | carbs: 20g | sugars: 10g | fiber: 17g | sodium: 186mg

Chai Pear-Fig Compote

Prep time: 20 minutes | Cook time: 3 minutes | Serves 4

1 vanilla chai tea bag
1 (3-inch) cinnamon stick
1 strip lemon peel (about 2-by-½ inches)
1½ pounds pears, peeled and chopped (about 3 cups)
½ cup chopped dried figs
2 tablespoons raisins

1. Pour 1 cup of water into the electric pressure cooker and hit Sauté/More. When the water comes to a boil, add the tea bag and cinnamon stick. Hit Cancel. Let the tea steep for 5 minutes, then remove and discard the tea bag. 2. Add the lemon peel, pears, figs, and raisins to the pot. 3. Close and lock the lid of the pressure cooker. Set the valve to sealing. 4. Cook on high pressure for 3 minutes. 5. When the cooking is complete, hit Cancel and quick release the pressure. 6. Once the pin drops, unlock and remove the lid. 7. Remove the lemon peel and cinnamon stick. Serve warm or cool to room temperature and refrigerate.

Per Serving:

calories: 167 | fat: 1g | protein: 2g | carbs: 44g | sugars: 29g | fiber: 9g | sodium: 4mg

Strawberry Chia Pudding

Prep time: 5 minutes | Cook time: 0 minutes | Serves 2

1½ cups frozen whole strawberries
3 tablespoons white chia seeds
1 tablespoon coconut nectar or pure maple syrup
1 teaspoon lemon juice
Pinch of sea salt
½ cup + 2-3 tablespoons plain low-fat nondairy milk

1. In a blender, combine the strawberries, chia seeds, nectar or syrup, lemon juice, salt, and ½ cup plus 2 tablespoons of the milk. Puree until the seeds are fully pulverized and the pudding begins to thicken. (It will thicken more as it cools.) Add the extra 1 tablespoon milk if needed to blend. Transfer the mixture to a large bowl or dish and refrigerate until chilled, about an hour or more. (It will thicken more with chilling, but really can be eaten right away.)

Per Serving:

calorie: 185 | fat: 5g | protein: 4g | carbs: 33g | sugars: 16g | fiber: 9g | sodium: 182mg

No-Added-Sugar Orange and Cream Slushy

Prep time: 5 minutes | Cook time: 0 minutes | Serves 2

½ cup (120 ml) unsweetened vanilla almond milk
½ cup (100 g) plain whole-milk yogurt
2 small oranges, peeled, seeds and pith removed, and frozen

1 small banana, frozen
1 teaspoon pure vanilla extract
2 tablespoons (10 g) unsweetened coconut flakes
1 tablespoon (12 g) chia seeds

1. In a high-power blender, combine the almond milk, yogurt, oranges, banana, vanilla, coconut flakes, and chia seeds. Blend the ingredients for 30 to 45 seconds, until a slushy consistency is reached.

Per Serving:

calorie: 203 | fat: 7g | protein: 8g | carbs: 29g | sugars: 17g | fiber: 7g | sodium: 67mg

Tapioca Berry Parfaits

Prep time: 10 minutes | Cook time: 6 minutes | Serves 4

2 cups unsweetened almond milk
½ cup small pearl tapioca, rinsed and still wet

1 teaspoon almond extract
1 tablespoon pure maple syrup
2 cups berries
¼ cup slivered almonds

1. Pour the almond milk into the electric pressure cooker. Stir in the tapioca and almond extract. 2. Close and lock the lid of the pressure cooker. Set the valve to sealing. 3. Cook on High pressure for 6 minutes. 4. When the cooking is complete, hit Cancel. Allow the pressure to release naturally for 10 minutes, then quick release any remaining pressure. 5. Once the pin drops, unlock and remove the lid. Remove the pot to a cooling rack. 6. Stir in the maple syrup and let the mixture cool for about an hour. 7. In small glasses, create several layers of tapioca, berries, and almonds. Refrigerate for 1 hour. 8. Serve chilled.

Per Serving:

(½ cup): calories: 174 | fat: 5g | protein: 3g | carbs: 32g | sugars: 11g | fiber: 3g | sodium: 77mg

Low-Fat Cream Cheese Frosting

Prep time: 5 minutes | Cook time: 0 minutes | Serves 8

3 cups fat-free ricotta cheese
1⅓ cups plain fat-free yogurt, strained overnight in cheesecloth over a bowl set in the refrigerator

2 cups low-fat cottage cheese
⅓ cup fructose
3 tablespoons evaporated fat-free milk

1. In a large bowl, combine all the ingredients; beat well with electric beaters until slightly stiff. 2. Place frosting in a covered container, and refrigerate until ready to use (this frosting can be refrigerated for up to 1 week).

Per Serving:

calories: 209 | fat: 7g | protein: 24g | carbs: 9g | sugars: 7g | fiber: 1g | sodium: 594mg

Oatmeal Raisin Cookies

Prep time: 5 minutes | Cook time: 15 minutes | Serves 6

3 cups rolled oats
1 cup whole-wheat flour
1 teaspoon baking soda
2 teaspoons cinnamon
½ cup raisins

¼ cup unsweetened applesauce
¼ cup agave nectar
½ cup egg substitute
½ cup plain fat-free yogurt
1 teaspoon vanilla

1. Preheat the oven to 350 degrees. 2. In a medium bowl, combine the oats, flour, baking soda, cinnamon, and raisins. 3. In a large bowl, beat the applesauce, agave nectar, egg substitute, yogurt, and vanilla until creamy. Slowly add the dry ingredients, and mix together. 4. Spray cookie sheets with nonstick cooking spray, and drop by teaspoonfuls onto the cookie sheets. Bake for 12-15 minutes at 350 degrees; transfer to racks, and cool.

Per Serving:

calories: 274 | fat: 4g | protein: 14g | carbs: 64g | sugars: 16g | fiber: 10g | sodium: 56mg

Lemon Dessert Shots

Prep time: 30 minutes | Cook time: 0 minutes | Serves 12

10 gingersnap cookies
2 ounces ⅓-less-fat cream cheese (Neufchâtel), softened
½ cup marshmallow crème (from 7-ounce jar)
1 container (6 ounces) fat-free

Greek honey vanilla yogurt
½ cup lemon curd (from 10-ounce jar)
36 fresh raspberries
½ cup frozen (thawed) lite whipped topping

1 In 1-quart resealable food-storage plastic bag, place cookies; seal bag. Crush with rolling pin or meat mallet; place in small bowl. 2 In medium bowl, beat cream cheese and marshmallow crème with electric mixer on low speed until smooth. Beat in yogurt until blended. Place mixture in 1-quart resealable food-storage plastic bag; seal bag. In 1-pint resealable food-storage plastic bag, place lemon curd; seal bag. Cut 1/8-inch opening diagonally across bottom corner of each bag. 3 In bottom of each of 12 (2-ounce) shot glasses, place 1 raspberry. For each glass, pipe about 2 teaspoons yogurt mixture over raspberry. Pipe ¼-inch ring of lemon curd around edge of glass; sprinkle with about 1 teaspoon cookies. Repeat. 4 Garnish each dessert shot with dollop of about 2 teaspoons whipped topping and 1 raspberry. Place in 9-inch square pan. Refrigerate 30 minutes or until chilled but no longer than 3 hours.

Per Serving:

calorie: 110 | fat: 3g | protein: 2g | carbs: 18g | sugars: 14g | fiber: 0g | sodium: 70mg

Mango Nice Cream

Prep time: 10 minutes | Cook time: 0 minutes | Serves 4

2 cups frozen mango chunks
1 cup frozen, sliced, overripe banana (can use room temperature, but must be overripe)
Pinch of sea salt

½ teaspoon pure vanilla extract
¼ cup + 1-2 tablespoons low-fat nondairy milk
2-3 tablespoons coconut nectar or pure maple syrup (optional)

1. In a food processor or high-speed blender, combine the mango, banana, salt, vanilla, and ¼ cup of the milk. Pulse to get things moving, and then puree, adding the remaining 1 to 2 tablespoons milk if needed. Taste, and add the nectar or syrup, if desired. Serve, or transfer to an airtight container and freeze for an hour or more to set more firmly before serving.

Per Serving:

calorie: 116 | fat: 0.5g | protein: 1g | carbs: 29g | sugars: 22g | fiber: 2g | sodium: 81mg

Chocolate Cupcakes

Prep time: 10 minutes | Cook time: 20 minutes | Serves 12

3 tablespoons canola oil
¼ cup agave nectar
¼ cup egg whites
1 teaspoon vanilla
1 teaspoon cold espresso or strong coffee

½ cup fat-free milk
1¼ cups quinoa flour
¼ cup ground walnuts
6 tablespoons cocoa powder
2 teaspoons baking powder
¼ teaspoon baking soda

1. Preheat the oven to 375 degrees. 2. In a medium bowl, beat the oil with the agave nectar, egg whites, vanilla, espresso, and milk. 3. In a separate bowl, combine the quinoa flour, walnuts, cocoa powder, baking powder, and baking soda. Add to the creamed mixture, and mix until smooth. 4. Spoon the batter into paper-lined muffin tins, and bake at 375 degrees for 20 minutes. Remove from the oven and let cool.

Per Serving:

calories: 113 | fat: 5g | protein: 3g | carbs: 15g | sugars: 4g | fiber: 2g | sodium: 43mg

Oatmeal Chippers

Prep time: 10 minutes | Cook time: 11 minutes | Makes 20 chippers

3-3½ tablespoons almond butter (or tigernut butter, for nut-free)
¼ cup pure maple syrup
¼ cup brown rice syrup
2 teaspoons pure vanilla extract
1⅓ cups oat flour
1 cup + 2 tablespoons rolled

oats
1½ teaspoons baking powder
½ teaspoon cinnamon
¼ teaspoon sea salt
2-3 tablespoons sugar-free nondairy chocolate chips

1. Preheat the oven to 350°F. Line a baking sheet with parchment paper. 2. In the bowl of a mixer, combine the almond butter, maple syrup, brown rice syrup, and vanilla. Using the paddle attachment, mix on low speed for a couple of minutes, until creamy. Turn off the mixer and add the flour, oats, baking powder, cinnamon, salt, and chocolate chips. Mix on low speed until incorporated. Place 1½-tablespoon mounds on the prepared baking sheet, spacing them 1" to 2" apart, and flatten slightly. Bake for 11 minutes, or until just set to the touch. Remove from the oven, let cool on the pan for just a minute, and then transfer the cookies to a cooling rack.

Per Serving:

calorie: 90 | fat: 2g | protein: 2g | carbs: 16g | sugars: 4g | fiber: 2g | sodium: 75mg

Watermelon-Lime Granita

Prep time: 15 minutes | Cook time: 0 minutes | Serves 10

1 pound seedless watermelon flesh, cut into 1-inch chunks
2 tablespoons agave syrup

2 tablespoons freshly squeezed lime juice

1. Line a baking sheet with parchment paper. Spread the watermelon chunks in a single layer on the sheet and freeze for at least 20 minutes. 2. Once the chunks are frozen, transfer them to a blender with the agave syrup and lime juice. Blend until liquefied and pour the mixture into a 9-by-13-inch shallow baking dish. Return to the freezer and freeze for 2 hours. 3. Every 30 minutes or so, take a fork and scrape the crystals into a slush consistency. Keep in the freezer for up to 1 month.

Per Serving:

calories: 23 | fat: 0g | protein: 0g | carbs: 6g | sugars: 5g | fiber: 0g | sodium: 1mg

Crispy Pistachio Chocolate Bark

Prep time: 5 minutes | Cook time: 0 minutes | Serves 16

1 cup (180 g) dairy-free 70% dark chocolate chips, melted

¼ cup (6 g) crisped rice cereal
½ cup (50 g) crushed pistachios

1. Line a large baking sheet with parchment paper. 2. In a medium bowl, combine the chocolate and rice cereal and stir to combine. 3. Spread the mixture out evenly on the prepared baking sheet to your desired thickness. I recommend ¼ inch (6 mm). 4. Sprinkle the pistachios on top of the chocolate mixture and press them lightly with your hands or the back of a spoon to ensure that they stick to the chocolate. 5. Place the bark in the freezer for 1 hour. 6. Remove the bark from the freezer and break it into 16 pieces.

Per Serving:

calorie: 101 | fat: 7g | protein: 2g | carbs: 11g | sugars: 8g | fiber: 2g | sodium: 8mg

Banana N'Ice Cream with Cocoa Nuts

Prep time: 10 minutes | Cook time: 12 minutes | Serves 4 to 6

For the Cocoa Nuts:
¼ cup freshly squeezed orange juice
1 tablespoon coconut oil
2 teaspoons cocoa powder
½ teaspoon kosher salt
¼ teaspoon ground cinnamon

¼ teaspoon ground cardamom
½ teaspoon orange zest
1 cup raw almonds
For the Banana N'ice Cream:
2 frozen, diced bananas

Make the Cocoa Nuts: 1. Preheat the oven to 350°F. Line a baking sheet with parchment paper. 2. In a small saucepan, bring the orange juice to a boil over medium-high heat, reduce the heat to low, and simmer until the juice is reduced to about 2 tablespoons, 5 to 7 minutes. Add the coconut oil, stir until well combined, and remove from the heat. Whisk in the cocoa powder, salt, cinnamon, cardamom, and zest. Then add the almonds and stir to coat them. Spread the mixture onto the prepared baking sheet. 3. Bake the nuts for 10 to 12 minutes, stirring halfway through, until toasted. Allow to cool. 4. Store the nuts in an airtight container at room temperature for up to 2 weeks. Make the Banana N'ice Cream: 5. Put the frozen bananas in a food processor and pulse. Scrape down the sides, then pulse once more. Continue to do this for several minutes until the texture resembles ice cream. Serve immediately with the cooled nuts.

Per Serving:

calories: 199 | fat: 14g | protein: 6g | carbs: 16g | sugars: 7g | fiber: 4g | sodium: 195mg

Apple Crisp

Prep time: 10 minutes | Cook time: 45 minutes | Serves 4

Fruit Mixture
3 tablespoons freshly squeezed orange juice or pressed apple juice
2 tablespoons coconut nectar or pure maple syrup
2 tablespoons water
1½ tablespoons freshly squeezed lemon juice
2 teaspoons arrowroot or tapioca powder (can substitute organic cornstarch)
1 teaspoon cinnamon
Pinch of allspice

⅛ teaspoon sea salt
4-4½ cups apples, cored, cut into small chunks (peeling optional)
Crisp Topping
1½ tablespoons almond or cashew butter, raw or roasted
3 tablespoons coconut nectar or pure maple syrup
¾ cup rolled oats
½ cup oat flour
⅛ teaspoon sea salt

1. Preheat the oven to 350°F. 2. To make the fruit mixture: In a large bowl, combine the orange or apple juice, nectar or syrup, water, and lemon juice. Stir to combine. Add the arrowroot or tapioca powder, cinnamon, allspice, and salt, whisking thoroughly. Add the fruit and stir to coat. Transfer the mixture to an 8" x 8" (or similar size) glass baking dish. 3. To make the topping: In a medium bowl, combine the nut butter with the nectar or syrup, stirring until fully incorporated. Add the oats, oat flour, and salt, and mix until crumbly, using a spoon or your fingers. Sprinkle the topping evenly over the fruit. Cover with foil and bake for 35 minutes, or until the fruit is tender. Remove the foil and bake for another 10 minutes, to crisp the topping slightly. Let cool a little before serving.

Per Serving:

calorie: 292 | fat: 6g | protein: 6g | carbs: 59g | sugars: 30g | fiber: 7g | sodium: 166mg

Appendix 1 Measurement Conversion Chart

MEASUREMENT CONVERSION CHART

VOLUME EQUIVALENTS(DRY)

US STANDARD	METRIC (APPROXIMATE)
1/8 teaspoon	0.5 mL
1/4 teaspoon	1 mL
1/2 teaspoon	2 mL
3/4 teaspoon	4 mL
1 teaspoon	5 mL
1 tablespoon	15 mL
1/4 cup	59 mL
1/2 cup	118 mL
3/4 cup	177 mL
1 cup	235 mL
2 cups	475 mL
3 cups	700 mL
4 cups	1 L

VOLUME EQUIVALENTS(LIQUID)

US STANDARD	US STANDARD (OUNCES)	METRIC (APPROXIMATE)
2 tablespoons	1 fl.oz.	30 mL
1/4 cup	2 fl.oz.	60 mL
1/2 cup	4 fl.oz.	120 mL
1 cup	8 fl.oz.	240 mL
1 1/2 cup	12 fl.oz.	355 mL
2 cups or 1 pint	16 fl.oz.	475 mL
4 cups or 1 quart	32 fl.oz.	1 L
1 gallon	128 fl.oz.	4 L

TEMPERATURES EQUIVALENTS

FAHRENHEIT(F)	CELSIUS(C) (APPROXIMATE)
225 °F	107 °C
250 °F	120 °C
275 °F	135 °C
300 °F	150 °C
325 °F	160 °C
350 °F	180 °C
375 °F	190 °C
400 °F	205 °C
425 °F	220 °C
450 °F	235 °C
475 °F	245 °C
500 °F	260 °C

WEIGHT EQUIVALENTS

US STANDARD	METRIC (APPROXIMATE)
1 ounce	28 g
2 ounces	57 g
5 ounces	142 g
10 ounces	284 g
15 ounces	425 g
16 ounces (1 pound)	455 g
1.5 pounds	680 g
2 pounds	907 g

The Dirty Dozen and Clean Fifteen

The Environmental Working Group (EWG) is a nonprofit, nonpartisan organization dedicated to protecting human health and the environment Its mission is to empower people to live healthier lives in a healthier environment. This organization publishes an annual list of the twelve kinds of produce, in sequence, that have the highest amount of pesticide residue-the Dirty Dozen-as well as a list of the fifteen kinds ofproduce that have the least amount of pesticide residue-the Clean Fifteen.

THE DIRTY DOZEN	THE CLEAN FIFTEEN
• The 2016 Dirty Dozen includes the following produce. These are considered among the year's most important produce to buy organic:	• The least critical to buy organically are the Clean Fifteen list. The following are on the 2016 list:

THE DIRTY DOZEN

Strawberries	Spinach
Apples	Tomatoes
Nectarines	Bell peppers
Peaches	Cherry tomatoes
Celery	Cucumbers
Grapes	Kale/collard greens
Cherries	Hot peppers

• *The Dirty Dozen list contains two additional itemskale/collard greens and hot peppers-because they tend to contain trace levels of highly hazardous pesticides.*

THE CLEAN FIFTEEN

Avocados	Papayas
Corn	Kiw
Pineapples	Eggplant
Cabbage	Honeydew
Sweet peas	Grapefruit
Onions	Cantaloupe
Asparagus	Cauliflower
Mangos	

• *Some of the sweet corn sold in the United States are made from genetically engineered (GE) seedstock. Buy organic varieties of these crops to avoid GE produce.*

Made in the USA
Coppell, TX
17 December 2022

89901332R00070